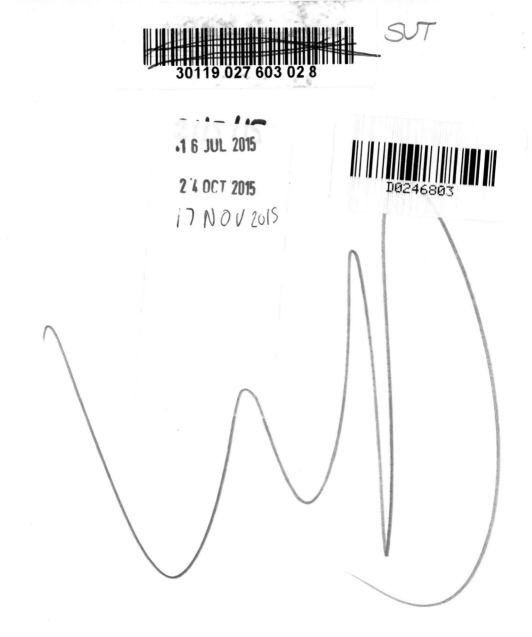

Build Your Own Brick House

Build Your Own Brick House

GERALD COLE

THE CROWOOD PRESS

First published in 2013 by
The Crowood Press Ltd
Ramsbury, Marlborough
Wiltshire SN8 2HR

www.crowood.com

British Library Cataloguing-in-Publication Data
A catalogue record for this book is available from the British Library.

ISBN 978 1 84797 485 3

Typeset by Jean Cussons Typesetting, Diss, Norfolk
Printed and bound in Malaysia by Times Offset (M) Sdn Bhd

Contents

Preface

If you're looking for a definitive, or comprehensive, manual for building your own brick home, this book isn't it; but, then, neither is any other.

House-building is simply too large, too complex and too varied an activity to be described exhaustively, even in a whole library of manuals. Just as importantly, many of the skills it demands reside not in words, technical drawings or formulae, but in the hands, memories and imaginations of the craftsmen and designers who take part.

That isn't an excuse, by the way – rather, a cause for celebration.

Self-build – building your own home – is, after all, an extreme form of self-expression, if only because it will cost most of us the largest sum we will ever spend in one go.

This book, then, is an attempt to make that process a little simpler, easier and cheaper by following the activities it entails in, broadly, the order in which they occur. At the same time they are kept in the context of the project as a whole, taking account of what, typically, should happen next or simultaneously.

'Typically', of course, isn't really a word that should be applied to something so individual in nature, but brick is Britain's traditional building material and the skills that go into making it, and making homes out of it, are centuries old and have gathered a wealth of practical wisdom. Hopefully, this book will provide some insight into that wisdom, and enable you to appreciate some of the practicalities and possibilities of brick. At the very least, you should be able to communicate more clearly and effectively with the designers and tradespeople who will bring your dream home into reality.

The principle, then, is not so much to show you how to build a brick home, as to show you how it should be built. The approach is severely practical, with the emphasis on making the best use of your time, abilities and budget.

One thing that isn't stressed, however, is price, except in terms of relative costs. Prices change too frequently and the degree of accuracy you will need is better found elsewhere.

Good luck with your build; though, having made the very sensible decision to read this far, I'm sure you won't need it.

Gerald Cole is the former launch editor, and now consulting editor, of *SelfBuild & Design* magazine, for whom he writes a monthly column. He has completed his own self-build and numerous house and flat renovations.

Educated at Wadham College, Oxford, he has published thirteen books of both non-fiction and fiction, including the novelization of the film *Gregory's Girl*.

Acknowledgements

It's only when you are asked to write book on a subject on which you believe yourself to be knowledgeable that you discover how little you actually know. Grovelling thanks are due to the following, in particular, for their generosity, expertise and encouragement.

Bob Harris, MCIOB, 2006 Master Builder of the Year, lecturer on ecological building, building consultant and passionate advocate of high thermal mass construction. You can gain a flavour of Bob's philosophy and achievements at www.earthdomes.co.uk.

Andrew Pinchin, architect, serial self-builder and brick aficionado, whose elegant designs and imaginative use of brickwork have embellished south-west London for many years. Andrew's expertise is currently available through the advice pages of *SelfBuild & Design* magazine.

Norman Stephens, master bricklayer, builder, perfectionist and lecturer on bricklaying skills.

Thanks are also due to Hanson, Ibstock and Wienerberger, the UK's leading brick manufacturers, who provided both advice and numerous images of brick homes and brickwork, and to Sketch3D (www.sketch3D.co.uk) for images in Chapters 10, 11 and 17.

Photographs and diagrams contributed by other companies and individuals are credited in context.

CHAPTER I

Why Build in Brick?

Walk down virtually any modern British street and you walk down an avenue of brick. Brick is Britain's most ubiquitous and most conspicuous building material for new homes. Even if the internal structure is timber or steel frame, chances are the outside walls will be brickwork. That's partly because the great majority of local planning authorities prefer it that way, partly because mortgage lenders and insurers grow irrationally nervous at any hint of 'non-standard' construction, but mainly because that's the way we like it.

We may coo appreciatively over the picturesque clapboard of Essex coastal cottages or the organic curves of Devonshire cob houses, but when it comes to putting down roots, most of us opt for bricks and mortar. It's easy to see why – bricks have a solidity and a permanence matched only by concrete or stone; but stone is largely confined to areas where it occurs naturally, while concrete smacks of public works and wartime bunkers, and its appearance is not enhanced with age.

Ageing is what brick does particularly well. Over the years its colours mellow and improve, yet it needs no regular maintenance. Its strength provides exceptional protection against wind, rain, snow and flood. Its density enables it to retain the heat of the day or the cool of the night, evening out internal temperature variations. It also provides excellent sound insulation and protection against fire.

This self-build, from Wimbledon-based architects Andrew Pinchin Associates, combines elements of brickwork and clay tile to create a style that's both modern and wholly traditional.

Traditional clamp fired brick-making at Ibstock's Chailey Brickworks in the Sussex Weald, where local clays have been used since 1711.

Despite all these qualities, however, brick remains breathable. Unlike timber-frame construction – brick's main rival – the structure of the house is not contained within an air-tight, plastic vapour barrier, designed to prevent water vapour from penetrating the timber and causing it to rot. Moisture passes through brickwork, albeit slowly, contributing to a naturally comfortable and healthy interior atmosphere.

More significantly for the builder, brick is one of the easiest of building materials to use and the most forgiving. The size of individual bricks is small compared to that of an entire home. As a result, variations from plumb that would prove disastrous for a precisely calculated timber- or steel-frame building can be compensated for with relative ease.

But it's in the look and the feel of brick where its appeal is greatest. Bricks can range in colour from bright yellow to red to dark blue, with every variation in between – sometimes within the same brick. Yet combinations of even the plainest and most common varieties can create striking effects out of all proportion to the costs involved.

Bricks can also range in texture from silky smooth to the roughness of naked rock – and here, perhaps, is where their appeal is most basic. Brick, in essence, is

the clay at our feet turned to stone, the artificial acceleration of a process that occurs naturally over millions of years.

Today most brick-making is concentrated among a small number of large manufacturers whose products are used countrywide. But less than a century ago, Britain was dotted with much smaller, brickworks using locally available clays to make bricks for local building. They produced the hard red, blue and yellow bricks of the South Wales valleys, the cream and light red bricks of Nottinghamshire and Leicestershire, and the grey and yellow bricks of London stocks. Homes built with these materials were rooted in the landscape from which they sprung. They expressed its colours and its texture, its unique character. If you're planning a home that will look and feel 'right' for its location, that promises stability and permanence, is low maintenance and economical to build, brick is hard to beat.

WHY BUILD YOUR OWN HOME?

Perhaps a more relevant question is: why not? That would certainly be the response of would-be home-owners in other European countries, as well as

What Do We Mean by a 'Brick' House?

To the building trade, a traditional brick house means 'brick and block'. In other words, it consists of an inner wall built with concrete blocks, which supports the floors and the roof, and an outer wall built from bricks. This supports the doors and windows, keeps out the wind and rain, and presents, hopefully, an attractive face to the world. The two walls are separated by a cavity, which prevents any moisture that penetrates the brickwork from reaching the interior. More recently, it's also been used to accommodate insulation.

The blocks used in construction are essentially bricks made from cement mixed with water and aggregates. The aggregates can include sand, stone or pulverized fuel ash (PFA), a waste product from power stations. Blocks are cheaper than clay bricks and larger, the standard size being the equivalent of six bricks, making them quicker and easier to lay. They can also be used to build floors, a method known as 'beam and block' (see Chapter 17 for details).

Aerated or 'aircrete' blocks are their latest development. Because they are honeycombed with air pockets, they provide good insulation and are so light they can even form solid roofs.

Walls built entirely of brickwork fell out of favour after 1945, largely because of a post-war shortage of bricks and bricklayers.

Self-build is the major form of house-building in Germany where companies like WeberHaus and Baufritz specialize in designing and building bespoke prefabricated homes. At their factories, customers can view demonstration houses and visit permanent exhibitions, where they can choose virtually every aspect of their new home from the interior design to details of roofing, guttering and even door and window handles.

Australia, Japan, Canada and the United States. In Germany, for example, a common wedding gift for a son or daughter is a serviced building plot, one of a number set aside periodically by local authorities for individual home-builders.

The plot owners can do much of the building work themselves, engage their own architect and builder, or approach one of the Germany's 100-plus catalogue house-builders. Typically, a manufacturer might have up to seventy house designs to view in a show village. Depending on the company, customers can buy a standard design, request a variation or commission a house based on their own design.

Customers can then view displays of every aspect of their new home, from heating systems to roof tiles to door knobs and window catches – all on the same site and usually at discounted prices. By the end of the process, the new home will be planned and priced to a level of detail we would find astonishing in the UK.

In fact, the nearest British equivalent has nothing at all to do with houses; it's how we would expect to buy a car.

SO WHY ARE THINGS SO DIFFERENT IN THE UK?

In Germany, self-build accounts for around 55 per cent of the house-building market. Speculative building by commercial developers is around 30 per cent.

In Britain the situation is reversed. Speculative developers account for around 80 per cent of the market, which is dominated by a small number of large companies. Self-build accounts for around 8 per cent, the lowest proportion in Europe.

Many of the reasons for this can be traced back to the 1930s. Before then most Britons rented their homes, but rising incomes and cheap credit fuelled a home-owning boom. Speculative house-builders rushed to meet the demand, setting a pattern that survives to this day.

Commercial builders have undoubtedly been successful at producing large numbers of homes, but it's been at a price. Individuality has not been a hallmark of the average 'executive' estate. Stereotypically, buyer choice has been limited to a small variety of bathroom suite colour schemes.

More importantly, most buyers have not been satisfied. In 2009 a survey by the now defunct Commission for Architecture and the Built Environment (CABE) found that 80 per cent of all new housing was regarded

Serviced plots, where the developer simply provides plots with utilities in place, leaving design and construction of the house to the buyer, are common in the USA, Australia and much of Europe, though they are slowly becoming more available in the UK.

by its owners as mediocre or poor. The most common complaint was lack of space. With an average size of 76 square metres, new British homes are the smallest in Europe.

Meanwhile, a highly conservative planning system ensures a continuing shortage of building land, which keeps house prices high and gives little incentive to developers to improve their products.

As an architect once told me: 'House-builders in the UK do not build homes; they add value to land.' So, if you're intent on obtaining a new house that meets all your needs from day one, is built to the highest standards and is genuinely the best value for the price you can afford, there really is only one option. It's time to swap sides, to move from being a consumer to a producer – of your own home.

HAVE I GOT WHAT IT TAKES TO BE A SELF-BUILDER?

Little more than a decade ago most people would have regarded wealth or a building background as the main qualifications for building their own home. But today we've been educated by a decade of television's *Grand Designs* and similar shows. We have three national monthly magazines devoted to self-build, *SelfBuild & Design*, *Build It* and *Homebuilding and Renovating*, a rash of annual self-build shows, even a National Self Build and Renovation Centre. Potentially the most significant development of all, however, is the government's first recognition of self-build in its 2012 National Planning Policy Framework. For the first time, local authorities are obliged to assess local demand for self-build and include plans for meeting it in their housing policies. A small but increasing number of councils has already begun releasing land for self-build use, while, at the time of writing, central government has just nominated seven sites of public sector land for the same use. The declared aim is to double the self-build market within a decade.

Meanwhile, the building trade has woken up to the potential of self-build. Many builders' merchants, including leading companies, now offer self-build advice and often quantity surveying services, too. Specialist mortgages are available and even specialist insurance schemes that allow home-owners to live in their existing houses until their new projects are completed.

German-style self-build may still be some way off, but building your own home has never been so easy for so many. That said, certain qualities are undoubtedly useful. If you haven't got them already, think seriously about acquiring them.

An ability to organize If you can run a busy home, stay on top of your finances or arrange a successful social occasion, you're halfway there.

An ability to communicate Most building professionals speak a language of their own and assume their clients are equally fluent – until you inform them otherwise and ask for explanations. Don't be embarrassed about continuing to ask until you're both clear what's being agreed. It's amazing how easily mutual misunderstandings can arise.

An ability to research An extension of the above. The more you research your project, the less likely you are to make a mistake. In self-build, preparation is all.

An ability to keep records Building professionals will only do what you ask them – and pay them – to do. Quotations and contracts are only the start of this process. Learn to keep track of every piece of paperwork and to make regular notes of every request made to those involved, and every agreement reached.

Flexibility Nothing as complex as a house-build will ever go exactly to plan. Learn to regard setbacks as opportunities for a re-think or an even better solution.

Patience Major building projects always take longer than you think. Always.

Self-Build Pros and Cons

Pros
- The design of home you want.
- The location of your choice.
- A higher standard of building.
- Saving yourself a developer's profit – typically 10 to 30 per cent of the value of an equivalent home.
- Saving yourself the VAT payable on building materials (see Chapter 24 for details).
- A smaller mortgage.
- The unique sense of achievement of building your own home and leaving something valuable behind you.
- Comprehensive knowledge of your house, unlike a home bought from a developer or second-hand – invaluable for maintenance, repair and any additional works in the future.

Cons:
- Having to cope with a new and unfamiliar environment.
- Competition from professional house-builders.
- Requirement for hard work and commitment.
- A degree of pressure – both on yourself and on your partner.

What you don't need Unless you have a specific building skill, practical ability is not necessary. Most self-builders limit their involvement in this aspect to painting and decorating at the end of the build.

SO WHO IS A TYPICAL SELF-BUILDER?

Very broadly, the market splits between families keen to jump a rung or two in the housing ladder and down-sizers planning for retirement. Most are couples and most already own their own homes.

But the joy of self-build is that there are always exceptions, from individuals doggedly constructing a dream home over several years to low-wage earners with no savings and little hope of a mortgage who invest their own time and labour – 'sweat equity' – in a community self-build (see Chapter 6).

In other words, if you want to self-build and you're willing to give it a try, you're a self-builder.

CHAPTER 2

How to Self-Build

Most home-buyers are used to viewing completed homes – either show homes or those still owned by their vendors. They tend to concentrate on the look of the house, the number of bedrooms, the state of the kitchen and bathrooms. Unless there are obvious problems, such as damp smells or a sagging floor, the condition of the structure is usually left to the mortgage-providers' surveyor. Surprisingly, given the scale of the investment, relatively few of us go to the expense of a more detailed survey from an independent surveyor. As a result, there can be surprises later on when an apparently solid wall turns out to be plasterboard or the attic space proves so full of timber supports there's no room for storage.

In theory, self-building, rather than buying a new home, can save you the 10 to 30 per cent profit that would otherwise go to a developer, but in practice, most self-builders use this saving to create a home with a higher specification or in a more desirable location.

It's a sign of how dependent we have become on volume producers – and how brainwashed we have been by the rising value of our homes – that we've either lost interest in the way they are built or we regard construction as the province of experts.

The truth is that, although house-building does demand skills, experience and, at certain points, specific expertise, the basic principles are well within the understanding of most of us.

Or they will be by the end of your build.

THE SEVEN STAGES OF SELF-BUILD AND HOW LONG THEY TAKE

1. **Decide what you can afford** You can do this in a spare evening.

2. **Find and buy a building plot** This can take from a few months to several years, depending on the availability of land in your chosen location or locations, and your willingness to compromise. You'll also need to make all the legal checks you would normally do for a property purchase.

3. **Choose a design** Allow several weeks for working out the details with your architect or designer and then having plans drawn up. Even if you have a very clear idea of what you want, or are choosing an existing design, it will still need to be adapted to fit your plot.

4. **Obtain detailed planning permission** This is dealt with by the planning department of the local authority in which your building plot lies. It is statutorily obliged to respond to applications within a set period, usually eight weeks, but it may be very

Adequate research is key to a successful self-build: The Building Centre in London's Store Street houses the UK's most comprehensive self-build bookshop, as well as a wealth of information and displays of building products and materials.

busy and ask for more time. If there are objections to your design, the plans may need to be revised and re-submitted and perhaps considered by the planning committee of elected councillors. All this can take up to several months.

5. **Obtain building regulations approval** Though there are alternatives, this is typically handled by the relevant local authority's building control department. Its job is to ensure that all new buildings comply with the technical requirements of the building regulations. Allow around a month.

6. **Choose a main contractor or sub-contractors** Allow at least a fortnight for builders to provide full quotations based on your plans. In practice, you should be considering builders from the design stage. Good, reliable contractors and sub-contractors are likely to be booked up several months in advance.

Self-Build Approaches – Pros and Cons

DIY

Pros:
- Minimal or zero labour costs.
- Maximum sense of achievement.

Cons:
- Much longer build-time.
- Only advisable for those with building skills and experience.
- Reasonable fitness and physical strength needed.
- Additional material costs to allow for errors.
- Exceptional commitment.

Turn-Key

Pros:
- Good for cash-rich and time-poor or those unable to make regular site visits, e.g. returning expatriates or self-builders building abroad.
- Reduced anxiety – let the professionals take the strain.

Cons:
- Most expensive method.
- Heavy dependence on professionals and their skills.

Project Management – Single Contractor

Pros:
- Good for those with organizational skills but limited experience of building.
- Single price for entire build.
- One point of contact for build process.
- Main contractor hires and manages sub-contractors.
- Main contractor will obtain reduced 'trade' prices for supplies and materials.

Cons:
- Reliance on one professional – firing a main contractor is hugely disruptive and finding a replacement difficult.
- A mark-up will be added to sub-contractors' fees and materials.
- Possibility of high costs for extra work not included in the fixed price.

Project Management – Several Sub-Contractors

Pros
- Exercise full control over all aspects of the build.
- Avoid a single-contractor's profit.
- Freedom to hire and fire sub-contractors of your choice.
- Freedom to negotiate costs of each aspect of the build.
- Potentially one of the most cost-effective approaches.

Cons:
- Heavy dependency on the organizational and management skills of you and your spouse/partner.
- Possibility of missing poor workmanship or bad practice that a professional would spot.
- Higher likelihood of errors due to inexperience.
- Constant pressure.
- High levels of stress likely on partner/family relationships.

7. **Build your home** Between 6 and 8 months is a typical build time for a traditional brick and block house, though problems, delays or an innovative or complex design can easily stretch it to twice that.

FOUR WAYS TO MANAGE YOUR PROJECT

There's no single way to tackle a self-build, rather a spectrum of approaches based on the degree of involvement you are willing, or able, to make.

DIY Few people, including professional builders, boast all the skills a house build requires – at least, to the satisfaction of a building control inspector. Maximizing your own contribution will, of course, dramatically reduce your labour costs, but at the expense of time and personal effort. An alternative approach is to hire a main contractor to build a watertight shell, which you then fit out yourself or with the help of sub-contractors.

Turn-key Here, the entire project is handed over to a professional. Traditionally, this is an architect who creates the design, gains the necessary building consents, puts the plans out to tender, recommends a main contractor, supervises the build and hands over the keys of the completed house. Other professionals, including chartered building surveyors, quantity surveyors and design and build companies, can do the same. Unsurprisingly, it is the most expensive option.

Single main contractor An architect or designer produces an approved design, but then the build is handed over to one main contractor.

Project management Instead of hiring a main contractor, you take that role, engaging sub-contractors and specialist firms to carry out the work and supervising the build yourself. Alternatively, you might hire a project manager, or project management company, to do it for you.

Most self-builds combine aspects of all four approaches. It's worth pointing out, however, that whichever route you choose, the sheer number of decisions involved makes some degree of 'hands on' involvement unavoidable, which is really the point of such a personal project.

CHAPTER 3

Making a Budget

Working out how much you can spend on a self-build is, in principle, no different from budgeting to buy an existing property. In other words, you tot up your available funds, add the likely proceeds from the sale of your current home, deduct expenses, such as stamp duty, legal fees and moving costs, and then judge if you can afford the mortgage you need to complete the deal, assuming that you actually need one.

With this 'ball park' figure in mind, you then choose a property, and make an offer. If it's accepted, that is pretty much that, barring a disappointing survey or a last-minute gazump. Your budgetary concerns now switch from acquiring your property to maintaining and holding on to it.

Self-build isn't quite like that.

Buying a building plot may be no different from buying a house – the procedures are much the same – but that's only the first stage of the process.

Stage two is, of course, the construction of your new home. The usual rule-of-thumb is to allow between a third and a half of the total budget for plot purchase, though in some highly desirable locations it may be considerably higher. The bulk of the rest is taken up by materials, labour and ancillary costs.

And here the complications start. Until you have detailed plans, and have had them accurately priced, your build budget can only be an approximation of the actual expenditure.

In theory, it should be possible to draw up detailed plans from the moment you have a clear idea of your new house. Equally theoretically, you should then be able to acquire a level plot on which to set your dream home, orientating it in exactly the way you've planned. That may happen, but don't count on it. Most self-builders start with a vision of their ideal home, but the most important factor in determining the house they actually end up with is the plot.

Plots come in all shapes and sizes, and all sorts of conditions. You may find your ideal location with your ideal view, but the area may be too small for the home you have in mind, or the ground may be steeply inclined, or the local planning department may place restrictions on size or roof height. Any of these factors can affect your plans, demanding minor or major revisions. That's a normal, if frustrating, part of the process. The good news is that it can inspire all sorts of design improvements, which might otherwise never have occurred to you.

So how do you decide your budget?

The quick answer is that you start with your best estimate of the total costs and then refine it as you obtain further and more detailed information. But first you need to know the most expensive aspects of your budget.

NINE KEY FACTORS THAT DETERMINE BUILD COST

1. Size
Most home-owners are used to discussing house size in terms of the number of bedrooms – one reason why they, along with all rooms in new homes, have been shrinking steadily over the past 80 years. But the professionals who build those houses think in terms of square metres (m^2). They are measured externally, ignoring internal walls, and the figures for each floor are added up to achieve a total floor area. A typical four-bedroom detached home, then, has a total floor area of around 150m^2. A small two-bedroom bungalow will be closer to 75m^2.

Having a clear idea of the size of your proposed home now allows you to calculate a price per square metre.

The major attraction of timber-frame construction – brick and block's main rival – is the degree of prefabrication, allowing the shell of a house to be erected swiftly. Michele Meyer

Luckily, there are a number of regularly updated construction industry price guides that can help you with this information. There are also a number of computer programs that do the same.

2. Build Quality

The industry price guides base their figures on average costs for standard quality building. For that, floors will be covered with sheets of chipboard, internal walls are likely to be timber studwork covered with plasterboard, and kitchen and bathroom fittings will be 'trade' models.

This isn't to say these products and materials won't be perfectly functional, but if you picture your dream home with hand-made clay roof tiles, solid oak floorboards and a designer kitchen, your budget will be significantly enlarged. For that reason, you need to gain an idea of the prices of these items as early as possible, otherwise you may have some unpleasant financial surprises, and possible disappointment, down the line.

In practice, most builds turn out to be a balance between size and specification. Deciding where the balance lies will depend on your personal wants and needs. For example, if you are building a home for retirement, it may be sensible to opt for a smaller floor plan with a high specification – for comfort, convenience and lower maintenance costs in the future.

If you are younger, with a large family – or one planned – a bigger house with a more moderate specification may be more practical. High-quality fixtures and fittings don't always survive young children, and you're still likely to have time, and earning capacity, to upgrade your home later, if you wish.

A common compromise, however, is simply to pick and mix, balancing, say, chipboard flooring against an eye-catching kitchen; or, more creatively, blending materials and items from a variety of sources – designer, trade, second-hand or salvaged – in a very personal, eclectic mix.

3. Building Method

Brick and block is Britain's 'traditional' method of house-building, even though the technique has only been well-established for the last half-century. It does, however, mean that it's a method known to all building professionals and its ubiquity helps to keep material costs reasonable. As a result, it tends, on balance, to be the least expensive building method, though, as in all building matters, that may vary with individual projects.

Building Industry Price Guides

An authoritative price guide is The Building Cost Information Service (BCIS) from the Royal Institution of Chartered Surveyors (see Contacts). As well as an online rates database, BCIS publishes Wessex Price Books, which provide average price details from day rates for trades to all aspects of major building works. Similar price books include Spons, Griffiths and Laxton's.

The data can allow for small, medium and large houses, standard, good and excellent qualities of build and adjustments for labour rates in different areas of the UK.

The main drawback of these services is their high price, aimed as they are at the professional sector. Much of their information, however, is available in build-cost calculators published in monthly self-build magazines. BCIS also offers a free online house-rebuilding calculator, intended primarily for insurance purposes.

Computer estimating software can provide detailed estimates. Some, like EstimatorXpress from HBXL or Sirca home Developer (see Contacts), are aimed specifically at self-builders. The learning curve, however, may be steep, though demonstration versions give you the opportunity to try them out.

Its main rival is timber frame. Here, the structure of the house – what supports the roof and floors – is made from a wooden framework. Invariably, though, this is then covered with an external wall, or 'leaf', of brick, stone or timber cladding.

Timber frame's big advantage is that the frame is usually produced in a factory. Once it's delivered to site, the structure of a house can then be erected very rapidly, enabling work to start on the interior sooner than with brick and block.

Timber frame's disadvantages are that it's more expensive and that a frame manufacturer will expect to be paid before delivery, which can account for up to 40 per cent of an entire budget – a big ask for so early in the build.

In theory, the additional cost can be recouped by a shorter build time, but the complexity of house-building means that projects are rarely completed on schedule, regardless of their building method.

Alternatives to Brick and Block

Walls of brick and block separated by a cavity may be the UK's most common form of house-building, but there are other methods of masonry construction you may consider.

Solid Walls

This is how brick houses were originally built, with single-leaf walls as thick as a brick is long. Doing the same today would not be permitted under the energy efficiency requirements of the building regulations, nor would it be very comfortable for the occupants.

However, solid masonry does have its advantages. For example, its density gives it a high thermal mass, which means that it can act as a kind of heat 'battery', storing warmth for long periods. It also means that the heat of summer takes much longer to penetrate thick masonry walls, keeping the interior cool. As a result, over the year, internal temperatures tend to be relatively even. This saves heating bills in winter and air-conditioning bills in summer. But this only works if the masonry is suitably insulated, and the most effective way to do that is on the outside. External insulation helps to lock winter warmth within the masonry, while slowing down the penetration of the sun's heat.

To meet current building regulations, and to be cost-effective, solid walls are built with blocks, either dense concrete or, more typically, larger, more thermally efficient aircrete blocks. Because there's only a single leaf, and no need to install cavity ties or cavity insulation, construction can be much faster, especially if 'thin joint' mortar systems are used (see Chapter 18 for details).

An alternative form of masonry build: insulated concrete formworks are hollow polystyrene blocks, assembled Lego style, then filled with fresh concrete to create a permanent, highly insulated structure. ICFA

Insulation is then attached to the exterior, using a variety of materials and systems. But isn't the end result a block rather than a brick house?

Certainly, the majority of solid-walled homes tend to be rendered, but 'brick slip' systems are available, where brick faces are applied, rather like tiles, and, once jointed, are indistinguishable from a solid brick wall.

Insulating Concrete Formwork (ICF)

Here, the walls are built with hollow forms made of rigid foam insulation, which are then filled with fresh concrete. The forms, typically expanded polystyrene, can be panels, held together with steel or plastic ties, or individual blocks, which are assembled Lego-style. The end result is a solid concrete wall, sandwiched between two layers of permanent insulation. The interior can then be plastered, and the exterior usually rendered, though brick slips could also be applied.

The method achieves high levels of insulation and airtightness and, since the initial assembly of the forms is semi-skilled, it has a particular appeal for self-builders. ICF is also used for basement construction.

Contact the Insulating Concrete Formwork Association for more details (see Contacts).

Solid-wall houses, built entirely out of blockwork with external insulation, can be exceptionally energy efficient; brickslips, like this, allow the exterior to appear indistinguishable from a conventional brick home.

Property details

Plot type   Single Building Plot
Location   Lochawe, Torran Farm, Argyll & Bute
Price   £50,000 - £99,999
Details   A plot of approx. 1 acre with outline planning permission for the erection of a dwellinghouse. Located in a enviable elevated position with panoramic views towards Loch Awe. Offers Over £89,000.
Agent   Bell Ingram (e-mail them)
   D M Mackinnon Estates, Oban, Argyll & Bute PA34 4AY
Telephone 01631 566 122
Fax   01631 564 764

Please quote PlotBrowser when contacting the agent.

Property details

Plot type   Single Building Plot
Location   LLANGOLLEN, Wrexham County Borough
Price   £50,000 - £99,999
Details   Elevated plot on the edge of Llangollen town centre with views of the River Dee.0.15 acres with Outline Planning consent for the erection of a single dwelling and new access.GUIDE PRICE £75000.
Agent   Thomas C Adams (e-mail them)
   8a King Street, Mold, Flintshire CH7 1LB
Telephone 01352 752 222
Fax   01352 759 112

Please quote PlotBrowser when contacting the agent.

Prices of plots in remote, and often highly attractive, areas of the British Isles, like these examples from *SelfBuild & Design*'s Plotbrowser pages, can be remarkable bargains, but taking advantage of them will usually involve a significant change of lifestyle.

4. Location

Anyone who has glanced through the plots for sale in self-build magazines and seen the prices in remote parts of Scotland, Wales or Northern Ireland is usually pleasantly surprised. But relatively few us are willing, or able, to take advantage – at least, without a significant change in lifestyle.

Unsurprisingly, plot prices follow the prices of existing property, making London, the south-east and fashionable holiday and retirement spots the most expensive areas. That said, the self-builder has options denied to the straightforward house buyer.

Problem plots, for example, which might deter a commercial developer, can offer an opportunity to an ingenious self-builder. Existing houses in poor condition may be candidates for demolition and replacement. Business or commercial premises may also have potential.

Alternatively, it may be more cost-effective to buy on the outskirts of a popular area, where prices are lower but the desired amenities are still within reach. One advantage of a less fashionable area is that labour costs may be substantially lower. Materials costs, however, are likely to be much the same in most parts of the country.

rightproperty

**Custom Home Build Index
England and Wales, 3Q2012**

The quarterly guide to Custom Home Build costs and land budgets

Plot prices per hectare and building costs for three-, four- and five-bedroom houses across England and Wales are available in *Rightproperty*'s quarterly index of custom-built homes.

A useful indication of plot prices and building costs throughout England and Wales is the quarterly Custom Home Build Index from Rightproperty available free through its website (*see* Contacts).

5. Personal Contribution

If you have a professional building skill – and with a brick house, bricklaying is hard to beat – you can make substantial savings on labour costs.

If you don't, treat your DIY input carefully. Ask yourself:

* Will the savings outweigh any consequent loss of income, e.g. through unpaid holiday time or work turned down?
* Is it likely to delay the progress of the professionals?
* Will it put me at physical risk?

This is why painting and decorating after the professionals have finished is the most common self-builder DIY task.

Don't forget, you already have a central and demanding role as the developer, hopefully reaping a developer's rewards.

6. Ancillary Costs

First-time buyers are often shocked by the number of additional fees that materialize during an apparently straightforward house purchase – stamp duty, legal fees, mortgage arrangement fees, survey fee and so on. Self-build ancillaries trump those easily, and it's important to allocate sufficient funds to deal with the extras that occur.

The most common ancillary costs are:

* Architect or designer – for a comprehensive service (preparing plans, submitting them for planning approval, tendering for contractors and managing the build) expect to pay between 6 and 10 per cent of the total budget; or an hourly rate for smaller, specific services.
* Structural engineer – required to produce recommendations, calculations and designs for non-standard aspects of the design, including foundations. An hourly rate is normally charged for site visits, including travel time. Otherwise, charges can be per beam calculation (because structural engineers invariably work out the size and strength of supportive beams).

* Project manager – an individual or company can take on the architect's traditional role of managing the build, and with similar payment arrangements.
* Stamp duty – due on land in the same way it is on property, and at the same rates.
* Planning application – the government's online planning and building regulations' resource, the Planning Portal (*see* Contacts), contains current fees for England and Wales.
* Building control application – traditionally this is arranged through the relevant local authority building control service, but other Approved Inspector building control services are also available.
* Party wall surveyor – only necessary if the excavations for your build will be close to a neighbouring property (*see* Chapter 9 for full details) and the neighbour objects. By law, he or she can then appoint a surveyor to ensure their property will not be damaged, and their fees will be charged to you.
* Quantity surveyor – a qualified professional who will draw up a 'bill of quantities', detailing all the materials you will need for your build and producing an accurate estimate of costs. He, or she, can also draw up a final account at the completion of the build.
* Utility connections – water, sewerage, electricity and gas supplies are local monopolies and connection charges reflect this. In addition, water companies in England and Wales will make an infrastructure charge of several hundred pounds each for mains water and sewerage. This doesn't apply in Scotland or Northern Ireland where water and sewerage have not been privatized.
* To connect your drains to a sewer beneath a public highway, you will need a Street Works Licence from the local authority highways department in order to dig up the road. This, again, is likely to cost several hundred pounds.
* Where a main sewer connection isn't possible, off-mains drainage is likely to run to several thousand pounds, depending on which system is most suitable (*see* Chapter 5 for details).
* Telecoms connection – relatively minor in cost compared to other utilities, largely because you have the option of a landline, cable, satellite dish or nothing at all (i.e. a mobile).
* Insurance – three types are essential: public liability, contract works or 'all risks' and employers' liability, if you employ sub-contractors (*see* Chapter 6 for details). Lenders will require this.

Builders' Merchants

Many builders' merchants, both local and national, provide specialist self-build advice. Their aim is to sign you up for a trade account, which you will need, and some offer build-cost estimating services, based on architect's plans. Often the fee charged can be recouped from your first large order; sometimes the service is free.

- Warranties – cover against structural defects, usually up to 10 years after completion (see Chapter 6). Also required by lenders.
- Accommodation costs – only required if you plan to sell or move out of your existing home; temporary accommodation in a caravan or mobile home on site may be an economical, if not entirely comfortable, alternative.

7. Contingency Fund

However comprehensive your budgeting, there will inevitably be items of unexpected expense. Ten per cent of the total budget is typically put aside to cover this. More is advisable if problems are anticipated: for example, where ground conditions are known to be poor, or where the design is innovative or unconventional.

8. Interest on Borrowing

Before you take out any loan for your project, you should know full details of monthly interest payments, including early repayment charges and penalties if you default.

Some self-builders take out mortgages at a higher interest rate than they would prefer – usually because that's all they are offered. Their plan is to switch to a lower rate once the house is completed and is a more attractive proposition to lenders.

Your budget, then, should include an allowance for additional repayments that may be necessary if your build takes longer than scheduled – which most do. The same applies, of course, to any other temporary loan, including overdrafts, bank and building society loans, and credit card debts.

9. VAT

Just when you thought your cash could head in only one direction, here's a piece of good news. Value added tax (VAT) is charged on most products and materials used in construction – with a few exceptions we will cover later (see Chapter 24); but new house-building is zero-rated. This means that VAT is not, or should not be, charged by a main contractor or sub-contractors involved in your build, while the VAT you do pay on the great majority of construction items you buy can be reclaimed. There are only three provisos to this:

- You must keep every VAT invoice you receive to prove your claim.
- You can only make one claim.
- It must be within three months of completing your build.

These are a small price, however, for receiving a substantial sum at the end of your project. Typically, your reclaim can pay for carpeting, landscaping, perhaps even a garage, or it could eliminate or cut debt.

Building it into your budget from the start, perhaps to reduce your contingency fund, is tempting but inadvisable. It's wiser to treat it as a well-deserved bonus.

Thinking About Budgeting

When we buy an existing house, we take an enormous number of things for granted. Obviously we expect it to be structurally sound, along with a functioning kitchen, toilet and bathroom. But, unless something is in clear need of repair, or the decoration truly horrific, it's unlikely to demand swift attention. After all, once we've moved in, we can attend to it at our leisure.

A new build isn't like that. Every item in every room has to be thought of in advance, selected and purchased. That includes the window frames, glazing and catches, the doors, door frames, architraves, handles and locks, the skirting, light switches and fittings, power points, central heating radiators and so on. Even in the smallest room, that can amount to an extraordinary number of items.

In a self-build those choices are up to you, and the sooner you make them – preferably when you first draw up your budget – the wider your choices will be, the fewer the financial surprises later and the smoother running your build.

You can, of course, leave them to your main contractor or sub-contractor, but in that case, you're likely to end up with standard trade quality items, which may not be to your taste at all.

CHAPTER 4

Finding a Plot

Finding the right plot – or, indeed, any suitable building land – is the first big hurdle in self-build, and one that proves insurmountable to many. That's understandable, but no indication of your likely experience.

There's no escaping the fact that Britain is a relatively small country with well-established communities who are keen to maintain the status quo (often with good reason), and who are largely supported in this by planning laws. Overcoming, or bypassing, these obstacles to any significant degree usually takes the political and financial clout of large commercial developers.

But self-builders are developers, too. In fact, collectively they are the UK's single largest group of house-builders, though they operate as individuals. As such, they have been generally regarded as rather amateur versions of small house-builders or budding property entrepreneurs. Public recognition has largely been confined to designated self-build lots in the post-World War II 'new towns', notably Milton Keynes, or 'affordable' community self-builds, usually organized by housing associations.

But in 2012 this changed. For the first time, government recognized the role of self-build in its planning policies and pledged to double the size of the market within 10 years. The government's aim is to use self-build to kick-start a depressed house-building market.

Hopefully, this enthusiasm will survive a reviving economy and allow self-build to become as widespread and entrenched as it is in the rest of Europe. But it's important to appreciate that, even without official support, an estimated 14,000 self-builders manage to complete their projects every year and there is absolutely no reason why you shouldn't join them.

It's also worth noting that recessions, like the current one, can be the best times to start a project. Any property you plan to sell may be worth less than it was during the last boom, but so will most of the plots you are considering. With work in short supply, main contractors and tradesmen may be much more

National Planning Policy Framework

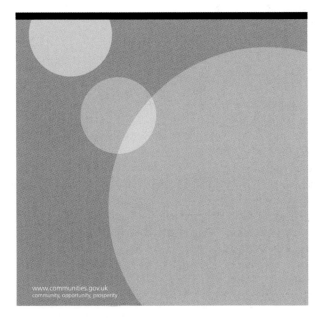

In 2012, for the first time ever, the government recognized the role of self-build in its National Planning Policy Framework.

inclined to negotiate charges, while frequent sales, not to mention bankruptcies, will ensure keen prices for household fixtures and fittings.

You may be lucky enough to find the right plot very quickly – you may even own it already – but for many people, locating suitable land takes many months and even years. The key to success is not so much the availability of plots, as the way you approach the search and the criteria you set yourself.

For that reason the most useful attributes are persistence, flexibility, ingenuity, imagination and possibly a little low cunning. Get those right and luck will invariably follow.

WHERE TO FIND BUILDING LAND

Contrary to many people's perceptions there is a great deal of land for sale in Britain at any given moment, and at reasonable prices, too. It includes single plots, fields, pastureland, woodland, forest and great swathes of open countryside. Unfortunately, the vast bulk of it is classed as countryside and not available for building, except in very limited circumstances (*see* Chapter 8).

For most practical purposes, then, house-building is confined to areas of cities, towns and villages defined by 'Local Plans'. The Local Plan is a policy document, drawn up by the relevant local authority, which sets out the area in which development will be considered. It also includes details of the policies that apply to new housing. The Local Plan can be found at the local planning department's offices or on the council's website.

Development outside the Local Plan boundary is usually not permitted. Rare exceptions might be when a council is about to enlarge the boundary and your potential plot falls within the new area. But don't count on that happening very often.

For this reason, the focus of your search should be plots that have planning permission, either outlined or detailed. Without that, the land is effectively pasture, and worth accordingly.

House building is normally only permitted within areas defined by the local authority's Local Plan, which is viewable in the planning department. In a small village, however, its extent can usually be clearly seen.

'Bungalow eating' involves buying existing houses and replacing them with something larger, though planners may restrict the size of the replacement.

Strategies for Plot Searching

- Visit your area of interest, preferably at weekends or holidays when you have time to explore. Get to know it well, not just in terms of building opportunities but as a place to live.
- Buy a local Ordnance Survey map: a scale of 1:1250 shows individual buildings. Look for open ground in or adjacent to residential areas.
- Tour the area, ideally on foot or by bicycle. Travelling by car, it's much easier to miss things; even if you don't, parking within a reasonable distance isn't always possible.
- Take a compact digital camera or smartphone with a good camera and photograph likely plot opportunities.
- Check the small ads in local shops.
- Place 'building plot wanted' advertisements in local shops, newspapers, magazines and on local websites.
- Mention to anyone who'll listen that you are plot searching in the area. Keep cards on you with your name, mobile phone number and/or email address, ready to hand out.

WHAT IS BUILDING LAND?

An empty 'greenfield' plot – i.e. one that has never been built on before and has planning permission – may sound ideal, but if you confine your search to land bearing this description there are opportunities you will miss.

Plots that already have houses on them can have even more potential. For a start, planning permission is no longer a major issue since it's already been granted for the existing property. Second, all the utilities are in place, saving a considerable amount in infrastructure charges.

The main drawback is that you are paying for a property you don't want, and you now have the additional cost of demolition. But if that's the only opportunity you can find in the location of your choice, it may be worth taking.

This is, of course, the principle of 'bungalow eating' – the developer's trick of buying a small property on a large plot and replacing it with two or more properties, perhaps even a small 'executive' estate.

You don't have to go that far, though; if you're lucky enough to acquire a larger plot than you need, you may be able to divide it up, gain planning permission for the newly created plots and sell them off to finance your own build.

Meanwhile, you can try to reduce your initial outlay by looking for properties in poor condition, which, hopefully, will be reflected in the price. Look for estate agents' ads offering homes 'in need of modernization' or 'updating' or 'would suit DIYer'.

If you're able to make a cash offer, you might also consider houses with unconventional methods of construction. Older forms of concrete or prefabrication induce deep paranoia in lenders, making mortgages hard, if not impossible, to find. Cash buyers may be the vendors' only option and your offer can benefit from that.

Plots that have already been developed are known as 'brownfield' sites. As well as existing housing, they also include commercial properties, from huge former gasworks – such as the site of the O2 arena in London – to small, shop-sized premises. Many of the latter are found in residential areas. Former corner shops, small workshops, builder's yards, scrapyards and rows of garages may be marketed as development opportunities with planning permission already in place. If not, a change of use can be applied for, though you should check with the local planning department whether this is likely to succeed before making any offer. Here, the chief drawback is site contamination. Even the least industrial pursuits can, over time, result in hazardous chemicals leaking into the ground, and decontamination may prove costly.

Not all plots, however, are recognized as such by their owners. The classic example is the large back garden with either rear or side access. This is known as 'garden grabbing' to those who disapprove. In this case it will be up to you to approach the owner, persuade them to sell and sell to you.

Usefully, you can apply for planning permission on land you don't actually own, though you are obliged

Rows of garages in residential areas are sometimes sold off with planning permission for a new house or houses.

An extended garden with good road access can be a good prospect for a building plot.

may to able to track the owner down by asking locally or consulting the local electoral roll or the Land Registry (*see* Contacts).

WHERE TO START

Estate Agents

Estate agents sell land as well as property, but, unless they have a specific land sale department, only a handful of plots are likely to be marketed every year.

Nevertheless, agents are keen to discover development opportunities, largely because they can produce at least two sets of commission, one for the site and another for the new property, or properties, built on it. In fact, agents have been known to contact developers they know as soon as they hear of such opportunities, enabling them to negotiate mutually advantageous deals before the property even reaches the market.

If this only confirms your low opinion of estate agents, think again. You are now a developer. You may only be developing one plot, but the estate agents you register with don't need to know that. They do, however, need

Partly because most estate agents seldom deal with land sales, and partly because such sales are offered first to commercial developers, boards like this are comparatively rare.

to inform the owner. It's also essential to reach a legal agreement beforehand. This involves either exchanging contracts (just as in a house sale) 'subject to receipt of satisfactory planning consent', or agreeing an 'option to purchase', which obliges the owner to sell only to you for a specified time. Once planning permission is granted, it's attached to the plot, not to the applicant. Without safeguards there would be nothing to stop a grateful owner deciding to sell to a higher bidder.

All this becomes irrelevant, of course, if the garden happens to belong to your existing home.

Other potential plots include gaps between terraced houses and waste ground of any kind in residential areas. If the ownership isn't immediately obvious, you

to know that you are a player, i.e. you are in the market to buy as soon as the right opportunity arises. So meet them in person, talk knowledgeably about the kind of property you plan to build, leave full contact details, follow up with a letter or email confirming your interest and call them regularly to discuss current or upcoming prospects.

Remember, most people tend to do favours for people they know and like or, at least, respect. Who knows – you may be tempted to build again, and again. This could be the start of a lucrative friendship.

Auctions

Auctions have traditionally been the marketplace for 'problem' properties. Typically, they are houses in poor condition or in need of major repair, repossessions, probate sales and so on. All these, of course, may be good development opportunities.

Land also appears regularly, and with similar variations. A recent London auction, for example, included a plot with a partially completed house that had breached building control regulations and a double plot with lapsed planning permission for two four-bedroom houses.

Each auction item is given a guide price, usually designed to stimulate interest rather than reflect an acceptable purchase figure. The vendor, meanwhile, will have a reserve price, which will not be disclosed. This is the minimum amount he or she is prepared to accept.

Auctions provide good plot opportunities, not just in terms of building land, but also for sites, like this former car showroom, which can be converted to residential use.

Auctions are designed for quick sales, with the fall of the hammer marking a legally binding contract. You may only have a week or two beforehand to visit the plot you have in mind, initiate legal searches, commission any surveys and arrange the finance. If your bid is successful, a 10 per cent deposit has to be paid immediately and the rest within 28 days. If you can't raise it, you risk being sued for the full amount, plus compensation.

Some auctioneers, however, run conditional auctions. In return for a non-refundable deposit, successful bidders are allowed up to 28 days to obtain finance and another 28 days to complete.

The whole process can sound very hairy, with the possibility of losing substantial sums if your bid fails, but it's not all as black and white as it seems.

If an item fails to reach its reserve price, it is withdrawn. But, if you're still interested, you can inform the auctioneer and it may be possible to negotiate a price with the vendor. Alternatively, you can make an offer before the auction takes place.

Auctions are clearly best suited to cash buyers, though bidders with firm mortgage offers can do equally well. Success, as in most aspects of self-build, goes to those who have thoroughly researched their field of interest and can spot a bargain before the less prepared bidder. It's not unknown for a plot or property that a buyer has pursued unsuccessfully on the open market to reappear at auction at a bargain price after a sale has fallen through.

Plot-Finding Agencies

In exchange for yearly or quarterly subscriptions, these provide regularly updated lists of plot, renovation and conversion opportunities across the UK, generally by county. The best known is probably PlotSearch from Buildstore (see Contacts), which also includes larger sites for multiple self-builders to buy jointly and divide up into individual plots.

There are, however, a large number of free services, both online and included in the self-build magazines, such as *SelfBuild & Design*'s Plotbrowser and *Homebuilding and Renovation*'s Plotfinder.

The main advantage of plot-finding services is the size of their databases, which is also their main disadvantage. With so many opportunities on offer from so many sources, it's inevitable some will be sold or withdrawn before you make contact. But agencies provide a useful overview of prices in unfamiliar areas and, as with all plot finding, they may have – or be about to have – just the plot you're looking for.

Another source of information on plot prices and local planning policy is the Valuation Office Agency's bi-annual property market report, which you can download from the VOA's website (*see* Contacts).

Newspapers and Magazines

Subscribing to local newspapers – both free and paid for – in the areas where you are looking is important in several ways. You not only keep track of the local property market through estate agents' advertisements, you may also see opportunities in personal ads and announcements of planning applications.

Being aware of local events is always useful. Any proposals to expand the boundary of the Local Plan are likely to be hot topics long before they are adopted or rejected. Stories that involve property – schools or libraries closing down, fires or flood damage rendering homes or other buildings uninhabitable – may be plot opportunities.

Similarly, subscribing to self-build magazines not only eases you into the self-build world and provides regular doses of advice and inspiration, but also keeps you up to date with the latest developments.

Planning Applications

Every local authority's planning department has a database of planning applications, which can be consulted at their offices or online. It includes both applications and the council's decisions.

Why would these interest a plot-finder?

When planning permission is granted, it applies for three years, during which time the project concerned must be started, or the consent lapses. Most successful applications go ahead within that time, but not all. Funds might not be available, the applicant's circumstances may change or there may simply be a change of mind.

If you find an application for a new build that is approaching its three-year deadline, it may be worthwhile contacting the applicant and discovering what the position is. If the project has been shelved, would they consider an offer for the plot?

This, of course, requires some digging into planning application files, and compiling and maintaining a database of likely possibilities. But, in popular locations where building opportunities are rare, it can be worth it.

This approach also applies to failed applications. It may be possible to adapt a rejected design, or replace it, in a way that counters the objections. If you believe you can succeed where the applicant failed, it may be worth approaching them and making an offer.

Public and Corporate Landowners

Large bodies, such as local authorities, utility companies, Network Rail, British Waterways and so on, sometimes sell off land. Contact their estates departments and enquire if they have anything available now or coming up soon.

Builders, including mass-housing developers, occasionally dispose of land they can't profitably develop or when they need to boost cash flow. Smaller builders may only sell if you engage them to build your house. If you know their work and are impressed by it, it may be worth agreeing to this, but you are likely to pay a premium for not getting a competitive tender.

Word of Mouth

As in so many aspects of life, serendipity can play a decisive part. A chance conversation with a friend, a relative, a work colleague, a pub landlord, a shopkeeper, can point the way to a plot opportunity. Let them all know you're looking.

After generations of rising house prices, most Britons know the value of property but are less aware where land is concerned. Your vigilance, and your increasing knowledge, can fill in the gaps.

Legal Alert

As with a house purchase, purchases of land require a solicitor to handle all the legal aspects of the transaction. But don't assume you can simply use the solicitor you have previously used for house purchases. Land purchase is a specialized area and not all solicitors will have experience of it.

Early in your plot search, make time to research legal practices with land-purchase experience, preferably in the area where you are searching, since local knowledge could be invaluable. You can do this online or by quizzing local estate agents or auctioneers.

It could also be worthwhile giving a likely solicitor a brief call to confirm their experience and to alert them to your intentions. When you find the right plot, you are likely to need to them to move quickly.

CHAPTER 5

Assessing and Buying a Plot

You have a strong suspicion that this is the spot. The location looks good. The plot seems about the right size for the house and garden you have in mind. And the asking price doesn't make you wince.

Chances are, however, that you aren't in the company of your designer, a surveyor or structural engineer, and you probably can't get them on site in the next day or two. But, if the plot looks this good to you, it's going to look equally good to a rival buyer. Clearly, you need to act quickly.

How do you go ahead?

GROUND RULES FOR THE INITIAL VISIT

Rule 1: Walk the ground – don't settle for a once-over from the nearest boundary. Put on some Wellingtons or sturdy footwear and explore as much of the plot as you can physically reach.

Rule 2: Take photographs from every angle – preferably with a digital camera, which will record the date and time. You may think you remember the plot vividly, but photographs will immediately show you points you've missed or forgotten.

Rule 3: Make a sketch map. You don't need to be a Da Vinci – simply mark the main features, especially boundaries, trees and access points. Add brief notes of any special details, such as power lines, damp ground or dumped rubbish that might devalue the site. This will be more than just a useful reminder for later. It will help to focus your attention now.

Rule 4: Check out the neighbourhood. You're not only concerned with your potential new neighbours (though that's useful), look at the size and design of the existing houses, especially newer ones. Are they a similar size or architectural style to the design

you have in mind? Is yours likely to fit in? This could make a significant difference to your success in any planning application.

Plot potential can sometimes be hard to spot. This small plot of just 0.025 hectares (0.061 acres) has good access to a busy residential road and a disused building already on it, but it is backed by a steep railway cutting and so overgrown that close inspection is extremely difficult.

WHAT TO LOOK FOR AND WHY

Size

Most self-builders start with a broad idea of the size of house and garden they would like, but it's wise to be flexible. A plot in the right location and with stunning views may be too small or too narrow for the design you have in mind. Your design may be out of scale in comparison with neighbouring houses, or the position or orientation you prefer may not be acceptable to local planners. None of these need necessarily rule out the plot. There are almost always ways round problems of this kind, but it's helpful to start out with a clear idea of what is most important to you.

Is it the right location, the right view or the house itself? Is a good-sized garden crucial, or could you be content with a small patio area?

Considering these alternatives in advance may prevent you from missing a golden, though not immediately obvious, opportunity.

Access

Two types of access are important: for you, and the

vehicles you own, and for builder's and supplier's vehicles visiting the site.

If the plot adjoins a typical residential street, neither should be a problem. Note, however, that the local authority's highway department will have standards for visibility for leaving the plot. In other words, the driver of a departing vehicle should be able to see clearly to left and right before entering the roadway.

You can judge this by stepping a couple of metres back from the boundary. Typically, in a 30mph zone, you should have unimpeded views 60m up and down the roadway. Faster roads will require much longer distances. Problems immediately arise if the plot lies on sharp bend or near the crest of a hill.

Another common concern of highway authorities is the ability of vehicles to leave the site facing forward. In other words, will there be enough room on the plot, once the house is built, for a vehicle to turn easily?

If the plot is approached by a private road or track, it's important to establish whether or not the approach is included in the purchase. If it's shared with neighbours, what precise rights and responsibilities do you have?

This is one for your solicitor to investigate, but it's also of concern for the build process. Will the approach be wide enough and in good enough condition to take delivery lorries and JCBs? If repair or upgrading is needed, the cost should be reflected in the sale price.

Boundaries

Obvious as it seems, you should be entirely clear about exactly what you are buying. Where plots have been neglected for some time, or are bounded by unruly hedges or poorly maintained fences, boundaries can become blurred.

Ask the vendor or his agent for a copy of the plan from the title deeds and check it out on the ground. If there appears to be any confusion, ask the vendor for clarification. One way to be absolutely sure is to walk the boundary with the vendor, or their agent, getting them to mark it with wooden pegs and taking measurements.

This may seem picky, but boundary disputes with neighbours, either existing or potential, can be time-consuming and costly, not to mention seriously damaging your enjoyment of your new home.

Party Wall Issues

Even where the boundaries are well defined, problems can still arise where a neighbouring property lies close to one, especially if you plan to build on the boundary or close to it. This occurs most often, though not exclusively, on tight urban plots where you need to make maximum use of the space.

In these cases, the Party Wall Act of 1996 can come into play, and it's important to deal with any issues it causes as soon as possible. More than one plot purchase

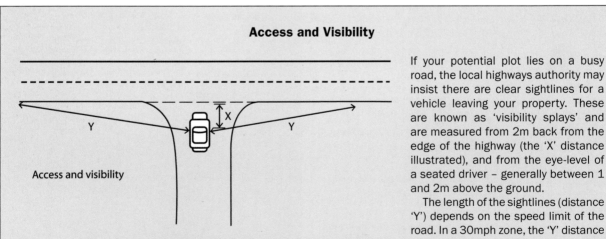

Access and Visibility

Access and visibility

If your potential plot lies on a busy road, the local highways authority may insist there are clear sightlines for a vehicle leaving your property. These are known as 'visibility splays' and are measured from 2m back from the edge of the highway (the 'X' distance illustrated), and from the eye-level of a seated driver – generally between 1 and 2m above the ground.

The length of the sightlines (distance 'Y') depends on the speed limit of the road. In a 30mph zone, the 'Y' distance can be up to 90m. On a road with a 70mph limit it can be close to 300m.

Any obstruction, such as a tall hedge or trees, may need to be trimmed or removed. If it lies on your plot, this should not be a problem (unless any tree is subject to a Tree Preservation Order or lies in a conservation area). But if the obstruction belongs to a neighbour, its removal will have to be negotiated with them.

RIGHT: **Boundaries are not always clear, so ask the vendor or his agent to walk the boundary with you, marking it with wooden pegs and taking measurements you can both agree.**

BELOW: **Party wall agreements with neighbours are necessary for narrow plots like this one, where an existing semi-detached house has been demolished and the replacement design includes a full-height basement.**

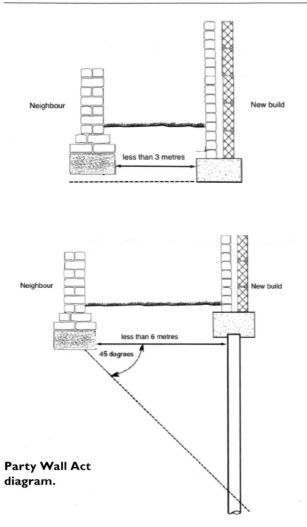

Party Wall Act diagram.

The basic idea is to ensure that neighbouring structures aren't undermined or made unstable by your building works, right from hairline cracks appearing in the neighbour's walls to partial or total collapse. Before the Act reached the statute books, such occurrences could lead to lengthy, costly and acrimonious legal disputes.

The act requires that you give your new neighbours 2 months' notice in writing of the start of your build. Your letter should include details of the work and explanatory plans. It also gives the neighbours 14 days to write back, confirming that they have no objections.

If they write, declaring they have no problem, that's the end of it. But if their letter says they're not that keen, you are officially in dispute. Worse, if they don't reply at all, the law assumes you are in dispute.

To resolve the problem, you jointly have to appoint an 'agreed surveyor' to draw up an 'award'. This is a document that sets out the works to be done and at what times, takes note of the current condition of the neighbouring property and gives a surveyor the right to make inspection visits to your site. You must also undertake to pay for any damage your works cause.

Don't Be Taken for Ransom

Very occasionally a small strip of land along the boundary of a plot is retained by a previous owner. It may be only a few centimetres wide, but it still restricts access. In order to develop the site, you will need to buy both the plot and the strip. Since the owner of the 'ransom' strip is in a pivotal position, this could add significantly to your plot costs.

The vendor should, of course, make this clear to you before you view, but sometimes no record remains of the previous owner, they are untraceable or there is doubt that the strip actually exists – it could simply be a drafting error in previous conveyancing documents.

In these cases, it may be worthwhile taking out defective title insurance (see Contacts). This guarantees that your insurer will negotiate a sale if a vendor appears subsequently, or offer you compensation if negotiation fails.

One indication of a ransom strip may be an unusually large verge on the access boundary to the plot. It's also important to check the dimensions of the plot against those marked on the title deeds or at the Land Registry.

has fallen through because plot buyer and neighbour haven't been able to agree.

It applies when:

- You build within 3m of a neighbouring property and your foundation trenches are deeper than the neighbour's foundations.
- You build within 6m of a neighbouring property and your foundations are lower than a 45-degree line drawn from the bottom of the neighbour's foundations.
- You build up to a boundary wall and your foundations need to pass under the wall, if only by a few inches.
- You are building off a neighbouring property's wall.

A sun-position compass can show you how much sunlight a plot will receive throughout the year and the effects of shading by neighbouring buildings or trees.

The 'agreed surveyor', incidentally, must be independent, i.e., not one you happen to be employing anyway. If you and your neighbour can't agree on one, they are entitled to appoint their own. If the two surveyors can't reach an agreement, the surveyors have to appoint a third to adjudicate between them.

If all this strikes you as a fee bonanza for surveyors, you wouldn't be alone. What's worse is that all those fees have to be paid by you.

It should also be obvious by now that the Act can be a joy to a vexatious neighbour – another reason to keep your new neighbours fully informed of your plans from the design stage and on good general terms. Or, failing that, build well within your boundary.

Orientation

Does the plot lie on a north–south or east–west axis, or something in between? A house with an unimpeded southern aspect will be able to take maximum advantage of the sun, both for light and energy-saving warmth, including solar heating and photovoltaic panels.

Use a sun-position compass to find out how much sunlight the plot will receive throughout the year, and if it's likely to be shaded by neighbouring buildings or trees.

Steep slopes need either shoring up with retaining walls, as here, or excavation of the incline – often both – adding substantially to building costs, though the price of the plot should reflect this.

Slopes

Even quite mild slopes will add to your costs, and steep slopes will be substantially more expensive.

Coping with a steep slope involves either digging into the incline, building it up to create a platform or creating split levels within the house – or variations of all three. All involve a great deal of excavation and the construction of retaining walls, which will add significantly to costs.

On the plus side, this makes sloping plots much less attractive to commercial developers and, therefore, a good prospect for the self-builder, especially in locations you might otherwise be unable to afford. You may also end up with stunning views from your hillside eyrie.

Poor Ground Conditions

The great imponderable in all building is what lies beneath the surface. All builders breathe a sigh of relief when they get 'out of the ground'. Poor ground conditions – i.e. ground that may not support your house adequately – will need to be made good and that will involve extra expense.

Watch out particularly for:

- Boggy ground – indicated by damp soil, standing water, reeds or marsh plants. The area may need draining and excavating to a depth where it can support foundations. It may also indicate that the area is prone to flooding. In a location with no main sewer available, a high water table is also likely to rule out the use of a septic tank, and more inconvenient and expensive methods of sewage disposal may be necessary (see Chapter 15 for details).
- 'Made up' ground – ground that has been excavated previously and infilled with other material, making it unstable. It may be a buried pond, well or soakaway or the remains of a previous building. Look for piles of rubbish or mixed material in the ground.
- 'Telltale' road or street names – anywhere called 'Brick Lane', for example, suggests clay may have been excavated locally for brick making and the resulting holes infilled.
- Contamination – more usually found in 'brownfield', i.e. previously occupied, land, such as former

BELOW: **Marsh plants indicate boggy ground that may need draining before foundations can be laid.**

A 'telltale' street name may indicate infilled ground and perhaps contamination in the past.

factories or petrol stations, but more rural plots could also be affected by, for example, leaking drums of fuel oil or pesticides. Owners of contaminated land are legally required to inform the local authority, but not all do, or realize that they should. If you have any reason to suspect contamination – perhaps by odd smells, ground discoloration or knowledge of the site's previous use – ask the vendor for clarification. If contamination is detected, the affected soil may have to be removed or capped with a layer of concrete or clay. Usually those responsible for the problem are obliged to pay for this but, if they

can't be traced, the bill will fall on the land owner. In this case, remedial costs should form part of the purchase negotiations.

- Natural contamination – in some parts of the UK, particularly where granite and limestone are common, a radioactive gas called radon can build up inside enclosed areas of homes. It's easily dealt with, however, by fitting a gas-tight membrane over the ground slab and ensuring underfloor spaces are well ventilated.
- Methane – similar measures can guard against this natural gas, which can combine explosively with air. Invisible and odourless, it's normally produced by rotting organic matter. A common source is landfill sites. Any house built within 250m of one is officially regarded as at risk.

Trees and Vegetation

Mature trees can be an attractive aspect of a plot, but not if they happen to be exactly where you want to build. Removing them is straightforward, but, once the roots are no longer extracting moisture, the ground may swell or 'heave', becoming unstable. Some soils are more prone to this than others.

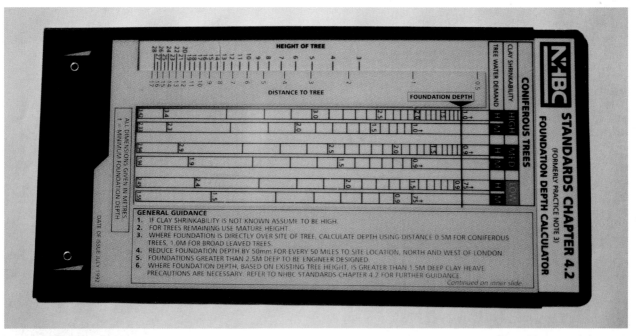

Roots from a nearby tree can damage foundations. A calculator like this one from the National House Building Council (NHBC) enables you to establish the correct depth of foundation according to the species of tree, its height, demand for water and the ability of the soil to shrink.

Trees are sometimes protected by Tree Preservation Orders, meaning they cannot be removed, or even pruned, without planning permission; if it cannot be obtained, the design or position of the house may have to be changed.

Trees may also be protected by a Tree Preservation Order (TPO) imposed by the local authority. This means that the tree, or trees, in question can't be felled, or even pruned, without planning permission. If you do so, it's an offence, incurring a fine of up to several thousand pounds, and the felled trees will have to be replaced.

Services

The availability of mains services, or their lack, can be an important factor in a plot purchase. In a residential area, making new connections to water, sewerage, electricity and gas shouldn't be a major problem, though always check. The nearest main sewer, for example, may be relatively close but higher than your plot, ruling out a connection dependent on gravity.

In a more isolated spot, however, fewer services are likely to be available, or those that are may be too

Manhole covers can indicate public or private drains, which may need to be bridged or moved.

A small concrete post with a metal descriptive plaque – missing in this case – may be the only indication of a buried power cable.

Good foundations depend on the compressed, and largely lifeless, subsoil below. Broadly, there are three types:

- Rock, such as granite, limestone, sandstone and strong shales, can't be beaten in terms of support, but will need heavy equipment to excavate sufficiently deep foundations.
- Non-cohesive soils, such as gravels and firm sands, may not sound particularly stable, but they consist of large particles held together by their own weight and can carry heavy loads.
- Cohesive soils, such as clay, loose sand and soft silt, consist of much smaller particles, which trap water and stick together. As inhabitants of central and southern England will know, clay soils can expand and shrink dramatically as their water content changes through the seasons. To avoid these effects, soils with high shrinkability will need deeper than usual or piled foundations (*see* Chapter 16 for details).

Dense clay soils are also largely impermeable, making them unsuitable for absorbing the effluent from septic tanks. If you are unable to connect to a main sewer, and obliged to use a septic tank instead, your local Building Control Department will require you to prove that your soil is suitable. You can do this with a percolation test.

distant to connect economically. There are, however, ways of coping with all these eventualities.

For now, check whether any existing services cross the land. You may be able to tie into them, which will save you money. But you may need to have them moved in order to build where you wish and you will need to contact the owners.

Poles carrying above-ground power lines are obvious enough. Buried cables can be indicated by a small concrete post with a metal plaque. A manhole cover may reveal the existence of a sewer.

GOOD AND BAD SOILS

The first foot or so of soil, known as topsoil, contains large amounts of organic material as well as minerals, compounds, air and water. This makes it too unstable for supporting buildings, but ideal for growing plants – a good reason why it should be retained when the site is cleared.

The Percolation Test

- Dig a hole to the depth of the drainage pipework for a septic tank – typically, about a metre. Make it big enough to dig a further hole in the bottom. This should be 300mm square and 300mm deep.
- Fill the second hole with water to the top. Leave overnight.
- The next day refill the hole and time how long it takes the water to drop to a depth of 150mm. Divide this time by 150. This will give you the average time in seconds it takes the water to drop 1mm.
- Repeat three times. If the average result is between 12 and 100, the ground is suitable for handling septic tank effluent. If it's outside these limits, the ground may still be suitable if the effluent is given additional treatment before it's discharged.

If You Can't Connect to a Main Sewer

Even when a main sewer runs next to your plot, it still needs to be at least 800mm below ground-floor level to ensure a suitable flow by gravity. Where this isn't possible, a pumped system can be used.

If the nearest main sewer is higher than a plot, or too distant for a conventional connecting drain to be economical, a pumped system can be installed; it uses an underground holding chamber, large enough to hold 24 hours' worth of discharge. Klargester

In the example illustrated, the house's sewage drains into an underground holding chamber, large enough to hold 24-hours' worth of discharge in case of emergency. It also contains an electrically powered pump, which propels the contents uphill to a suitable drain or directly to a main sewer.

Adding a macerator or grinder allows the sewage to be pumped along a much smaller diameter pipe, which is cheaper and easier to lay than a conventional drain. Even when the nearest main sewer is downhill but a long distance away, it may be more cost-effective.

For all other situations there are three main options:

Septic Tank

A septic tank is the most common method of off-mains' sewage disposal. It consists of a large sealed, underground tank, traditionally made of brick but now fibreglass or reinforced plastic and typically onion-shaped.

The sewage enters at one end and is broken down by anaerobic (i.e. non-oxygen-breathing) bacteria, leaving a sludge at the bottom, a crust on top – which usefully masks smells – and a moderately clean effluent. This drains away into the ground, typically through a network of perforated pipes buried in gravel-filled trenches.

The process is natural and automatic, so, once the tank is buried and connected up, the only maintenance required is pumping out the sludge once or twice a year – a task undertaken by specialist tanker lorries.

Building control has to approve the system. If the ground is insufficiently permeable (see percolation test below) or the local water table too high, they may insist on a more thorough treatment system.

The same applies for any discharge within 10m of a stream or river, or anywhere near a water-catchment area. The Environment Agency (see Contacts) lists these on its website.

Mini Treatment Plant

This more thorough system also consists of a buried tank but uses both anaerobic and aerobic (oxygen-breathing) bacteria to produce a much purer effluent. It does so by stirring up the sewage to mix it with air and water, using a variety of methods, including slow-moving paddles, discs or a stream of air bubbles.

Treatment plants are several times more expensive than septic tanks and need electrical power and more maintenance, but they may be required in locations where the discharge from a septic tank will not be acceptable.

Cesspool

Only considered where no other system is workable, a cesspool is a large, fibreglass tank, which simply stores the sewage until a tanker empties it. Given that the minimum size is 18,000ltr – enough for two people for a month – a tank for a family household is likely to be very large and need emptying by tanker once a month.

Other Options

Reed beds can act as a further level of treatment for discharges from septic tanks. They come in two forms:

The most common form of off-mains drainage is a septic tank, typically a large, onion-shaped container, which is buried on site; its use has to be approved by the local building control department.

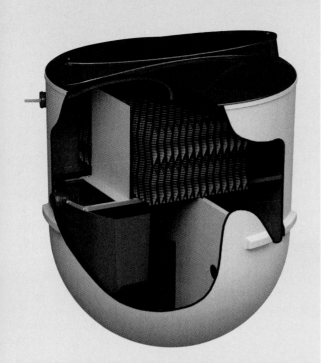

Where a septic tank is not acceptable, a mini-treatment plant may be used; by mixing air and water mechanically with the sewage, it produces a much purer effluent. Klargester

- A vertical flow bed consists of a container with layers of sand and gravel in which to grow the reeds, which provide oxygen for micro-organisms breaking down the sewage effluent.
- A horizontal flow bed is essentially a gravel-filled reed pond with an outflow. For the best results, both forms should be used.

Reed beds can be aesthetically appealing and attract wildlife, but you'll need a reasonably sized plot that slopes away from the house.

An entirely internal solution is a composting toilet, sometimes seen in remote visitor centres. In the best known – the Swedish Clivus Multrum – a shaft drops vertically from the toilet to a large, independently venti-lated double-chambered tank in the basement.

Each time the toilet is used, a handful of wood shavings is dropped down the shaft to aid the composing process. After six months or so, one of the chambers is emptied of odourless, non-toxic humus, which can be deposited on the garden.

You'll need a basement and a way of ensuring vertical drops from all toilets, but you can expect lower water bills, as well a rebate on the sewerage part of the bill.

A further complication is that ground is not always entirely consistent. Areas of firm subsoil may easily alternate with softer patches. The good news is that these can usually be compensated for by deeper foundations at that point or by bridging from firmer areas on either side.

DIGGING TO DISCOVER

Finding out exactly what lies beneath your plot can only be done by digging, but you'd be unwise to wait until the foundations are excavated. Instead, start with between two and four trial holes outside the proposed footprint of your house (holes dug inside will only need to be filled in again). The idea is to find at what depth firm subsoil begins, and in the process discover the composition of the ground.

Trial holes are typically between 2 and 4m deep, and will normally need a mechanical digger or mechanical augur, which can be hired with an operator. If you are confident that the ground is basically sound, you may only need your architect, builder or local building control officer to take a look and make a judgement.

If there is evidence of problems, hire a structural engineer to carry out a site survey. Your designer should be able to arrange this. It is likely to cost several hundred pounds, but it will save considerably more if conventional foundations later prove to be inadequate.

IS THE PRICE RIGHT?

The quick answer is: if it's right for you. That's to say, you have, at the very least, made the following calculation:

- estimated build budget +
- ancillary fees +
- contingency fund +
- estimated sum required to remedy any observed defect in the plot +
- the asking price of the plot.

If the total of these sums is equal to, or, preferably, lower than, the amount you have to spend, you are clearly in a good position. You are now reasonably sure that your project is achievable and, since you can meet the asking price, you are able to make a swift purchase and avoid any risk of losing the plot to a higher bidder.

BUT IS THE PRICE FAIR?

Again, fair for whom? A commercial developer, who will need to add between 10 and 25 per cent profit – depending on the cost of the project – in order to making a living, may not think so. But you are a home-owner as well as a developer. Your profit is going to be measured in the satisfaction you take in your new house for as long as you live in it.

But let's be realistic. We'd all prefer to pay less than we expect, not just to reduce our borrowing or to build at a higher standard, but simply for security's sake.

Unless you have been very lucky at the beginning of your search, you will probably have a good impression of the prices of plots in the area. Perhaps the most reliable indication is to find out the likely sale price of a newly built house of similar size and specification locally. Local estate agents should be helpful here. Talk to at least three, though not the one who is selling the plot.

At the end of the day, however, the decision will be personal. If you are convinced you have found your dream plot but the price is more than you allowed for and you can't persuade the vendor to reduce it, you may simply decide to bite the bullet. You may then be able to claw back the extra cost during the build; for example, by reconfiguring your design or postponing a desirable but non-essential feature.

This is an easier decision to make when you are relatively youthful with an on-going career. Downsizers, who may only have one pot of savings to invest, may not be so flexible.

Again, as in all aspects of self-build there's an upside, achievable through a little ingenuity and imagination. Might it be possible, for example, to divide the plot in two? Selling off one half with planning permission in place won't endear you to the original vendor, but it could provide a massive boost to your budget.

If you're in a location that appeals to holidaymakers,

The object of the exercise, but a successful purchase will involve a lot more research and calculation than buying the average property.

could you include a self-contained flat within your design and rent it out in the holiday season? Or rent it out long-term for an additional income and a means of reducing and eventually eliminating debt? Later, it could become a granny annexe or perhaps a home – temporary or otherwise – for offspring who haven't yet had your success in the property market.

HOW TO BUY

In England, Wales and Northern Ireland, land is bought in much the same way as houses – that's to say, either by private treaty, which is the most common method, by tender or at auction. However, because of the additional complexity of land purchase, two other approaches are available: the 'conditional contract' and the 'option to buy'.

Private Treaty

After a price has been agreed between you and the vendor, either privately or through an estate agent, you instruct your solicitor to prepare a draft contract, send preliminary enquiries to the vendor's solicitor and carry out searches at the local authority and Land Registry.

This may give rise to further enquiries being addressed to the vendor's solicitor, until details of the contract are agreed on both sides. At this point you pay a deposit – normally 10 per cent of the purchase price – and contracts are exchanged. Shortly afterwards – commonly four weeks, but shorter periods can be agreed – the balance of the purchase price is handed over and completion occurs. You are now a landowner.

Advantages: it's familiar to buyers, vendors and solicitors.

Disadvantages: gazumping – until the moment of exchange the vendor can accept another offer, forcing you to withdraw if you can't match or better it.

Tender

If several buyers are competing, estate agents can invite them to submit 'sealed bids' in an informal tender. It's 'informal' because the result is not legally binding.

Each buyer puts his or her 'best and final offer' in writing in a sealed envelope, which has to be received by a given date and time. The vendor then chooses which to accept and the sale proceeds normally.

Advantages: most belong to the vendor, but at least it's an opportunity for you to remain in the game. Though other buyers may outbid you, your source of finance may be more secure and you may still win as a result.

Disadvantages: a lot of anxiety, particularly if you distrust the estate agent. Delivering your bid personally just before the agreed time can reassure you everything is being handled correctly.

A variation of this is the 'contract race', where competing buyers are invited to submit contracts, the sale going to the individual who exchanges first. If you lose, you will still have to pay your legal costs. If you win, there's a possibility of an important detail being missed in the hastily produced contract.

Auction

The main attraction here is speed. Once your auction bid is accepted, you have made a legally binding contract. Normally a 10 per cent deposit – plus the auctioneer's fee – has to be paid immediately and you then have 28 days before the balance is due. (See Chapter 4 for further details of the auction process.)

Advantages: immediate certainty that have made your purchase.

Disadvantages: you will have only a short time to investigate the plot and carry out legal searches. You will also need either ready cash or a pre-arranged loan that can be activated at short notice.

The Scottish Method

Though sales by private treaty exist in Scotland, it's common for vendors of both land and property to invite offers over a stated figure by a certain date. Sealed bids are submitted and, once an offer is accepted and a contract agreed, it becomes legally binding. This effectively rules out English/Welsh-style gazumping and gazundering.

Land and property may also be offered at a 'fixed price', in which case it goes to the first person to meet that figure. If there is more than one interested party, a closing date is set. Even where 'offers over' are invited, it can be worth asking if a quick sale at the starting price would be accepted.

Conditional Contract

If there are uncertainties about the viability of a plot – such as obtaining suitable planning permission, a problem about boundaries or perhaps suspected soil contamination – a conditional contract can be agreed. Here, you commit to buying the plot but only on condition that the stated problems are remedied.

The vendor may insist on a specified cut-off date, after which the contract ends, so it's important to decide on a sensible estimate of the time needed to do what you require.

Advantages: you have the opportunity to sort out problems that might otherwise make you reject a plot, and reassurance that it will not be sold elsewhere in the meantime.

Disadvantages: unless the contract is carefully worded, you may end up buying a plot which does not serve all your needs.

Option

Though buying a plot without planning permission is almost always an ill-advised gamble, this is one method of making it work for you.

Where land is offered without planning permission, and the vendor is unwilling to go to the expense and effort of obtaining it, you can offer to do it for them. In exchange for an exclusive option to buy at an agreed price within a specified period, you pay the vendor a non-returnable sum – usually between 1 and 10 per cent of the purchase price.

The period needs to be long enough to cover what are likely to be extended negotiations with the planners. But the purchase price will take account of your efforts, being typically between 75 and 85 per cent of the value of the plot with planning permission.

Options are mainly used by commercial developers, who can write off any losses as a tax-deductible expense, and who are also likely to have more lobbying clout with local authorities.

Advantages: if your gamble pays off, you may have a bargain.

Disadvantages: you must be prepared to lose the option sum plus planning application fees and, very likely, architect's or designer's fees for drawing up plans.

ASSESSING A PLOT OFFSITE

Investigating a plot on the ground is only the start of the assessment process. Equally important – and often more so – are the planning and legal aspects. The bulk of this is done by your solicitor, but knowing what he or she should be doing, and why, will reduce the chances of misunderstanding and mistakes on either side.

PLANNING CHECKS

Buying a plot with either outline or detailed planning permission may be a priority, but it's important to realize that all consent comes with conditions, some of which may cause problems for you.

PLANNING CHECKLIST

1. How Much of the Planning Consent Period Remains?

Permission for both outline and detailed planning lasts for 3 years from the date it is granted. With outline planning permission, you have that time in which to submit an application showing full details of the approved plans, known as 'reserved matters', or you can submit full or detailed planning for an entirely new building. With detailed planning permission, you have the same period in which to start work. If you do nothing during that time, the consent lapses.

You can apply for an extension, but local planners will regard this as a new application and are under no obligation to approve it simply because they have done so before. Planning policy may well have changed in the interval.

If there are only a few weeks or days left of a planning consent, leaving you insufficient time to produce and submit a detailed planning application – or to decide whether or not to accept existing detailed plans – you need to know how likely it is that planning consent will be renewed. If there's a reasonable doubt, you could insist the vendor renews the permission before the sale goes ahead.

Alternatively, if you are happy with existing approved plans, but are not in a position to start building immediately, you need to know exactly what the local planners regard as a 'start'. To some authorities this means at least excavating and pouring foundations. Others are more flexible, especially if you can show clearly you are going ahead with the project.

Do make it a priority to discuss this with your local planning department. If you go ahead on assumptions, which later prove unfounded, you may end up losing a great deal of money.

2. What Conditions are Included in the Planning Permission, and Are They Acceptable?

Planning consent always comes with conditions. Typically, the materials and finishes used on the outside of the house have to be approved by the local authority, as do details of the drainage system, road access and sight lines, and the provision of car parking and turning space. Other conditions may restrict the height of the new house or forbid future extensions.

If any of these create problems, this is the time to discuss it with the planning department.

3. Are Other Developments Pending Nearby That Could Affect Your Enjoyment of the Plot?

Is a new bypass planned at the end of your garden? Does your neighbour have planning permission for an extension that will overshadow your new home?

The local planning department should have details of all proposed development in the area.

4. Is the Plot at Risk of Flooding?

Check the Environment Agency Flood Map, which is available free at the agency's website (see Contacts). For more accurate information, specific to the postcode, use the Flood Risk Indicator at the Land Registry website, which at the time of writing costs £65.50.

5. Does Your Plot Lie Within a Conservation Area?

This should be fairly obvious if your plot is surrounded by distinctive and well-preserved period buildings. Conservation areas are designed to preserve and enhance buildings and areas of architectural or historic interest. Any development, or indeed any change, comes under special scrutiny to ensure that it complements the character of the area. For example, planning permission is required to extend your home and the local authority must be notified before you can fell, or even prune, trees above a certain size.

If your new home is of a similar style to its neighbours, this may not be a problem. A more modern design may not necessarily be rejected, but approval is likely to involve protracted and complex negotiation.

6. Does Your Plot Lie Within Any Other Designated Area?

Conservation areas aren't the only locations where special planning restrictions apply. Others include Green Belt land, National Parks, Areas of Outstanding Natural Beauty (or, in Scotland, National Scenic Areas) and Sites of Special Scientific Interest. Some are covered by local authorities, others by specific bodies, though all will have strict planning policies. Typically, they are only likely to permit the demolition and replacement of existing houses.

7. Is Your Plot Near a Listed Building?

Listed buildings are single properties of special architectural or historic interest and any alteration or repair is very strictly controlled. These controls also apply to all structures within the 'curtilage', i.e. any surrounding land that formed part of the property when it was originally listed, even though it may now be owned separately.

If your plot includes land that was once part of a listed property, you will need planning permission to alter or remove any structure lying on it. That will include boundary walls, outbuildings and even statues. Even if your house is beyond the curtilage but still close by, this is likely to be taken into account when your design is considered.

Talk these matters over with the local authority conservation officer.

8. Does an Agricultural Tie Apply?

Living in the open countryside, outside local authority development boundaries, is regarded as a privilege usually reserved for those whose work demands it – in other words, those engaged in agriculture, horticulture and forestry.

Unless you can prove this applies to you, you won't be allowed to take up residence. Nevertheless, more than one self-builder has overcome this problem by combining their project with a new career on the land.

LEGAL CHECKLIST

1. Are There Any Planning Obligations?

An agricultural tie is also an example of a planning

ABOVE & LEFT: When a public footpath or bridle way crosses a plot, it can be very difficult to have it removed; to guarantee privacy, it can be more practical to shield it with hedges or a fence.

ABOVE: A 'wayleave' gives a service provider a right of way over land in order to carry out maintenance or repairs.

obligation, otherwise known as a 'planning agreement' or 'Section 106 agreement'. This is a condition that is attached not to the planning permission, but the title deeds of land, making it legally binding on existing and future owners. Typically, it imposes restrictions on the use or further development of the plot. You can apply to have it removed, but only after 5 years and if you can prove that it's now out of date or that removing it will not harm the area.

A more controversial obligation, however, is a demand for a financial contribution to mitigate the impact of new building on the local infrastructure. Traditionally, these have only been imposed on major developments, such as large supermarkets or commercial housing estates. But, more recently, increasingly cash-strapped local authorities have included one-off self-builds. As well as increasing a self-builder's costs, obligations of this kind have added a fresh level of uncertainty, since each contribution has to be negotiated individually.

In April 2012, however, the government introduced a new charge known as the Community Infrastructure Levy (CIL), which is designed to make these sorts of charges more predictable and transparent, and eventually replace Section 106 agreements. CIL is levied on the gross floor space of all new building, with the exception of social housing and buildings used by charities. If you're demolishing and replacing an existing structure, however, you can deduct its floor space from the total.

The charge can be made on the developer or the owner of the land being developed, depending on who takes responsibility. If no one does, the owner is liable.

Unlike Section 106 agreements, the rate a local authority charges for CIL can be discovered in advance, allowing you to include it in negotiating a plot price. The bad news – at least at the time of writing – is that CIL rates can sometimes be very high, especially in areas where land values are already elevated.

The worse news is that some councils are insisting on both CIL and Section 106 cash payments, effectively making many self-builds unaffordable.

There is allowance in the CIL legislation for arguing that it should not be imposed if it makes a development uneconomic, but presenting that case will clearly take time and expense with no certainty of success. That said, one current minister has insisted that CIL should not apply to individual self-builders. Hopefully, by the time you read this, the situation will be resolved.

2. Does a Covenant Apply?

A covenant is a binding private agreement made between individuals, including a vendor and a buyer of land. For example, as part of a sale, the buyer may agree to put up fences or improve a common access. Covenants can also be 'restrictive', i.e. the buyer agrees not to do certain things, such as build a house above a certain height or build at all on certain parts of the plot.

Because covenants are written into the title deeds, they continue to be enforceable long after the original reason for them has disappeared. You can negotiate with the person who now benefits from the covenant to have it removed or 'overturned', but if your project depends on their agreement, this may well prove expensive.

If a beneficiary can't be traced, you can take out indemnity insurance to cover you against the likelihood of one appearing and challenging you in the future.

3. Do Easements or Wayleaves Apply?

Where cables, pipes or sewers cross private land, the service providers involved will have either imposed or negotiated a right of way in order to carry out maintenance and repairs. Sometimes this includes a narrow strip either side of a buried pipe or cable to allow proper access.

If this is likely to obstruct your build, you can approach the owners and enquire if a diversion is possible.

On the plus side, service providers may pay you for these rights or allow you to connect to the services, saving you effort and expense.

4. Do Footpaths or Rights of Way Cross Your Plot?

Public footpaths or bridleways are protected by law. You can't apply to have them removed or diverted until you own the land, and opposition is likely to be fierce. A more practical approach is to ensure that any right of way can be shielded from your proposed home by hedges or fences.

Private rights of way – perhaps allowing a neighbour access to their property – will need to be negotiated privately.

CHAPTER 6

Obtaining Finance

Applying for a mortgage on an existing home is relatively straightforward, at least in principle. Once you spot a likely property, you approach a lender and fill out an application form, giving details of your current financial status and financial history.

Meanwhile, the lender despatches a surveyor to check that the property's market value is sufficient to cover the loan requested. Taking all the above factors into account, the lender then makes an offer, or declines the application.

The principle of a loan for a self-build is much the same, with one glaring difference: the property against which the loan is made doesn't actually exist yet.

Self-build mortgages are available on both land and building, typically providing between 75 and 90 per cent of the lender's valuation of each.

Despite the surety of a deposit, plus your proven ability to support a mortgage, you are essentially asking for a loan on the basis of a good idea – never an enticing prospect for a high street lender.

Banks and building societies overcome this unease in two ways. First, they estimate the likely value of the completed house. Second, the loan is not supplied in a lump sum, as it is for a house purchase; it's advanced in stages, the amounts being based on the value that the project has accrued with each stage.

It follows, then, that payments are only made after stages are completed – in other words, in arrears. It's up to you to finance the initial outlay. The only exception is the purchase of the plot, which will require your deposit.

The stages that trigger payments will depend on each lender's requirements but, typically, they are:

- Completion of foundations.
- Brickwork to roof level.
- Completion of roof and making the building weathertight.
- First fix (construction of internal walls, floors, ceilings, installation of all cabling and pipework and plastering).
- Completion of build.

As with most conventional mortgages today, lenders do not provide 100 per cent loans. The loan to value (LV) rate – i.e. the proportion of the valuation that the lender is willing to lend – is typically between 75 and 90 per cent on both land and building. Usually these are dealt with separately but variations can be wide.

Some lenders will not give loans for plot purchase. Others limit themselves to a third of the plot valuation. The broad majority vary between 75 and 85 per cent.

HOW TO APPLY FOR A SELF-BUILD MORTGAGE

Establishing your ability to repay your loan is only the beginning of an application process. Typically you will then need to provide:

- A copy of the planning permission relating to your plot. Initially, outline planning may be acceptable but detailed planning permission will be needed to finalize the loan.
- A copy of building regulations' approval.
- Details of the plot and its sale price.
- Scale plans of the proposed house, including floor plans and elevations, a brief specification and a site plan.
- Details of site insurance for the duration of the build.
- Details of the building warranty covering the build. If you are using an architect or other qualified professional to indemnify your project, their contact details, qualifications and a copy of their professional indemnity insurance will be required.

In practice, the more details you can provide, the better. The most convincing case would include a fully costed budget and build schedule, perhaps based on the estimates of your chosen main contractor. Showing a

good awareness of the build process and a reasonable estimate of the costs of each stage will undoubtedly improve your case.

DOWNSIDES TO SELF-BUILD MORTGAGES AND HOW TO OVERCOME THEM

Bigger Deposits/Higher Interest Rates

As we've seen above, self-build mortgages usually require larger deposits than those for existing property. Interest rates, too, tend to be higher than conventional mortgages. Partly this is the result of lenders' characteristic nervousness when faced with any degree of uncertainty; partly, because self-build lending is a niche market and borrowers have few other places to go. Consequently, it can be worthwhile switching to a less expensive, conventional mortgage once your home is completed. For that reason, choosing an interest-only self-build mortgage can minimize your loan costs for the period of the build when your finances are fully stretched.

Beware Stage Payments

Taking your loan in stages rather than in one hit is, of course, another way of keeping down costs. You only pay interest on the money you have actually borrowed. But it's also important to allow for the fact that payments are only made after a stage is completed, and that doesn't mean simply informing your lender that it's done. The work will need to be inspected by the lender's surveyor, and this can often take several days or even weeks. Furthermore, the surveyor's report will include a valuation of the project to date. The subsequent stage payment may be based on this figure rather than your actual expenditure. Over the course of the build this is likely to even out, but in the short term, your finances can be put under strain. It's important, then, to make the arrangements clear to any contractors or tradesmen you engage and alert them if any delay in payment is likely. Accounts with builders' merchants can also allow you at least 30 days' to pay bills – and up to twice that if you buy at the right time of the month.

There will, however, inevitably be times when bills, or tradesmen, can't wait and you will need a reserve to tide you over. If you don't have enough spare cash, arrange an extended overdraft or bridging loan with your bank and clear your credit cards.

The Value of a Valuation

Remember that when your plot and planned house are valued, the valuation is carried out by a surveyor employed by your lender. The value reached will be one that safeguards the lender's interests and is likely to be lower than the asking price of the plot or local estate agent's estimate of the price of the completed house. It's important, then, that the funds you bring to the purchase can cover any reasonable variation in the percentage of the loan you expect.

If the lender's valuation bears little relation to what you regard as reasonable, it's time to re-evaluate your project. Is the lender simply being excessively cautious or is the plot or house really worth less than you thought? If so, is it possible to re-negotiate the plot price or revise your design? Or should you approach a more accommodating lender?

If you already own a property, there is a way of overcoming this problem. The accelerator mortgage, pioneered by specialist self-build broker Buildstore (see Contacts), not only enables your stage payments to be made in advance, but allows you to stay in your existing home until the new one is completed. Even better, no valuations are required to trigger stage payments and loans can made up to 95 per cent of both land and build. The scheme also allows you to buy a plot with just outline planning permission. Some lenders only lend on land with detailed planning permission. In the time it takes you to obtain this, you could easily lose an opportunity.

How is all this possible?

Despite its name, the accelerator isn't actually a mortgage but an indemnity insurance, which underwrites your lender's advance stage payments. The insurance itself costs a few hundred pounds, depending on the size of your project.

Only a handful of lenders operate the accelerator scheme but, if your existing house contains a lot of equity while your funds are relatively limited, or if you simply don't want to sell up and move into temporary accommodation while you pursue your self-build dream, it can be an excellent solution.

Don't Forget Your Existing Mortgage

If you already have a mortgage on your current home, and won't be repaying it before starting your project, lenders will deduct the amount still owed on it from the amount you can borrow. For example, if you have a £90,000 mortgage and your income will support a £180,000 loan, the actual amount you can borrow will only be £90,000. Again, the accelerator mortgage can help out, by treating your existing monthly mortgage payment as simply another regular financial commitment.

The alternative is to sell your current property and bank the proceeds, ideally in a high-earning, easy access savings account. This not only hugely reduces your need for borrowing, but puts you in the ideal plot-buying position of being a cash buyer.

The only snag is having to find somewhere to live in the meantime. Rented accommodation will, of course, slowly deplete your nest egg but, once your plot is bought, it's always possible to move on site in a rented or second-hand caravan or mobile home (see Chapter 10).

Check Your Lender's Conditions

Each lender will have its own peculiarities. Some smaller building societies, for example, will only lend on projects within their locality. Others will insist you employ a single, main contractor or, if you decide to manage the build yourself, a supervising architect or professional project manager.

Eco Mortgages

Ever-rising fuel bills are making so-called 'eco-houses' – homes that are highly energy efficient and made from sustainable materials in sustainable ways – more and more popular. This is, in fact, the government's policy. All new houses must be 'zero carbon' by 2016 and the building regulations are growing ever more stringent to ensure that.

Choosing to go 'eco' won't just save energy bills, or the planet – it can also reap dividends with your mortgage. At the time of writing, at least two lenders – the Ecology Building Society and the Melton Mowbray Building Society (through BuildStore) – are offering discounted mortgages to self-builders building eco-homes. As the building regulations demand higher and higher energy efficiency for homes, offers like this may well become more common

Some building societies offer discounted mortgages on energy efficient and sustainably built self-builds, like this stone-built eco-house funded by the Ecology Building Society. Ecology Building Society

Other points to watch for include:

- Stage payments – do they correspond with your build schedule? Will they, for example, leave you with exceptional expenditure for an aspect of the build that spans separate stages? Can you negotiate a more acceptable staging arrangement?
- Valuation fees – what are they? Do they have to be paid when each stage is inspected, or can they be rolled up until completion?
- Redemption fees and early repayment penalties – what will you be charged if you swap your self-build for a conventional mortgage after completion and how long will these charges apply?
- Certification and warranties – these are guarantees that the build has been carried out correctly and insure against any major defects that may appear after completion (see details below). Which form of certification does your lender ask for, and will this affect your project?

- Time limits – are you obliged to finish your build within a certain period and are there any financial penalties if you don't?
- Any other charges and fees – ensure you know precisely how much you will be charged for all the lender's services and when you will be expected to pay.

Finally, the good news: some lenders will only consider houses built with traditional brick and block methods. Not a problem for the brick house self-builder.

WARRANTIES

One of the most common worries for self-builders is: how can I be sure my house is being built correctly? The easy answer is: by regular inspection by experts and the issuing of professional certificates.

Traditionally, site inspection has been carried out by the local authority's building control department.

Structural warranties provide guarantees against major defects in materials, design and workmanship for up to 10 years as well as protection against a main contractor going bankrupt.

A building control officer visits at key stages of the construction and checks that the build is following the agreed design and the relevant requirements of the building regulations. After the final inspection he, or she, issues a completion certificate.

This is still a common practice but most lenders, and therefore any future buyer of your home, will also insist on a building warranty, otherwise known as structural liability insurance.

Typically, this guarantees you against major catastrophes during your build – such as a single contractor going bust – and any serious defects in design, materials or workmanship that arise for up to 10 years after completion.

The best known is the Buildmark warranty from the National House-Building Council (NHBC). It can only be issued by an NHBC-registered contractor but, if you project manage your own build or use a non-NHBC registered contractor, the NHBC's Solo for Self-Build Warranty provides similar cover. The NHBC, incidentally, publishes a regularly updated manual of standards, which are generally higher than those required by the building regulations.

The UK's most widely used warranty, however, is the LABC New Home Warranty. Confusingly, the LABC is the representative body for local authority building control, though here operating as an independent service. Similar schemes are available from Premier Guarantee and Sennocke International Insurance Services with

its Build-Zone structural warranty, also known as Build-Care. Like the local authority building control department, all these providers make their own inspections.

Does that mean you have two sets of experts checking your build?

Yes, if you wish for that double assurance. But all the warranty providers also offer their own building control service as an alternative to that of the local authority.

The advantages are savings in costs and time – the rivals claim to be cheaper and react more quickly than over-pressed building control departments. They also tend to be more open-minded about less conventional forms of construction. This may be useful if you plan some innovative twists to your traditional build.

There is, however, another source of certification. This is the professional consultants' certificate (PCC) from the Council of Mortgage Lenders. The professional concerned is often the architect who has designed and supervised the project, but a chartered surveyor, a chartered builder or an architectural technologist (see Chapter 7) is equally capable. If you can be sure you will not be selling or remortgaging your property for at least ten years, this is a reasonable option that may you save you money in the short-term. Its main advantage is that your property can be certified by the professional who has supervised the build and knows it far better than a visiting surveyor.

But there are drawbacks. Not all lenders accept PCCs – a problem if you are obliged to sell or remortgage

Building sites are dangerous places, not just for workers but for visitors, passersby, trespassers and yourself. Ensure you have public liability and, if you are managing your own project, employer's liability insurance.

within a short time. PCCs only last 6 years and cannot be passed on to subsequent home-owners. A PCC also relies on the certifying professional maintaining professional indemnity insurance. If a problem arises, which your professional disputes, you may be forced to sue to obtain redress – and end up with a large legal bill. You can, however, guard against this with legal protection insurance (*see below*).

INSURANCE

Building sites can be hazardous places, not just for yourself and building workers but also neighbours and passersby. They can also cause serious damage to your finances if collapses occur, underground services are accidentally damaged or equipment or materials go missing. Taking out sufficient insurance, then, is essential – not least because lenders will insist on it. Essentially there are three types.

Public Liability

In all the excitement of acquiring your plot, it can be easy to forget that from the moment of completion you are now liable for any damage or injury caused to others arising from that plot – for example, children playing on the land and falling into a forgotten trial hole.

Those hazards increase exponentially once building works begin. Plant or materials may damage a

---

The Community Self-Build Route

For those on low incomes, with little prospect of raising a conventional mortgage, community self-build offers an alternative. At the most basic level, a group of would-be self-builders forms or joins a housing association or co-operative, which jointly buys a plot and finances the builds. Members of the group agree to contribute unpaid labour – typically, 25 to 35 hours a week – in exchange for a low rent or part ownership in a shared equity scheme.

A leading source of schemes like this is the Community Self-Build Agency (*see* Contacts), which also organizes training in building skills.

Community self-builds can also be organized privately. A group of like-minded individuals can use their combined resources to buy a single, large plot more cheaply than they might buy smaller individual plots. After dividing it up, they then undertake their own builds.

A developer might do the same, offering plots to self-builders, agreeing a range of designs and hiring a contractor to build the houses. The builds might be fully completed or simply watertight shells, which the self-builder finishes off, thereby reducing costs.

Schemes like these are currently being pushed by the Coalition Government. It's set up a £30 million Custom Build Homes Fund to provide start-up finance to ease the current mortgage famine. It's also releasing packets of public sector land specifically for community self-build, starting with a minimum of five properties.

At the time of writing, several local councils, including Swindon, Plymouth and Cherwell in Oxfordshire, are doing the same.

Community self-build involves self-builders joining together to maximize their resources. The government has recently offered £30 million in start up finance for projects providing a minimum of five homes.

neighbour's property. Mud from the site may cause a passerby to slip and fall. Even trespassers and thieves who suffer injury on your site have been known to sue.

Public liability insurance protects you against any claim for compensation for bodily injury or death from third parties or damage to property. As an indication of the risks involved, the standard cover is up to £5million.

Employers' Liability

If you are managing your own project and employing sub-contractors, this is a legal requirement, covering you against any claims for bodily injury, death, disease or nervous shock suffered by employees on your site. Incidentally, 'employees' includes anyone helping out, whether paid or not.

Contract Works or 'All Risks'

As the 'all risks' label suggests, this protects you against a range of hazards, from fire, flood and storm damage to the theft of tools, materials and fittings. Generally, insurers allow you to add options, such as personal accident cover or cover for on-site accommodation and its contents. Some insurers offer blanket site-cover, bundling together all three forms of insurance.

If you are hiring a single contractor to build your house, the contractor should have their own site insurance. Check, that they do, that it's up to date and that the sums covered by the contract works policy will cover the value of your completed house. You will, of course, still need public liability insurance until your contractor starts work on site.

Other Insurance to Consider

- Legal expenses – arising from any contractual dispute, e.g. with a professional, local authority or supplier.
- Personal accident and/or critical illness – insuring you against delays or losses caused by your own incapacity.
- JCT insurance 21.2.1 – this fills in a gap in public liability insurance, which only covers you for damage caused by negligence. Sometimes work can be carried out expertly and still damage neighbouring properties, such as driving piles for foundations, demolition of an existing property or excavating a deep basement. Named after a standard clause in building contracts (see Chapter 11), this provides protection if you feel there's a risk of such an eventuality.
- Defective title insurance – where the title deeds to a property are lost, missing or inadequate, or there may be reasons to believe there is an undisclosed right of way or easement, giving someone access to your plot for a specific purpose.
- Restrictive covenant indemnity insurance – a covenant is a legally enforceable deed, which typically restricts activity on land, e.g. building a house. It can date back centuries. If the owner of the deed cannot be traced, this insurance will indemnify you for any loss in value of your property if an owner subsequently appears and decides to enforce the covenant. It will also cover you against legal expenses incurred in defending your case.

CHAPTER 7

Choosing a Design

Welcome to the fun part.

For once, all the normal restraints of budget, location, rules and regulations don't apply – at least for a while. Every self-builder has a vision of an ideal home. It might be an idyllic thatch-roofed cottage, a neo-Georgian townhouse or a gothic castle. It might simply be a home with more space for a growing family, a low-maintenance retirement residence or just somewhere with a superb view. Whichever is yours, now is the time to bring it into focus.

Many of you may already have idled away hours over the years sketching out versions of your perfect home; but if you haven't, and visualizing things has never been your strong point, don't worry. Successful design has as much to do with deciding what to put into plans and sketches, and what to leave out, as it is with how those

... **to modernist minimalism** ... Hanson

... **to country manor** ... Ibstock

Whether or not you have a clear vision of your ideal home, the design stage is the time to explore options, from traditional thatch ... Wienerberger

... to prefabricated ecohome ... Hanson

... to compact urban detached. Hanson

ingredients are put together. That, after all, is why you pay for the expertise and experience of a designer or architect.

HOW DO YOU START?

Design is essentially a mixture of two things:

- form – how a building looks, and
- function – what it's meant to do, both inside and out.

Ideally, one should reflect the other. A sprawling mansion that looks perfect for large parties and communal gatherings won't be very successful if the interior is a maze of small rooms linked by narrow corridors. Alternatively, a small house dominated by one large, open-plan living area, with the kitchen, bathroom and bedrooms squeezed into corners, is likely to have limited appeal.

It's perfectly possible to start with either looks or function. For example, you, or your partner, may have a passion for steeply sloping roofs with plenty of dormer windows, or broad verandas or tall Elizabethan-style chimneys. If you're determined, those elements have a good chance of ending up in the finished design.

Even if your ideas seem certain, it's often more productive to start with function. That steeply sloping roof may be ideal for how you plan to use an upper storey, but it's equally possible that it just won't allow the amount of room you discover you need upstairs.

Good Design Begins at Home

Your present home may suit you perfectly and you're only leaving because you have to, but chances are you can't wait to move somewhere that better meets your needs.

So what are those needs? Refresh your memory by walking through and around the house, preferably making notes as you go.

Are certain rooms too small or too large? Would you like more bedrooms for a growing family? Are you fed up with washing baskets in the kitchen and desperate for a proper utility room? Do you long for a quiet sitting-room away from the kids, or an entrance hall that doesn't instantly fill up with clutter? Has storage always been a problem?

Don't forget to note your likes as well as your dislikes – the light-filled kitchen, the pleasantly secluded garden, the convenience of an en suite bathroom and so on.

The idea isn't to enjoy a nostalgia fest or have a general moan. It's to get you thinking about the way you live and your actual needs for a successful living space, which may not always coincide with your desires.

And, while you're at it, consider your existing furniture and which you'd like to keep. It will save time later if you jot down the measurements – height as well as width and length. The place to keep those details is in your design file (*see below*).

Creating a Bubble

Here's a technique for judging the number of rooms you'd like, their size and their relationships to one other.

Take a blank sheet of paper and draw a circle to represent the most important room in your new house. Typically, it's either a living-room or a kitchen or

kitchen/diner or possibly a mixture of all three. Label the bubble, then decide what's the next most important room and where it should be in relation to the first. Sketch it in, label it and connect it to the main room with a line. For the purposes of the exercise, include bubbles for outside features such as the garden, porch, conservatory, detached garage and so on. Once you've finished one floor, do the same for the next, and an attic floor and a basement, if that's your preference.

By the end you may find everything slots together quite easily. Or you may find that, after your partner and family members have made their contributions, you really need a house that's a great deal larger and more expensive than you'd ever thought of or could possibly afford.

Don't worry, and don't give up in despair. You're only in the development stage and every apparent dead end or source of frustration improves your ability to reach a successful conclusion.

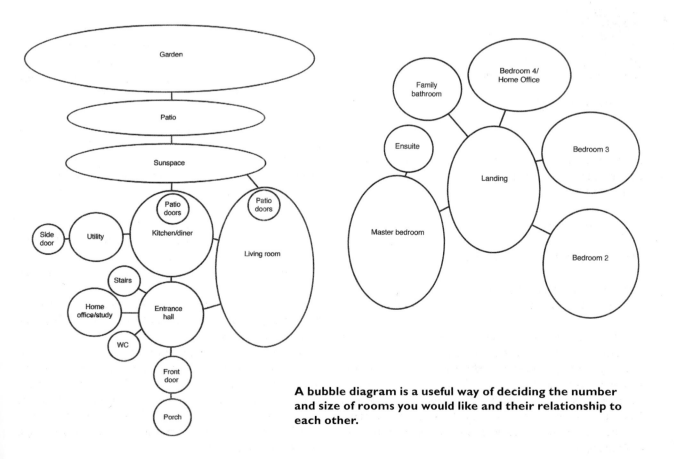

A bubble diagram is a useful way of deciding the number and size of rooms you would like and their relationship to each other.

The Design File

In practice, it can be a scrapbook, a ring-binder with clear plastic sleeves or a box of different coloured folders – whatever works for you. The idea is to collect together all the features that appeal to you and inspire you in terms of your new home.

They can range from photographs of attractive houses you find in books, magazines, newspapers or online, photographs you've taken yourself, brochures, postcards – whatever seems a good idea, an eye-catching finish, an interesting material.

To save yourself from being swamped, and improve your chances of finding any single item again, divide the file into sections. These might consist of rooms or different elements of the house: external walls, roof, floors, landscaping and so on.

It quickly becomes clear that the subject of design covers pretty much everything involved in your house project – from thoughts of interior colour schemes to central heating systems to types of brick. Which is as it should be.

The secret to success in a project as complex as a house build is preparation, and that demands research, as much as you can afford in terms of time and effort. Knowledge in house building is power, the power to achieve as close as possible to what you want. It provides you with a much wider choice of products, materials and approaches than is likely to be offered by the average jobbing builder. It enables you to talk the same language as the professionals and get the best out of them. But, most importantly, it gives you an understanding of the building process, what it involves, what's possible and what isn't, and the huge variety of choices you have at almost every level.

All that you learn can go into your design file – product details, tear sheets from self-build magazines and newspapers, notes of conversations with professionals over the phone, at builders' merchants or at self-build shows. If it seems useful, file it and do it straightaway. If you don't, chances are you'll never find it again, especially six months later when it's suddenly the perfect solution to an apparently intractable problem. Besides, making this a habit is excellent training for the build diary you will need to keep once your project is underway (see Chapter 14).

Time Travelling

Every self-build is a journey into the future, and particularly so in the case of a brick house. According to research at Leeds Metropolitan University, brick structures can expect a lifespan of 500 years or more. That's a good reason to take special care with your design, and not simply for the satisfaction of achieving a little piece of immortality.

Until the 2008 recession and collapse in property prices, home-owners would typically spend around 7 years in a house before cashing in on its rising value and taking another step up the property ladder. Today, unless you're very lucky, that ride is over, at least for a number of years. Together with a mortgage famine, this has major implications for the way we live. Among them is the virtual disappearance of the first-time buyer. As a result, more people are renting and more offspring are staying on in the family home, while family home-owners themselves are finding it harder to move on.

Within a few short years we have effectively moved from the idea of a house as a rung on a property ladder to something much more fixed, and much closer to the traditional concept of a home: a multi-generational residence, and with the growth in home-based businesses, it has become multi-functional, too.

It's even more important than ever, then, to design your new home to meet future as well as existing needs. The checklist that follows includes some suggestions that may make that easier.

DESIGN CHECKLIST

Main Entrance

- A ramp (if the approach isn't level) and as wide a door as you can afford. Easy access is not only a requirement of the building regulations (see Chapter 11), it makes it much easier to move large objects in and out, including shopping, buggies, bikes and furniture.
- A porch with glazing on three sides. This acts as shelter from the elements while you fumble for keys, an airlock limiting loss of heat from the house and somewhere secure to leave deliveries (as long as the glazing starts at waist height). It also means potential intruders are visible to passers by.
- A shelf on which to rest bags, shopping, etc. as you look for those keys.

Entrance Hall

- An alcove, corner or cupboard deep and wide enough to take a dozen coats without intruding into

One way of creating a dramatic entrance is to mix a full-height hall with a feature staircase, like this example made from Limeira limestone.
LimeStone Gallery

the main circulation space. (You need a clear space approximately 1.5m in diameter to take off a coat.)

- A waist-high shelf for post, keys, gloves or temporary storage.
- A boot and shoe store attached to the wall (leaving the floor uncluttered and easy to clean).
- A full-length mirror.
- A WC accessible to a wheelchair user. It could also be a bath/shower room (to allow for downstairs living in the future and/or separation of the house into two flats).
- For maximum impact consider an entrance hall open to the roof with a galleried landing.

Home Office

- Access through a door opening directly off the entrance hall. This makes it easier to keep home and business separate. It also eliminates the need for last-minute tidy ups when clients visit. If they don't, work in the most remote bedroom or build a garden office or workshop.
- A home office can double up as a bedroom for any

occupant who can't manage stairs – visitors, a parent or, eventually, yourself.

Stairs

- Staircases are the most theatrical part of a house – think of grand entrances in Hollywood movies – so treat them as a key feature of a hallway. Leave the balusters open or transparent to show off the staircase fully and the wall beyond.
- Don't try to minimize stairs or hide them away (which will only make moving furniture upstairs more difficult).
- Don't put them too close to the front door or they will dominate the hall and clutter up the entrance.
- To allow for separating the house into ground floor and first floor flats, site the staircase against an external wall (thus making it easier to create separate entrances).
- Make the staircase wide enough to incorporate a chair lift easily, or leave a corner of the entrance hall large enough to fit a small lift.
- Allow for handrails on both sides of the stairs.

Living Room

- An open-plan layout, perhaps incorporating the kitchen, suits small households, including those with young children, or those who entertain often.
- Households with teenagers, young adults and the elderly – who have different needs at different times – are likely to appreciate a more diverse living area, e.g.
  - a quiet room for reading, music listening or dozing;
  - an entertainment room for larger gatherings and with a television big enough for the whole household to watch together;
  - a playroom for young children.
- The kitchen should be separate so food preparation won't disturb other activities.
- Large open-plan layouts can also be divided up with temporary screens, folding or sliding doors or freestanding units such as bookshelves or display cabinets.
- For total flexibility, consider demountable partitions or much cheaper timber studwork and plasterboard walls, which can be removed and rebuilt as needs change.
- Plenty of unobtrusive storage throughout. A wall of handleless push open cupboards fades into the background but can hide a multitude of household clutter.

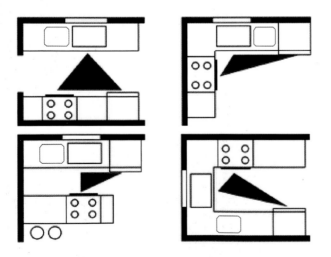

The kitchen work triangle links areas for food preparation, cooking and storage; they can be in several configurations, as long as each side is no longer than 2.7m or shorter than 1.2m.

Kitchen

- Use the work triangle rule: the main functions of a kitchen should take place between areas for preparation (a sink with at least 1m of work surface), cooking (oven/hob/microwave) and food storage (fridge/freezer). For optimum convenience, each side of this triangle should be no shorter than 1.2m and no longer than 2.7m.
- A double sink. (For wheelchair users make them wide and shallow, leaving space beneath to move up close.)
- A second sink – useful for larger households or for soaking or hand-washing clothes in a utility area. This could also form part of a second work triangle.
- Consider a pull-out spray tap for at least one basin. It makes filling and cleaning large pots and containers much easier.
- A large farmhouse kitchen-type table for additional food preparation and dining. Ensure at least 110cm of space between occupied seats and the worktop or wall to allow people to pass easily; approximately 75cm is needed to get up and sit down.
- An oven below worktop height with a side-opening door for easy access.
- An induction hob (for efficiency and safety since it only heats a suitable pot or pan placed on it).
- Shallow wall cupboards (to maximize access).
- Broad drawers, both shallow and deep, onfloor units (to maximize access and make all the contents immediately visible).
- Worktop concealers (shutters that either drop down under wall units or slide across open storage to hide worktop clutter instantly).
- A view of the garden (especially beyond food preparation areas).
- An external door or door to the entrance hall (for easy delivery of shopping and access to the garden for clothes drying).
- A pantry. This should be a walk-in area, ideally built out from a north-facing external wall and well ventilated to keep the internal temperature low. Incorporate a large stone or concrete slab to provide a cool surface on which to store perishables or wine. An insulated door to the rest of the kitchen will stem heat-loss.
- An extractor fan over the hob, either self-contained with an external outlet and, ideally, containing a heat-recovery unit or part of a whole-house ventilation system.

Broad yet shallow kitchen drawers both maximize access to the contents and make them immediately visible. Blum

Vertical drawers make good use of irregularly sized lengths at the end of work surfaces. PWS

Shuttered fronts to the wall units take up little space yet allow a cluttered worktop to be cleared quickly. Nolte

Utility

- Washing machine.
- Tumble dryer (gas-powered for economy; use an electric machine only if you have photovoltaic panels fitted and it's sunny. If the room is well ventilated, consider a Victorian-style clothes airer for maximum economy).
- A sink – preferably butler-style and capacious (for washing by hand and cleaning and filling of large items).
- Water-softener (to reduce limescale in hard-water areas).
- Central-heating boiler.
- Laundry storage – room for at least one dirty basket and one for freshly cleaned items.
- Ironing board – either retractable or simply space for a board to be erected and used.
- Storage for brooms, brushes, ironing board, vacuum cleaner, cleaning products, spare bulbs, fuses, vacuum cleaner bags, boots, grubby working clothes, etc.
- Pet feeding bowls, litter trays, dog leads.
- An external door (with cat flap, if needed).
- An extractor fan, either self-contained with external outlet and heat recovery or part of a whole-house ventilation system.
- A laundry chute. Specialist systems exist, but essentially they involve the following: cut a circular hole in the utility ceiling and the floor above, ensuring it opens into a built-in cupboard or wardrobe. Line the opening with a dustbin with the bottom cut out. Fix a bottomless laundry basket over the hole. Dirty laundry can now be dropped directly into a waiting basket in the utility.
- Services duct access point. Running the main services – rising main, soil vent pipe, gas pipe, plumbing and electric cabling – through a duct that can be accessed behind a panel in this room makes maintenance and repair much easier.

Landing

Landings, like entrance halls, are so-called 'circulation' areas, spaces that enable you to move from room to room. It can be tempting to skimp on them in order to maximize room space, but this can make a house feel cramped and even claustrophobic. It also creates difficulties in moving furniture and wheelchairs.

Add to their utility by:

- Lining one wall with shallow bookshelves.
- Making a large, open landing an upstairs sitting-room with a television and relaxation space or a home office (but only using one wall or it will take over the space).

Wet-room bathrooms are relatively easy to install in new builds and provide a flexibility for both the very young and the elderly. Aqualisa

- Filling it with light, ideally from two directions. If only one external wall is accessible, consider adding a roof light, lantern light or sunpipe (*see below*).

Bedrooms
- Master bedroom with ample storage and en suite bath/shower room/WC.
- Sound-proof adjoining bedrooms with back-to-back built-in wardrobes or en suites.
- Consider two or three large bedrooms that can be divided by demountable partitions or timber stud-work and plasterboard. This allows more flexible use than a larger number of smaller bedrooms.
- Make the bedroom above the kitchen a possible upstairs kitchen in the event of separating the house into two flats. (Ensure there is ample window space, preferably a good view, sufficient wiring to power kitchen appliances, blocked off pipe runs to hot and cold feeds and waste pipe.)
- Black-out blinds.

Bathroom
- Wet room/walk-in shower (with sufficient room for seating).
- Twin basins.
- Deep bath.
- An extractor fan, either self-contained with an external outlet and heat recovery or part of a whole-house ventilation system.
- Mirror with in-built light.
- Heated mirror (to eliminate condensation).

Loft Space
Good for quiet home office/music room/teenager's bedroom, or master bedroom with star-gazing roof light. If you don't need this space immediately, or can't yet afford to fit it out, specify attic trusses (*see* Chapter 19 for details). These allow you to make the space habitable at a later stage for minimal cost.

WCs
- One on each floor, accessible to a wheelchair user.
- Hand-basin.
- Book shelf.
- Magazine/newspaper rack.

Sunspace
- A glazed area covering all or part of a south-facing wall. It can be a conventional double-glazed

Making the loft space habitable can create a separated space within the home – for an office, music room or even self-contained accommodation for a teenager or lodger. Velux

A sunspace, covering all or part of a south-facing wall, yet separate from the main house, provides a recreational, drying and growing area, as well as trapping solar warmth in winter.

conservatory, a partially solid-walled orangery with extensive glazing, roof lights or lantern lights, or a large, single-glazed greenhouse. This:
- provides 'room-in-the-garden' sitting/dining space;
- warms the wall of the main structure throughout winter by the greenhouse effect, reducing fuel consumption;
- provides sheltered growing space for flowers and vegetables;
- makes a drying area in winter or when it's raining;
- provides shelter for pets (especially when they come in wet or messy from outside).
- To gain maximum heating benefit in winter, ensure there is an insulated barrier between the sunspace and the main house (e.g. double-glazed patio doors/ French windows), which can be closed when there is no sun.
- For an orangery, consider folding, sliding doors onto a patio/decking.

Basement
- Central heating biomass boiler (which will require storage for wood pellets or other solid fuel and an access to the outside for deliveries, e.g. a traditional delivery chute).
- Hot-water cylinder.
- Rainwater harvesting tank (see Chapter 16).
- Grey water collection tank (see Chapter 16).
- General storage.
- Workshop.

- Basements can, of course, function as any other room, including habitable accommodation, though in that case care should be taken to provide daylight and adequate ventilation.
- Installing a basement in a new build is relatively economical, especially if deep foundations are required. They can maximize the use of a restricted plot and swallow much of the functional clutter of a home.

The garage dilemma: incorporating a car-sized integral garage into a human-sized house demands design ingenuity. This solution uses a section of roof as a unifying feature. Hanson

If deep foundations are necessary, installing a basement becomes relatively economical; prefabricated systems like this one make the job quicker and easier. Basement Information Centre

A barn-style design conceals a double garage as a traditional feature. Wienerberger

A detached garage, which mirrors the design and materials of the main house, is often the most successful, but most expensive, solution. Wienerberger

Garage

- An integral garage is cheapest to build but difficult to accommodate architecturally. (A matter of scale: doors and windows are human-sized, garage doors vehicle-sized. Its impact can be reduced either by setting the garage towards the back of the house or at right angles to the main façade, accessed by a driveway down the side of the house.)
- An integral garage needs a fire door to give access to the rest of the house. An intervening lobby provides additional protection against fire and smells and can double as a utility room.
- Detached garages are more expensive to build but easier to make architecturally pleasing by mirroring the style and proportions of the house.
- A large, detached garage can incorporate a workshop, home office or even extra accommodation.

OTHER THINGS TO CONSIDER

Internal Walls

Normally, in a traditional brick and block house, only one internal wall has to be masonry to support upper floor joists and avoid making them too deep to span large distances. In most commercial builds, other walls are usually made from timber studwork covered in plasterboard, for speed of construction and economy.

Plasterboard, however, provides poor sound insulation, while attaching heavy items means either using special fixings or extra timber supports between the

How to Benefit from the Sun

Orientate your house on a north–south axis and maximize the glazing on the sunnier, south-facing side. Site the rooms used mostly in daylight – kitchen, living room, play room, home office – on that side.

Minimize the glazing on the cooler, north-facing side and place rooms there that are used only for short periods or mostly at night – bedrooms, bathrooms, WCs, utility, store rooms, etc.

If only an east–west orientation is possible, place the rooms benefitting from morning daylight – master bedroom, kitchen, bathroom – on the east-facing side. Place the living room/conservatory on the west-facing side to enjoy sunsets and long, summer evenings.

Avoid glare in rooms with large amounts of glazing in one wall by fitting a window or windows in a second wall. Two or

Overhead glazing can be a useful and economical way to light areas that are without windows or too distant from direct sunlight. Velux

more contrasting light sources soften sharp shadows and create an attractive interplay throughout the day. They will also make the room seem larger and airier.

Consider overhead glazing – roof lights in sloping ceilings, lantern lights or toughened glass roof panels in flat roofs and sunpipes for virtually anywhere without sunlight. (A sunpipe is a metal tube with a highly reflective inner surface. One end is attached to a transparent collector attached to a roof or a south-facing side wall. The other end, which can be several metres away, is covered by a shallow, translucent dome set into a ceiling. On a bright day a 30cm-diameter tube can produce as much light as six 100W light bulbs.)

Overhead glazing is useful for rooms with little or no natural light and will boost light levels in areas such as kitchens, dining rooms or work rooms, where good illumination is important. Natural light from above not only lasts longer, but provides a different quality of illumination.

Avoid overheating in summer by building deep eaves or fitting a brise soleil over south-facing glazing. (This consists of parallel lines of angled blades projecting from the eaves; they admit sunlight at low angles but cut it off when the sun is highest and hottest.) Fit blinds, particular to roof lights and other forms of overhead glazing. These can be electrically powered and operated remotely or programmed to close or open automatically as temperatures change.

Fit the right sort of glazing. Double-glazing with low-emissivity (low-E) glass is virtually standard in new homes. It allows the sun's warmth to enter the house but reflects back warmth produced inside. This is fine when it's cold outside, but can lead to overheating in summer. Avoid this by fitting solar control glass, which lets in the sunlight but reflects back the sun's heat. (You can combine low-E and solar control to get the best of both seasons.)

Consider an atrium. This is a central, open area running vertically through a building from the lowest floor to the roof, which has glazing panels or a lantern light set into it. Light can then travel the depth of a house, lighting areas such as landings and staircases, which might not otherwise receive direct sunlight. It's particularly useful for tall, narrow houses – such as infills in terraces.

Consider a courtyard design. Here, the house encloses an internal space open to the sky, allowing light to enter through windows and doors facing onto it. The enclosing wings of the house can be on all four sides, three or just two, with walls providing the missing sides.

The design needs a spacious plot, but it can a useful way of keeping different parts of a house separate but linked, such as bedrooms, a teenage or granny annexe, or a home office. An enclosed courtyard also allows you to enjoy the outside longer into colder periods of the year. It can create a micro-climate equivalent to living up to 300km further south.

uprights, known as 'noggins' ('dwangs' in Scotland). Fitting enough noggins for every likely future use demands a degree of prescience denied to most of us.

Masonry walls are inherently more sound-proof and allow the heaviest items to be attached easily at any point. Their disadvantage is that they are not as demountable as studwork.

Think carefully, then, about which rooms or areas need to be all-masonry. A solid-wall kitchen, for example, gives you maximum flexibility in terms of placing or rearranging units. The sound-proofing qualities of masonry are ideal for a music room, an office, a cinema room or a granny annexe.

Ceilings

Be aware of the effect of ceiling height. A high ceiling creates a sense of space and airiness, particularly in a small room. One of the reasons why many commercially built homes are criticized for feeling box-like is that the ceiling heights are reduced as an economy measure. Being aware of a ceiling less than a couple of feet above your head gives a feeling of claustrophobia and can ruin the sense of space in a large room or open-plan area.

Lighting and Glazing

Sunlight is not only free, it's good for your health (a prime source of vitamin D), not to mention your sense of well-being. It also brings heat into the home, a process known as solar gain. Maximizing the use of sunlight, then, not only makes your home a brighter, healthier place, it helps to reduce your fuel bills.

The Integrated Home

Here, all the main functions of a home – heating, lighting, sound, vision and security – are linked electronically. This enables you to control them all from a single point, or points, such as a touchpad, computer or smartphone.

Home-automation systems are often sold in terms of personal luxury. Lighting, for example, can be programmed for various moods; centrally sourced TV,

A dedicated media room may be the most ostentatious aspect of home automation, but a wired network can also provide central, and remote, control of energy use, security and home monitoring of the elderly and infirm. Konextions

radio, music and video games can be enjoyed throughout the house. Increased security, too, is stressed. Locks, alarm systems and CCTV can be operated and monitored remotely.

In practice, systems of this kind are just as important in providing local networks, allowing several computers to share a common internet connection, printer and back-up hard drive: all useful for a home-based business.

Increasingly, however, home integration is being used for energy management, monitoring and controlling its use and automatically swapping energy sources to the most cost-effective as internal and external conditions change.

Other promising developments include monitoring the health and safety of the elderly and infirm, hugely increasing their ability to remain independent.

Much of this can be achieved wirelessly but, in general, radio waves can't match the speed and reliability of a wired network, particularly in a brick and block home, where the building fabric can often block signals.

Creating a wired network means running cabling from each connection point to a central hub. This is known as star wiring. A minimum of four cables is recommended for each point – for TV, audio, ethernet and telephone – though they can be combined in a single, multiple cable.

The result is an awful lot of cabling, not to mention allowing space for the central hub, built-in speakers and motors and control units for operating alarm systems, locks and blinds.

Your designer should discuss a network of this kind with a specialist at the design stage. You can find one and a lot of useful advice at the website of the Custom Electronic Design and Installation Association (CEDIA). (See Contacts.)

The Green Home

New homes are getting greener all the time, thanks to updates in the building regulations and the Code for Sustainable Homes (see Chapter 11 for details). But self-builders, for all sorts of reasons, often choose to go further. They include:

Increased Energy Efficiency
For a relatively small increase in construction costs, you can build a house that's so well insulated it requires only minimal space heating (a particular boon to the retired

Used sensibly, solar heating panels can supply a household's total domestic hot water needs during the sunniest months, and provide supplementary warmth throughout the rest of the year.

Electricity produced by photovoltaic roof panels not only feeds the domestic supply but attracts government subsidy. Sandtoft

on fixed incomes). You will, however, need to install adequate ventilation, either passive or mechanical (see Chapter 21 for details).

Energy costs can be further reduced by fitting renewable energy systems, such as photovoltaic panels and wind or water turbines. Government grants and subsidies are available for many of these systems (see Chapter 23 for details). Potentially, they can not only produce sufficient power to run the home, but also an operating profit through the sale of surplus energy.

Zero-Carbon Living and Sustainability

The government aims to make all new homes 'carbon neutral' by 2016. This means that all the energy needed to heat and light them does not result in the production of any additional carbon dioxide, thus helping to limit the effects of climate change.

It also requires the use of construction materials that are renewable, such as timber or sheep's wool (for insulation), or recyclable, such as brick or steel, which further reduces the burden on the planet's resources.

Water Security

Collecting rainwater and using it in washing machines and for toilet flushing makes good sense as water resources dwindle and prices rise. It also provides a secure supply for garden irrigation. The same goes for 'grey water' – water from washing and bathing – which can be filtered, stored and reused, though not for personal consumption.

Health

Modern homes are full of synthetic substances and concentrations of radiation unknown to our ancestors and their long-term effects have yet to be fully gauged. One way of minimizing internal pollution is to install a whole-house ventilation system. This extracts warm, moist air through a system of ducts and replaces it with fresh, filtered air from outside. Air filters can also be incorporated for asthma and hay fever sufferers (see below for details).

Systems like this form part of a well-established building standard, developed in Germany, and known as Passivhaus. It promises energy savings of 80 per cent on existing homes and high levels of comfort and internal air quality. So far only a handful of homes in the UK have been built in this way. You can learn about Passivhaus at the Passivhaus Trust (see Contacts).

There is also a home-grown low-energy building standard known as Carbon Lite. It was developed by the AECB, The Sustainable Building Association (formerly the Association of Environmentally Conscious

Builders), whose website contains a register of designers, builders and suppliers experienced in green and sustainable building.

CONSTRAINTS ON DESIGN

At the beginning of this process you were encouraged to let your imagination run wild, but there comes a point when that's no longer feasible. With a steeply sloping plot, for example, it's reached very soon. On a spacious, level greenfield site it may take much longer. But all designs eventually face three major constraints:

1. The Plot Itself

The physical constraints may simply be space, or the lack of it, the direction of the best views, the proximity of neighbours, trees that can't be removed because of preservation orders and so on, but your design will need to take account of them.

2. Planning

The local planning department will have policies and opinions concerning the size, position and specific design of your house.

3. Building Regulations

These are only concerned with the constructional details of a building, which can normally be accommodated by almost any design. But three regulations have a more direct effect on design issues:

Part M

This ensures that all new homes are accessible to all, including the disabled. It affects such things as the size of doors, the external approach to the main entrance and the use of space inside the house.

Part L

This is concerned with the conservation of fuel and energy. It imposes minimum levels of insulation and air-tightness to avoid warmth leaking to the outside.

How does this affect design?

Most of the requirements will be invisible, with the possible exception of double-glazing, which most of us would fit anyway. But increased insulation in the walls creates special problems for conventional brick and block cavity wall construction. Until fairly recently the typical 100mm width of the cavity could easily accommodate slabs, or 'batts', of mineral wool or fibre glass, the cheapest and most common form of insulation. But with the latest requirements, and those planned for the future, even filling the cavity with mineral wool is no longer enough.

The obvious solution is to widen the cavity. When this was first considered, there was concern among house-builders that it might threaten the wall's stability. Since then a number of houses have been built with cavities up to 300mm wide, helping to allay those fears. But adding 200mm to the dimensions of a house either requires a larger footprint or a smaller interior, both of which are likely to be significant on a tight site. And there's an additional concern that if moisture penetrates a filled cavity it will saturate conventional insulation and render it useless.

The most common answer is to stick with the 100mm cavity but only partially fill it with rigid boards of poly-urethane foam insulation. These are twice as efficient as mineral wool, though around three times the price, but enough of a cavity is left for penetrating moisture to seep or evaporate away harmlessly.

Problem solved? Not quite.

Foam insulation only brings us back to where we started, so the insulation needs to be further boosted. One way is to build the inner leaf with lightweight aircrete blocks. These contain thousands of tiny, air-filled holes, which provide better insulation than standard blocks.

Another solution is to line the walls internally with another layer of foam insulation. This is available with plasterboard attached to provide a ready-made surface for decoration or skim plastering. Again, it reduces the internal space, though only marginally. But it also means that the walls don't have quite the solidity of conventionally plastered blockwork, or the thermal mass.

Building in large amounts of insulation, however, is only useful if there are no gaps left for heat to escape. Consequently, new houses must also achieve minimum levels of air-tightness, which has implications for ventilation, dealt with, in England and Wales, by Part F of the building regulations.

Part F

Well-insulated houses with few draughts can easily get stuffy and produce condensation and mould, as well as a build-up of toxic chemicals exuded by many modern materials. To deal with this, Part F, requires two forms of ventilation: 'background', which provides a minimum number of air changes per hour, and 'purge', which

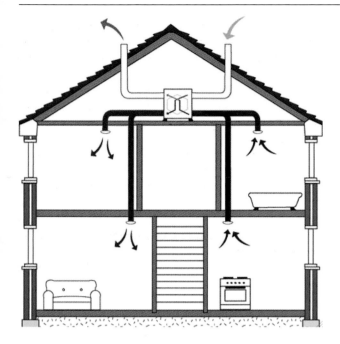

A mechanical whole-house ventilation system extracts warm, moist air from kitchens and bathrooms and delivers constant fresh into living areas via low-noise electric fans in an attic unit.

delivers a temporary boost to expel excessive moisture or nasty smells.

Typically, background ventilation has been provided by airbricks in external walls and 'trickle vents', small, closable slots in the frames of windows. Purge ventilation has been handled simply by opening windows and doors, and, in hot, moist areas, such as kitchens, bathrooms and toilets, by the use of extractor fans, vented to the outside.

When new houses were draughtier, this was adequate, but making it work under the current requirements will need some careful calculations by your designer regarding the size and positions of windows, and the size of trickle vents.

A more efficient answer is to build in a whole-house ventilation system, which provides constant fresh air throughout. There are two main methods, and both involve ducting, which extracts air from warm, wet areas, and expels it outside

In 'passive stack' ventilation the ducts exit at the ridge of the roof. They need to be as vertical as possible to allow the warm air to rise naturally. They also take advantage of the air flow over the house, which

creates a suction effect, drawing air up and out. Fresh air is then drawn into the house through wall vents and trickle vents in windows.

Some systems include flaps that open and close the ducts automatically as the humidity changes. The method is unpowered, but when there's no breeze, its effectiveness falls.

'Mechanical whole-house' ventilation gets round this by using low-speed, low-noise electric fans housed in a unit in the attic. They enable the extraction of the air to be continuous. They also draw in fresh air from the eaves and distribute it to the living areas through a second set of ducting.

Both systems, however, still lose heat via the extracted air. Adding a heat-recovery element to the mechanical system allows the outgoing air to warm the incoming, saving, it's claimed, over 70 per cent of the heat that would otherwise be lost. Systems of this kind are integral to the low-energy Passivhaus construction method (*see above*).

To be unobtrusive and installed in the most effective way, whole-house ventilation needs to be planned into your design from the earliest stages.

See Chapter 11 for fuller details of the building regulations.

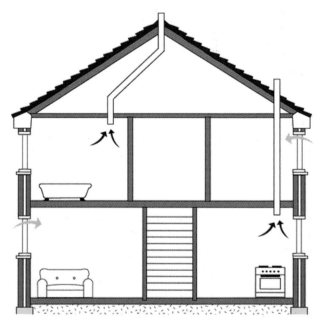

Passive whole-house ventilation depends on the natural tendency of warm air to rise through ducts in kitchens and bathrooms, a process aided by the suction effect of air moving over the roof.

CHAPTER 8

Designing with Brick

Bricks only represent around 4 per cent of your build cost – a relatively minor sum – but, in terms of the appearance of your new home, they can account for up to 70 per cent. It pays, then, in all sorts of ways, to think about your choice and use of brick as early as possible.

As the ultimate form of modular building, bricks may come in a standard size – 215mm × 102.5mm × 65mm – but their appearance can vary dramatically. Colour, texture, the way they are bonded together, the shape and colour of mortar and the patterns created by mixing different types of brick will all contribute to the final effect.

COLOUR

Bricks vary in colour from the palest grey through yellow and red to dark blue. They can also be multi-coloured or mottled, known as 'brindled'. The colours reflect the composition of the clays used to make them, the various chemical compounds that have been added to them and the way they are baked or 'fired'.

Iron oxide is the major colouring agent. The more a brick contains, the redder it will be, until the colour is so deep it becomes blue. If limestone or chalk is present, or is added, a buff colour is produced. Yellow shows the presence of magnesium oxide.

Brickspeak

Knowing, and using, the right technical terms in any aspect of building not only makes communication with professionals easier, it adds to your credibility – and sows the suspicion that you might know a lot more than you're admitting; always a good position to be in if you're negotiating with a contractor or tradesman. Don't overdo it, though. If you end up sounding like an idiot, all the effort is wasted.

Here are some basic bricklayer's terms:

Face – the side of a brick that's designed to be on show, i.e. the side that displays the intended colour and texture.

Stretcher – the long 'face' or side. Normally, it's the size of two faces placed together.

Header – the short 'face' or end.

Arris – any edge of a brick where two faces meet. Depending on the method of production, it can be square, rounded, lipped or distressed.

Bedding faces – the sides that are laid on or receive mortar, i.e. the top or bottom face.

Frog – a V-shaped indentation in a bedding face. Bricks are laid either 'frog up', so that the mortar fills the indentation – this is when maximum strength is required – or 'frog down'; this needs less mortar as it only covers the edges of the frog. Some bricks have single frogs, some have a frog in both bedding faces, others none at all.

Course – a single row of bricks.

Stretcher course – a row with the stretcher, or long face, showing. Each brick in it is known as a 'stretcher'.

Header course – a row showing the header or end face. Each brick in it is known as a 'header'.

Soldier – a brick laid vertically with the stretcher face showing.

Sailor – a brick laid vertically with a bedding face showing.

Bat – a brick cut across its width. It can be a 'half-', 'quarter-' or 'three-quarter-bat', depending on its length.

Closer – a brick specially cut to complete a bond at the end of a wall.

Queen closer – a brick cut along its length.

Perpend – the vertical mortar joint between bricks. Perpends should be aligned in a brick wall.

Creased brick. Ibstock

The sand used to mould the brick can also affect its colour, as can the temperature at which it's fired; the cooler the firing, the lighter the colour, and vice versa.

Brick colours are resonant not just because of their intrinsic appeal, they also provide a cultural and historical link to the areas where they were first produced. So-called 'white' bricks, for example, are made from 'gault' clay used widely in the south-east of England, outside of London. Blue bricks are made from clay found in and around the coal seams of Staffordshire and the West Midlands. London yellow stock bricks contain characteristic black specks, produced by ash from the coke used to fire them.

Modern brick-makers can produce all the traditional colours and distribute their products throughout the UK. In the late Middle Ages, when brick was first revived as a building material after the departure of the Romans, transport was difficult and costly. As a result, bricks were usually made on site, using local clays. This gave a distinctive character to the buildings, tying them to the surrounding landscape, both natural and man-made.

Dragfaced brick. Ibstock

Selecting a brick that reflects local traditions, then, can help to root your home more securely in its environment. It may also be a requirement of your planning consent.

TEXTURE

The texture of a brick's face can provide as much character as its colour. A smooth finish gives an

Rumbled brick. Ibstock

Rusticated brick. Ibstock

Sanded brick. Ibstock

Smooth brick. Ibstock

impression of neatness and control, and suits a clean, modern design. A textured finish suggests a traditional, hand-made brick, common to vernacular design.

Textures can range from small indentations (known as 'dragfaced') to printed irregularities, to a rippled or wave effect ('rumbled'). These can also be achieved by tumbling machine-made bricks in a drum to give them a distressed appearance.

Genuine hand-made bricks, characterized by a creased texture and a slightly irregular shape, achieve an instant traditional look, but the labour-intensive process makes them the most expensive.

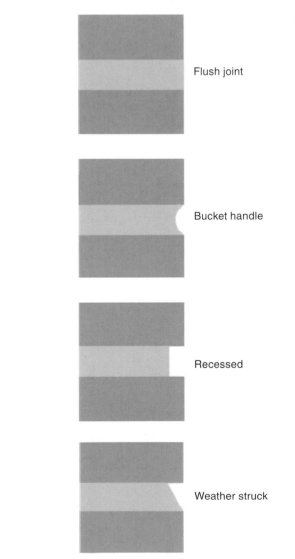

Flush joint

Bucket handle

Recessed

Weather struck

Types of mortar joint.

MORTAR

The glue that holds bricks together may seem of minor importance, until you realize that mortar constitutes up to 17 per cent of a brick wall. It can have a major effect on the appearance of brickwork.

Coloured mortars are available to tone in with, or set off, the brickwork. The way in which the mortar is applied – known as the jointing – can be equally effective in creating a look.

A 'flush' joint, where the mortar lies in the same plane as the brickwork, produces a smooth, seamless appearance.

In a 'recessed' joint, the mortar is applied then raked back to depth of around 5mm. This emphasizes the shape of each individual brick, creating a shadow effect. Because water can collect in the recess, it's not recommended for exposed locations.

More weather-resistant is the 'bucket handle' joint, which creates a shallower, semi-circular recess. It also helps to emphasize the texture of the brickwork.

The best weather protection is provided, appropriately enough, by the 'weather struck' joint. This is recessed at the top and slopes outward to meet the lower edge. As water enters the recess, it hits the angled mortar and is shed downwards. Used with well-formed regular bricks, it gives a neat, well-ordered appearance.

BONDING

The way bricks are arranged is known as a 'bond'. It's designed to maximize the structural strength of the brickwork and create a uniform appearance.

In most modern, brick-built homes, which have a cavity wall, a 'stretcher bond' is used for the external brickwork. All the bricks show the long or stretcher side, except at the ends of rows, where a header is typically used to make up the length of the final brick.

This is the simplest of all bonds, creating a wall just half a brick thick. It follows the basic rule of all brickwork: no brick should be laid directly on top of another one, so all the vertical joints are staggered. In the stretcher, the brick above is positioned halfway along the one below. This makes it easy to spot a cavity wall in an existing house.

Other bonds include:

- **Flemish** – this was the most popular bond when houses were built with solid walls. Each course consists of alternate headers and stretchers, with the next course laid so that the headers sit in the middle of the stretchers below. The result is a wall as deep as a brick's length. Its decorative effect depends on perfectly aligned vertical joints.
- **English** – this consists of alternative courses of stretchers and headers. Like the Flemish bond, it produces a brick-deep wall but much stronger,

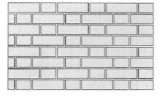

Stretcher bond

Flemish bond

English bond

Types of bond.

English garden wall bond

Herringbone bond

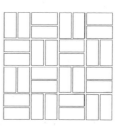

Basket weave bond

making it ideal for load-bearing situations, such as foundations, manholes or retaining walls.

- **English garden wall** – either three or five rows of stretchers alternate with a row of headers. It's not as strong as standard English bond, but more economical because so many stretchers are used.
- **Herringbone** – a course consists of a stretcher laid next to soldier (an upright brick with its slim edge showing) and so on. This creates the appearance of a stairway rising at 45 degrees. The pattern can also be laid on its side to give a look of rising and descending zigzags. This is a purely decorative bond, only practical as a panel set into supportive material. The Tudors used it widely as an infill in timber frame buildings. It's also popular for patios and pathways.
- **Basket weave** – another purely decorative bond, where a course is made from two, or three stretchers laid next to two or three soldiers, and so on.

PATTERNING

One of the great advantages of brick is that an almost infinite variety of decorative patterns can be created, often very easily and cheaply.

One of the simplest, and most effective, is known as 'banding'. Here, a single course – sometimes called a 'string' course – cuts across an area of brickwork and makes a decorative contrast, either with a different colour of brick, a different shape or a different kind of bonding. It can also project or be recessed from the main brickwork.

It's useful for adding interest to a large area of uniform brickwork, reducing its scale or simply marking the division between ground and upper storeys. The most familiar form of banding is probably the soldier course, a row of bricks laid on end above or below a window.

Here, 'banding' – horizontal lines of brick in a contrasting colour – adds decorative interest to an otherwise uniform façade and draws the different elements together. Wienerberger

Band courses can also be multiple and needn't be confined to a single shape, bond or colour. 'Polychromatic' brickwork, a kaleidoscopic blend of different colours, often emphasized by different coloured mortars, was hugely popular with the Victorians.

Other variations include:

- **Diaper work** – another Victorian favourite. Here, a pattern is picked out from uniform brickwork with different coloured, recessed or projecting bricks. It first became popular with the Tudors, who favoured diamond and square patterns. The Victorians went on to produce complex, often hugely flamboyant designs.
- **Dentil course** – it sounds tooth-like, because that's how it looks. A line of banding is produced by a row of bricks laid with alternate headers projecting. Traditionally it was used at the eaves or the verges to help support the roof timbers. A variation is 'dog toothing', where the bricks are laid at 45 degrees to the main brickwork, either projecting or recessed.
- **Quoins** – these are the outer corners of a wall and can be picked out in contrasting brickwork, typically with alternating full-length and half bricks.
- **Plinths** – these are projecting courses at the base of a wall, originally designed to increase its strength. The top course is formed with specially shaped bricks.
- **Corbels** – the opposite of a plinth, usually projecting outward at the top of a wall. Dentils are a form of corbel. Corbelling can also be used beneath window openings to provide a 'corbelled' sill.
- **Arches** – these can both create and frame openings for doors and windows, adding to the visual impact of both. The simplest versions are made from soldier courses, laid flat but with the ends cut at angles so they slope towards the centre (an effect known as 'skewback'). Arches can also be semi-circular, form a segment of a circle or complete a full circle (known as a 'bull's-eye'). The wedge-shaped bricks, which form the centre pieces of arches, are called 'voussoirs'.

Creating patterned brickwork on site requires skilful and experienced bricklayers, but many of these patterns can be supplied by brick manufacturers, either ready-made or fashioned to order.

This design features elaborate corbels below the first floor windows as well as eye-catching diaper work and banding for the storey above – but all using the same brick. Ibstock

Here, the eaves' decoration shows copious use of 'dog toothing', where projecting bricks are laid at 45 degrees to the main brickwork. Ibstock

Quoins embellish the outer corners of a building with contrasting brickwork. Hanson

A full circle arch, known as a 'bull's eye'. Hanson

A common use for corbelling in a gable end, but it's also used more subtly at the base of the chimney stack. Hanson

HOW ARE BRICKS MADE?

Most of the clay used in brick-making is extracted, or 'won', from quarries, ground into fine particles and mixed with water and other materials to produce a mix that can be easily shaped.

The bricks are formed either by extrusion or moulding. In extrusion the clay is squeezed through a die, from which it emerges in a continuous brick-shaped column. Different textures can be given to the surface before the column is cut by wire into single bricks.

Moulding is the traditional method of brick-making. A softer clay is pushed into a brick-shaped mould, where a dusting of sand, oil or water prevents it sticking. Then it's simply turned out. The process is fully mechanized now, but hand-made bricks are still produced and valued for their individual quality.

The bricks are then dried to remove as much moisture as possible. This typically takes place over one to three days at a temperature of between 80 and 120°C. The atmosphere needs to be kept humid to prevent the bricks cracking.

The dried bricks are now fired in a kiln – usually between 900 and 1,200°C – for between 2 and 4 days. Bricks are either loaded in one of a series of

Why Has Brick Become so Popular in the UK?

Brick was introduced into Britain by the Romans. After they left, it was largely abandoned until the late Middle Ages when refugees from the Low Countries helped to re-establish it, which is the reason why one of the most common bonds is called 'Flemish'.

Initially, the material was used mainly for fireplaces and chimneys. Buildings made entirely from brick were confined to the wealthy, notably Cardinal Wolsey who used it for Hampton Court Palace. But the 1666 Great Fire of London provided a boost. In its aftermath all new buildings in the capital had to be built of masonry.

In the seventeenth and eighteenth centuries, brick was championed by the rising middle class. They were attracted by its looks, durability and convenience. Clay was abundant in central and southern England. In London, for example, many Georgian townhouses were built with bricks made on site from the clay excavated for the foundations – a remarkable economy.

The industrial revolution created a huge market for brick, including the construction of the canals and railways, which for the first time allowed brick to be transported in large quantities throughout the country. Mechanized brick-making massively increased production.

Even so, it's likely that, largely for reasons of economy, Britain would eventually have adopted the European practice of building with hollow, clay blocks, which are then rendered. The fact that it didn't is down to the discovery of a new form of shale clay at the Huntingdonshire village of Fletton in the 1880s. Lower Oxford clay, as it is known, runs several feet down from Yorkshire to Dorset.

It has two exceptional qualities. First, it contains around 10 per cent of combustible material. As a result, when it's fired, it burns, more than halving the fuel costs. Second, its water content is so low it doesn't need to be dried after the bricks are formed; they can be fired immediately.

Cheaply produced Flettons were first used widely in London, and so became known as 'London' bricks. They had little aesthetic appeal, but their price meant they quickly dominated the British market. When a more attractive version, known as the Rustic, was produced in the 1920s, the Fletton's dominance was assured, and brick became firmly established as Britain's most popular and ubiquitous building material.

Today, Flettons are routinely fired with moulded facings on three sides, creating a huge range of colours and textures. The bedding face, with the frog bearing the distinctive Fletton stamping, remains untouched. Modern Flettons are made exclusively by Hanson Brick.

ABOVE: Georgian townhouses, like this example from London, were often built with bricks fired on-site from clay dug from the foundations.

BELOW: Diamond diaper patterns in brickwork first became popular with the Tudors, as shown here at Hampton Court, one of Britain's first major brick buildings.

Freshly machine-moulded bricks, still bearing the sand used to ease them out of the moulds.

After forming, bricks are dried for between 1 and 3 days before firing in a kiln.

chambers, which are heated in sequence, or they are carried on a slow-moving trolley through a single continuous kiln.

The traditional method of firing is with a clamp. It consists of up to 100,000 dried bricks, stacked around forty high in the open air. Small spaces are left between each brick, as well as fire holes around the base of the clamp, where the fuel is inserted. The clamp is then completely enclosed in pre-fired bricks, leaving vents at the top.

Once the fuel is ignited, the clamp will burn for around three weeks, slowly baking the dried bricks. The fire holes are designed to face the prevailing wind, providing a draught for the fire.

Given the vagaries of British weather, however, the firing is generally haphazard. Typically around 20 per cent of bricks end up either under- or over-fired and have to be discarded. But it's the individual character of the bricks produced in this way that make them highly valued.

TYPES OF BRICK

As we've seen above, bricks can be classified in all sorts of ways, but there are basic types and it's important to be aware of the distinctions to make full use of them.

All bricks, for example, are either solid, frogged (with a V-shaped indentation in one or both bedding faces), perforated or cored (where holes perform the same keying function as the frog).

Bricks can also be distinguished by function. 'Facing' bricks are the best quality, designed to be used externally to enhance the appearance of your home – the ones we are primarily concerned with when it comes to design. They come in four main varieties:

- **Wirecut** – usually the most economical because it's produced by the extrusion process, the most automated form of brick-making. Around 40 per cent of all bricks are made this way.
- **Stock** – a moulded brick, still produced by an automated process known as 'soft mud moulding', which uses more water in the mix than in extrusion. This causes the bricks to shrink more during manufacture. Sand is also used to ease the brick out of the mould, giving it a characteristic sanded surface and a wide variety of colours. The result is a softer, more irregular shape.
- **Water-struck** – this is also produced by soft mud

Wirecut bricks, shown here in a perforated form, are the most common, and most economical. Ibstock

Stocks are produced from a sanded mould, giving them a softer, more irregular shape. Ibstock

Waterstruck bricks are also moulded, but water is used to ease the brick free, giving it a smoother appearance. Ibstock

Individually produced hand-made bricks, characterized by the 'smile' on the stretcher face where the brick has sagged in the mould, are the most expensive. Ibstock

moulding but water, instead of sand, is used to free the brick from the mould. As a result the surface texture is smoother with a washed appearance.

- **Hand-made** – produced one at a time by craftsmen filling individual moulds, this is the most individual, and most expensive brick. A common characteristic is a creasing on the stretcher face known as a 'smile' where the clay has sagged slightly in the mould.

There are also other types of bricks:

- 'Common' bricks, for example, are a lower quality with a variable colour and appearance. They are used for concealed brickwork, such as internal plastered walls.
- 'Engineering' bricks are the strongest and most hard-wearing. Highly resistant to moisture and frost, they are used for foundations, damp-proof courses, drains and retaining walls.
- 'Specials' are essentially any non-rectangular brick, typically used to create or finish off decorative brickwork. They include 'bullnoses' (round edges), 'cants' and 'squints' (forms of angled edges), 'arch' bricks and virtually any other shape you can think of (which can usually be made to order). They even include bricks whose stretcher face looks like a traditional hanging tile.
- Reclaimed bricks are typically used to match existing brickwork in renovations or conversions of non-domestic buildings. They are more likely to be in older, Imperial measure and slightly larger than modern metric bricks – 230mm × 110mm × 70–80mm (9in × 4½in × 3in).

Not all bricks need to meet the same conditions, so it's important to know that your choice will be suitable. Two factors in particular need to be borne in mind.

The first is frost. If the moisture within a brick freezes, it will expand, causing the surface to flake off and crumble or 'spall'. Bricks are categorized by their resistance to frost:

- The most resistant are F2-category. They will not spall, even if they are fully saturated in freezing temperatures, making them ideal for exposed locations.
- F1-category bricks provide moderate frost resistance. They're suitable for most locations where they will not be subject to heavy weathering.
- F0-category bricks are for internal use only.

Factor number two is the soluble salt content. Bricks are a blend of several compounds, including soluble salts. If brickwork becomes saturated, the salts can react with cement mortar, causing it to crack or crumble. Again, there are categories:

- S0 bricks can only be used in completely dry locations.
- S1 bricks in moderate conditions.
- S2 is necessary when bricks are subject to constant moisture, such as foundations or retaining walls.

ALL ABOUT BLOCKS

Concrete blocks are the hidden face of construction, the work-a-day items that provide the structural support and much of the thermal and acoustic insulation for our homes. There are three basic types:

- Dense, concrete blocks are the strongest, heaviest and cheapest. They are used most often below ground. Their insulating qualities are poor, but their density gives them a high thermal mass.
- Lightweight, aggregate blocks are around half the weight and provide better insulation. They are most commonly used for the inner leaf of cavity walls and for internal walls, where they are particularly good for plastering. They're also used widely in 'beam and block' floors (see Chapter 16).
- Aerated or aircrete blocks are designed for thermal efficiency. Filled with tiny air bubbles, they're light and can be cut with a saw or rasped into shape.

Blocks can also be built with a special quick-drying adhesive, which provides a much slimmer joint than conventional mortar – just 3mm compared to the usual 10mm. Known as 'thin joint masonry', this technique enables laying to proceed up to three times faster than with conventional blocks, especially when large-format blocks, twice the normal size, are used. Because the adhesive isn't squeezed out by the load of blockwork above, whole storeys can be constructed at a time. The slimmer joints also provide improved thermal and acoustic efficiency.

The honeycomb structure of aircrete means that special fixings are sometimes needed to hang heavy items. It's also subject to shrinkage, which can lead to cracking if it's wet plastered. Nevertheless, the main manufacturers supply forms of aircrete to meet all uses, from high-strength foundation blocks to paint grade, smooth enough for decoration.

The standard size of a concrete block is 440mm long × 215mm wide × 100mm deep. But depths are available from 75mm (for internal walls) to 355mm (for foundation blocks that span the width of a cavity wall), as well as brick-sized coursing units for infilling around doors and lintels.

Blocks can be solid or hollow. Open-ended hollow blocks are used in steel-reinforced basements or retaining walls. Those with one end sealed can be filled with mineral wool to absorb sound, or they can be used as a lighter, cheaper alternative to solid blocks.

Blocks are measured by their compressive strength (the point at which they crumble under pressure). The measure used is Newtons per square millimetre

Aircrete blocks are a form of cement construction block made lighter and more thermally efficient by the inclusion of thousands of tiny air bubbles.

(N/m^2 or simply N), with 3.6N the basic strength, while foundation blocks may need to be a sturdier 7N. The precise compressive strength for blocks used in your build will be specified by your designer on the plans submitted for building regulations' approval.

Even more significant under the current building regulations is the thermal conductivity of the block. This is measured in 'U-values'. A U-value tells us the flow of heat, in Watts, through a square metre of a material for every 1°C difference in temperature between inside and outside. It's written W/m^2K ('W' for watts, 'm^2' for square metres and 'K' for kelvin, another term for centigrade). Essentially, the lower the figure, the better the insulating qualities (see Chapter 11 for further details).

A dense concrete block, for example, might have a U-value of $1.32W/m^2K$, compared to just $0.295W/m^2K$ for an aircrete block. Using aircrete blocks of this kind can make it much easier to meet the energy efficiency requirements of the building regulations.

CHAPTER 9

Finding a Designer

DO I NEED ONE?

Some self-builders act as their own designers, perhaps having their plans drawn up professionally by a qualified draughtsman. If the design is simple and conventional, this can be tempting, especially as the fees of a competent and experienced designer are not going to be cheap.

Before you take this step, though, it's important to appreciate what a designer actually does. Creating a design and drawing up professional plans based on your requirements is only part of their job.

WHAT A DESIGNER DOES

Essentially, the designer's role is to bring the needs and aspirations you want to express in your new home into actuality. To achieve this, he, or she, will:

- Carry out a site survey, gaining an idea of what is and isn't possible, taking into account the physical constraints of the plot, its surroundings, the likely attitude of the local planning department to the proposed development and, most important of all, your budget.
- Fully discuss with you the house you have in mind, perhaps with the help of your design file, and use this information to compile a brief.
- Prepare preliminary sketches based on the brief, which you will either reject or suggest amendments to until you are satisfied.
- Liaise with the planning department to find out what is, and isn't, likely to receive planning approval, and possibly make further amendments to the plans, in consultation with you.
- Prepare detailed plans and submit them with a full planning application.

- In the event of a rejection, or a strong indication that one is likely, agree amendments to the plans and re-submit an application.
- Prepare detailed technical drawings with a full specification and any structural calculations, and submit a building regulations' application to the local building control department.
- Negotiate, if necessary, with building control to make the plans acceptable.
- Invite tenders from at least three building contractors to carry out the project, providing them each with detailed drawings and specifications.
- Recommend the most suitable tender and draw up a contract for you and the contractor to sign.
- Project manage the build, visiting the site regularly to ensure that the work is being carried out according to the approved plans and the terms of the contract.

Only architects registered with the Architects Registration Board can call themselves by that title and become chartered members of the Royal Institute of British Architects (RIBA) or its national equivalents.

- Certify that work has been completed satisfactorily at agreed stages of the build (something mortgage lenders may insist on), and issue a council of mortgage lenders' professional consultants' certificate (pcc) to the same effect, at the completion of the project.
- Ensure that a completion certificate is issued by the building control department, confirming that the build has been completed in accordance with the relevant building regulations.

Of course, it isn't necessary to buy the whole designer package. You could, for example, simply hire a designer to draw up your plans and obtain planning permission and building regulations' approval. You can then either engage your own main contractor or project manager, or project manage the build yourself. This is a popular option with architects who prefer not to get involved in the day-to-day complexities of site work.

WHERE DO I FIND A DESIGNER?

An architect is the traditional source of house design expertise, not least because seven years' hard slog are needed to qualify – five years' academic study and at least two years' practical experience. Only then can you register with the Architects Registration Board, enabling you to call yourself an architect and become a chartered member of the Royal Institute of British Architects (RIBA) or its Scottish, Welsh or Northern Irish equivalents (see Contacts).

RIBA has a directory of architects and practices, categorized by location and speciality, which you can search online. ASBA, formerly the Association of Self Build Architects (see Contacts), is a national network of domestic architects – typically small, independent practices – who specialize in self-build, renovations, extensions and conversions.

Alternatively, as in much construction work, personal recommendation is always valuable. If you see a one-off home you admire, contact the owners for details of its designer, or find them on the planning application at your local authority planning department.

For a unique vision, an architect is undoubtedly your best bet. His, or her, approach is as much artistic as practical. In fact, the most common criticism of architects is that their designs look wonderful but disregard practicality or budget. On the other hand, a good architect should save you at least the cost of their

fees, and both satisfy and delight you with their design solutions.

For a relatively straightforward design, or one that demands a high degree of technical expertise, you might also consider an architectural technologist. Architectural technologists are as capable as architects at designing and project managing a house build, but their expertise is more in the scientific and technological aspects of design and construction.

The Chartered Institute of Architectural Technologists (CIAT) has a directory of members that can be viewed online. Some of the members are also chartered environmentalists – useful if you are planning an eco-home. Others are accredited conservationists, useful again, if your project includes the renovation or restoration of a listed building.

You might also choose an architectural designer or an individual or company offering architectural services. Such companies may well include an architect who has qualified but chosen not to become a member of RIBA, or someone qualified in other fields of construction, such as surveying.

Another alternative is to buy a design and build package. These are best known with timber-frame homes, where the company that manufactures and erects the frame also provides a design service. A couple of companies offer the same service with brick and block (see Contacts), and main contractors sometimes do the same. Their disadvantage is that you can't choose your designer, so you have to be happy with what's provided. The advantage is that, if design services are included in the price of an overall package, you can reclaim the VAT charged on them at the end of your build. VAT on designer's fees isn't otherwise reclaimable.

HOW DO I CHOOSE THE RIGHT DESIGNER?

This is a bit like asking how to choose the right home. Most of us know instinctively if a property is right for us within moments of crossing the threshold. That's not to say, of course, there won't be a good deal of research and selection before that point, and choosing a designer is no different. To ease that process, a first step is to decide what is most important to you in design terms. This might include:

- Experience and success with the style of house you want.

- A good track record for planning applications with the local authority covering your plot.
- Knowledge and experience of the sort of construction method you'd like, e.g. very traditional, highly energy efficient or low maintenance.
- Economy – not so much cheapness as capability of producing good and imaginative solutions within tight budgetary constraints.
- Openness to clients' ideas and flexibility of approach.
- Experience of project management and willingness to do the same for you.

Likely prospects can be identified through their websites, examples of their work, personal recommendation or success with local planning applications. For the latter, browse the local register of planning applications for houses or sites that resemble your own.

It's a good idea to pick three candidates and set up meetings, which should be cost-free. Apart from discovering if you're likely to work well together, you'll need to know:

- The services they offer – a design service, planning and building regulations' submissions or full project management.
- Their charges – for example, a fixed fee, a percentage of the total build cost (6 to 10 per cent is typical) or an hourly rate.
- Whether or not they have professional indemnity insurance – this should be a given, but it's wise to check that it's up to date.

Incidentally, don't expect a designer to do a trial sketch or two for free based on your conversation. If they do, fine, but it suggests a worrying shortage of work.

RIBA's art deco London headquarters features a bookshop, exhibitions and a library.

CHAPTER 10

Obtaining Planning Permission

If acquiring a plot is the first major hurdle in self-build – which it is – obtaining planning consent for the home you want to build on it is the second.

You're likely to have some idea of the complexities involved from the conditions of the planning consent that came with the land (assuming it did). Typically, local planners will want to approve the external materials and finishes, and arrangements for drainage, road access and car parking. They may also be very specific in terms of the size of the proposed property, its orientation or layout.

While these conditions might seem designed to thwart you, it's important to realize that gaining planning permission is much more than a straightforward bureaucratic procedure. There is, of course, a whole stack of rules, regulations and policies, which sometimes, very annoyingly, contradict one other. In essence, it's a negotiation. It's designed, however imperfectly, to reach a balance between your desires as an individual, building and living on land you own, and the desires of the larger community, of which you will form a part.

Having, then, a clear vision of the house you want to build is always valuable, but flexibility and compromise can be just as important in realizing your aims. In other words, obtaining planning permission is something of a game and success often depends as much upon the individual players as it does on the rules.

TYPES OF PLANNING PERMISSION

'Outline' planning permission is essentially consent in principle to build a new dwelling on a plot. Before any building can take place, however, a detailed or full planning application has to be submitted, giving precise details of the particular house you have in mind. These details are also known as 'reserved matters'.

Outline planning permission is granted for 3 years. Once reserved matters are approved, you have 2 years to start building or the consent lapses.

The alternative is a detailed or full planning application, which can also be made directly. This really only applies where you already own the land or, if you're buying land without consent but on condition that consent is granted. In this case, it's quicker and cheaper to go for full planning permission rather than spend time and money on an outline application. Like the outline version, full planning consent lasts for 3 years in England and Wales, though in Scotland it's 5 years.

Some plots, of course, come with detailed planning permission already in place. This may be because the vendor wanted to build for themselves, then had a change of mind. Or it may be that the site is so sensitive, local planners insisted on seeing full details of the proposed development before making a decision.

If the approved design happens to correspond exactly with your dream home, or as near as makes no difference, you may simply choose to go with it and save yourself the cost of another application. Most people, however, will want to submit a new application. Generally speaking, unless your design is radically different, you should be successful.

Be warned, however, that few things are certain in the planning system. If, for example, planning consent lapses, it doesn't mean that a fresh application will automatically succeed, even with an identical design. Local and national planning policy is in constant ferment and even within a few months attitudes can change.

HOW PLANNING WORKS

A planning application is submitted to the local planning department, which then publicizes it, inviting

Details of planning applications are published online, in local newspapers, letters to neighbours and on notices like this at the site of the proposed development.

comment. This can be via letters written to neighbours, details published on the local authority website or in a local newspaper, or a notice displayed on the site of the proposed development. Meanwhile, the planning department consults other council departments and outside bodies, such as the highways and drainage authorities and the parish council.

If there are no objections, or only minor ones, the planners may decide to make a 'delegated decision', in other words granting consent themselves. If, however, a number of issues are raised, the planning department will write a report and make a recommendation for acceptance or rejection.

This entire process is supposed to take a maximum of 8 weeks. Given the workload of many planning departments, however, it's likely to be longer, and you will often receive a letter requesting more time.

The planners' report and recommendation then go to the local authority's planning committee, where elected councillors will make a final decision. This can be a further cause for delay since the meetings only happen once a month. The committee will accept the application, reject it, 'delegate' it or 'defer' a decision.

A delegated decision is essentially an acceptance, but minor amendments or further details may be needed for a final approval, and these can be handled by a senior planning officer. A decision is deferred for similar reasons, but the committee wants to see the revised version before making up its mind.

If an application is rejected, or only granted with conditions the applicant considers unacceptable, an appeal can be made to the Secretary of State. This can be done in three ways: a written representation, an informal hearing or a public enquiry. You have 6 months after the rejection to lodge an appeal.

HOW TO MAKE A PLANNING APPLICATION

Even if you decide to hand the whole process over to your designer or other professional, it's important to know what's involved – partly to avoid nasty surprises later, partly because you can play a crucial part, but mainly because you're going to get involved anyway. Complying with planning requirements can have as dramatic an effect on your design as the plot itself.

The application process starts well before any forms are filled in, and typically follows the pattern described below:

1. Preliminary Meeting with Planning Officer

This may be with you, your designer or both of you, ideally on-site. It's essentially a fishing expedition, to gain an idea of what is and isn't likely to be acceptable, so specifics shouldn't really be discussed, unless they are absolutely crucial to your project. Don't take it to heart if the planning officer appears unenthusiastic or even downright discouraging. Giving hope to applicants is not part of their brief. Remember this is only the start of a negotiation process, so discovering the reasons for a poor reaction will be valuable.

2. Checking the Planning Register

Look up the planning history of your plot. If a previous application has succeeded, but then lapsed, this can give useful clues on what's likely to succeed again. Alternatively, if one or more previous applications have been rejected, study the reasons given and see if your design can overcome them. For the same reasons, check out successful and failed applications for similar designs to yours in the same locality.

3. Second Meeting

By now you should have sketches or initial plans, which should have picked up on the pointers given, or deduced, from the first meeting. The best result is something along the lines of 'there seems no obvious cause for

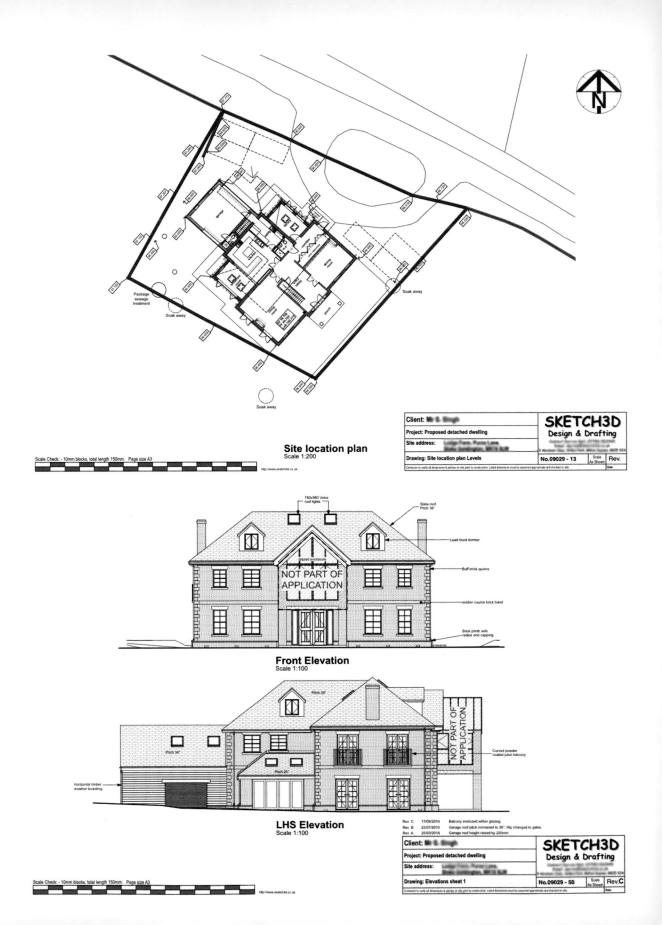

Site location plan
Scale 1:200

Scale Check: - 10mm blocks, total length 150mm. Page size A3

http://www.sketch3d.co.uk

Client: Mr S. Singh

Project: Proposed detached dwelling

Site address: Lodge Farm, Pincor Lane, Stoke Goldington, MK16 8LW

Drawing: Site location plan Levels

No.09029 - 13

Scale As Shown

Rev.

SKETCH3D
Design & Drafting

Contractor to verify all dimensions & pitches on site prior to construction. Listed dimensions must be assumed approximate and checked on site.

780x980 Velux roof lights

Slate roof Pitch 38°

Lead lined dormer

glazed enclosure

NOT PART OF APPLICATION

Buff brick quoins

soldier course brick band

Brick plinth with radius end capping.

Front Elevation
Scale 1:100

Pitch 38°

Pitch 38°

NOT PART OF APPLICATION

Pitch 25°

Curved powder coated juliet balcony

Horizontal timber weather boarding.

LHS Elevation
Scale 1:100

Rev C   17/08/2010   Balcony enclosed within glazing.
Rev B   23/07/2010   Garage roof pitch increased to 38°; Hip changed to gable.
Rev A   25/03/2010   Garage roof height raised by 225mm

Client: Mr S. Singh

Project: Proposed detached dwelling

Site address: Lodge Farm, Pincor Lane, Stoke Goldington, MK16 8LW

Drawing: Elevations sheet 1

No.09029 - 50

Scale As Shown

Rev.C

SKETCH3D
Design & Drafting

Contractor to verify all dimensions & pitches on site prior to construction. Listed dimensions must be assumed approximate and checked on site.

Scale Check: - 10mm blocks, total length 150mm. Page size A3

http://www.sketch3d.co.uk

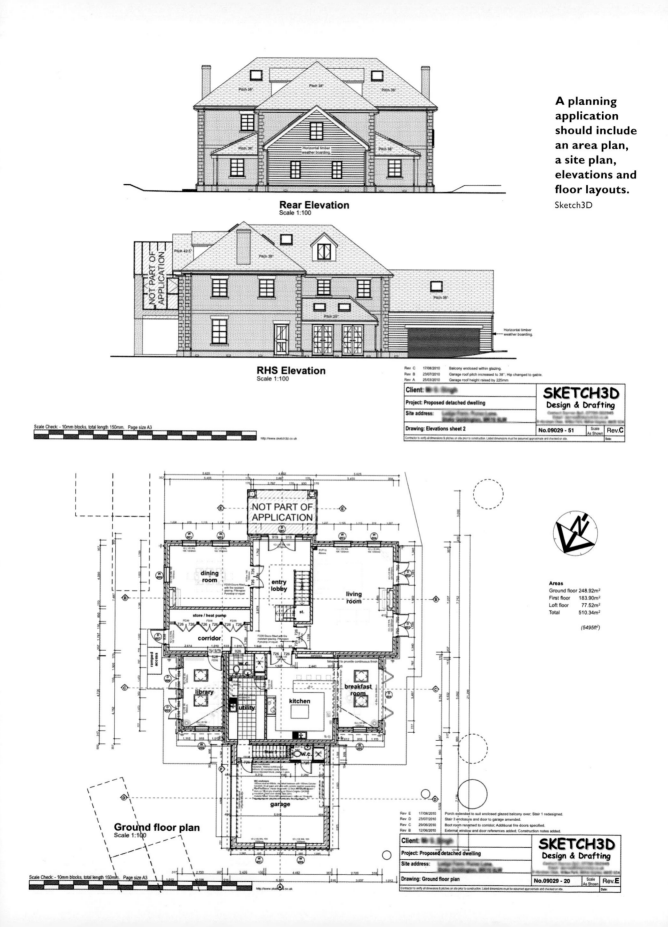

Rear Elevation
Scale 1:100

A planning
application
should include
an area plan,
a site plan,
elevations and
floor layouts.
Sketch3D

RHS Elevation
Scale 1:100

NOT PART OF APPLICATION

Scale Check:- 10mm blocks, total length 150mm. Page size A3

Rev C   17/08/2010   Balcony enclosed within glazing.
Rev B   23/07/2010   Garage roof pitch increased to 38°; Hip changed to gable.
Rev A   25/03/2010   Garage roof height raised by 225mm

Client:
Project: Proposed detached dwelling
Site address:
Drawing: Elevations sheet 2

SKETCH3D
Design & Drafting

No.09029 - 51 | Scale As Shown | Rev.C

NOT PART OF
APPLICATION

Areas
Ground floor 248.92m²
First floor   183.90m²
Loft floor   77.52m²
Total   510.34m²

(5495ft²)

dining room
entry lobby
living room
store / heat pump
corridor
w.c.
library
utility
kitchen
breakfast room
w.c.
garage

Ground floor plan
Scale 1:100

Scale Check:- 10mm blocks, total length 150mm. Page size A3

Rev E   17/08/2010   Porch extended to suit enclosed glazed balcony over; Stair 1 redesigned.
Rev D   23/07/2010   Stair 3 enclosure and door to garage amended.
Rev C   29/06/2010   Boot room renamed to corridor; Additional fire doors specified.
Rev B   12/06/2010   External window and door references added. Construction notes added.

Client:
Project: Proposed detached dwelling
Site address:
Drawing: Ground floor plan

SKETCH3D
Design & Drafting

No.09029 - 20 | Scale As Shown | Rev.E

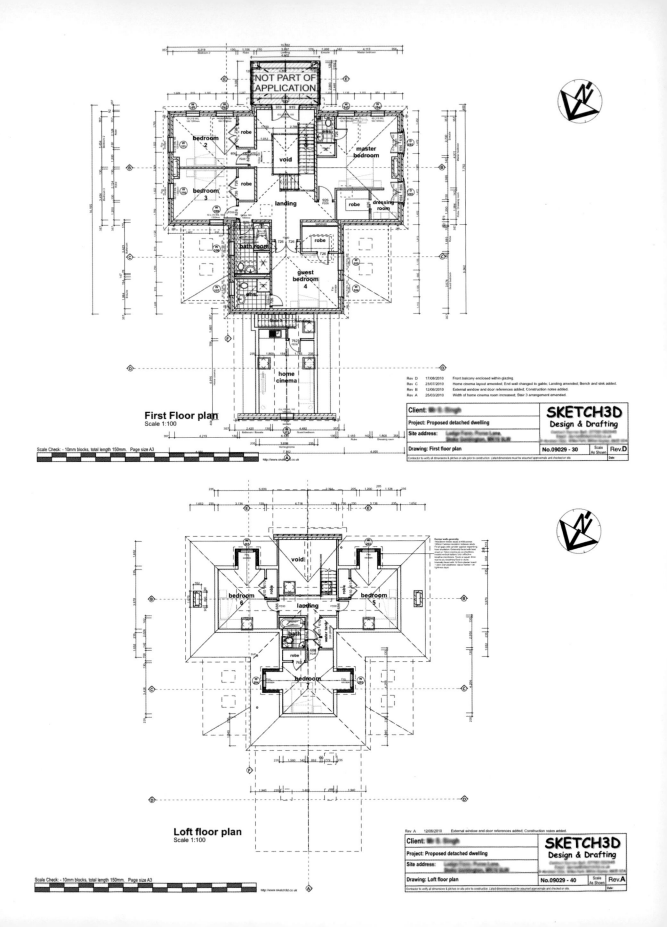

First Floor plan
Scale 1:100

NOT PART OF APPLICATION

bedroom 2

robe

void

ens.

master bedroom

robe

bedroom 3

landing

robe

dressing room

bath room

robe

ens.

guest bedroom 4

home cinema

Rev D 17/08/2010 Front balcony enclosed within glazing.
Rev C 23/07/2010 Home cinema layout amended; End wall changed to gable; Landing amended; Bench and sink added.
Rev B 12/06/2010 External window and door references added; Construction notes added.
Rev A 25/03/2010 Width of home cinema room increased; Stair 3 arrangement amended.

Client: Mr S. Singh	**SKETCH3D**
Project: Proposed detached dwelling	Design & Drafting
Site address: Lodge Farm, Plume Lane, Stoke Goldington, MK16 9LW	
Drawing: First floor plan	No.09029 - 30	Scale As Shown	Rev.D

Contractor to verify all dimensions & pitches on site prior to construction. Listed dimensions must be assumed approximate and checked on site. Date:

Scale Check: - 10mm blocks, total length 150mm. Page size A3

http://www.sketch3d.co.uk

Loft floor plan
Scale 1:100

void

bedroom 6

robe

robe

bedroom 5

landing

bath

water tank

robe

bedroom 7

Rev A 12/06/2010 External window and door references added; Construction notes added.

Client: Mr S. Singh	**SKETCH3D**
Project: Proposed detached dwelling	Design & Drafting
Site address: Lodge Farm, Plume Lane, Stoke Goldington, MK16 9LW	
Drawing: Loft floor plan	No.09029 - 40	Scale As Shown	Rev.A

Contractor to verify all dimensions & pitches on site prior to construction. Listed dimensions must be assumed approximate and checked on site. Date:

Scale Check: - 10mm blocks, total length 150mm. Page size A3

http://www.sketch3d.co.uk

Upcoming Changes

The current government has pledged to make the planning process simpler and more straightforward, so do check that the details outlined here still apply when you come to make your application. Given the usual breakneck speed of the planning system, however, don't expect dramatic changes, though one likely casualty is said to be the design and access statement.

rejection, in principle, but nothing can be guaranteed before a formal application'. The worst result will be a strong indication that it's probably not worth proceeding. At this point you begin to appreciate the value of an experienced local designer who deals with the planners on a regular basis and knows how to counter setbacks of this kind.

3. Preparing the Application

The application form is available either directly from the local planning department or online through the Planning Portal (see below and Contacts). Typically, it consists of around thirty sections. As well as a description of the proposed development, it asks for details such as the parking and pedestrian access, sewage disposal method, the number of trees and hedges on site and whether or not you've consulted your neighbours. You're also required to sign a certificate stating you are the owner of the land. If you're not, you can still apply, as long as you've informed the real owner or, if the owner is untraceable, you've taken reasonable steps to find out who they are. You'll also need a set of clearly labelled plans, scaled to fit onto either A4 or A3 size paper. If you're posting or hand-delivering your application, between three and six copies of each will be required, depending on the local authority. If you're applying online, you'll only need a digital copy of a master plan. These plans are:

- Location or area plan on a scale of 1:1250 with the site boundary outlined in red – this is taken from an Ordnance Survey Map of the area, which your designer should be able to provide; otherwise, you'll need to buy a map online or from the Planning Portal.
- Site or block plan on a scale of 1:200 or 1:500 – a more detailed view of the site, showing the positions of the proposed house, boundaries, adjoining roads and buildings, trees, hedges and drains.
- Proposed front, rear and side elevations of the finished house, on a scale of 1:50 or 1:100.
- Proposed layout plan of each floor with the rooms clearly labelled.

Finally, you will need to make a 'design and access' (D&A) statement. This is a brief report setting out the thinking behind your design and covering six aspects: amount, layout, scale, landscaping, appearance and context.

- 'Amount' means the number of proposed units (effectively, one plus, perhaps, a detached garage).
- 'Layout' should talk about the relationship between the proposed building and the buildings and public spaces around it, including its accessibility for the elderly and disabled.
- 'Scale' refers to the height, width and length of the house and how they relate to the surrounding buildings.
- 'Landscaping' should include proposed hard and soft landscaping, i.e. paving and pathways and planting, the reasons for each and plans for maintenance.
- 'Appearance' should summarize the visual impression of the new house, including the materials, colours and textures used and the reasons why.

Design and access statements
How to write, read and use them

A useful guide on design and access statements is available from the Design Council (see Contacts).

- 'Context' should indicate the ways in which the design is likely to affect the surrounding area in physical, economic and social terms. This is unlikely to be relevant in residential areas, though it might become so if you're building in a rural area in order to follow an agricultural occupation (see 'agricultural tie' in Chapter 5).

Plans and photographs can be included in the statement to illustrate your points.

If you're making your own planning application, the design and access statement can induce a degree of panic. It appears to demand information you've already included elsewhere, while the rest seems designer-type waffle. This is a good reason for handing it over to a designer.

On the other hand, it gives you an excuse to examine your design more critically and articulate the reasons for your decisions – in other words, make a more personal pitch. It could, for example, allow you to explain the need for an annexe to house an elderly parent, or that an apparently unusual aspect or material is, in fact, a revival of a local traditional building practice.

The Planning Portal has advice on writing design and access statements, including a useful guide from the now defunct Commission for Architecture and the Built Environment (CABE). It's also useful to look at D&A statements for successful planning applications on the local authority website.

4. Dealing with Neighbours

Once you have a complete set of plans, but before submitting your application, it's wise to alert your new neighbours – especially the immediate ones – and talk through your design. If you live close by, one time-saving approach is to invite them in for an evening or a weekend afternoon and ply them with wine and nibbles. Not everyone, of course, can read plans, so if you or your designer can produce a model, or a 3D visualization you can display on a laptop, it will be worth it.

Be sympathetic and conciliatory, without actually conceding anything (unless you really want to). If you can persuade anyone to write a letter in support of your development, so much the better; written material will go into your application file and be taken into consideration.

Don't be too disappointed if a neighbour happily accepts your hospitality then immediately dashes off a letter of outrage. Nobody likes change, especially close to home. You will at least have proved yourself to be a good future neighbour, which may deter objections from the marginally less outraged, and you can tick the neighbourhood consultation box on your application.

Incidentally, local objections, even in large numbers, aren't in themselves a valid reason for rejecting an application. If, however, enough objectors lobby the local district councillor or parish council, this could sway the views of the planning committee who make the final decision. This is why it's useful to get in touch with your local councillor and lobby them first.

Living On Site

One way to maintain the closest supervision of your project, and also save mortgage or rental outgoings, is to live on site in a caravan or mobile home. Normally, planning permission isn't required, since the accommodation is self-evidently temporary – but check with your local authority. If they think otherwise, you may need to include planning permission for temporary accommodation in your application.

However, if your plot includes an existing residence, which you are replacing, you're perfectly entitled to site temporary accommodation in your own garden.

Living on site saves money and allows close supervision of your build; if the temporary accommodation is as appealing as this shepherd's hut it can stay on as a garden feature, office or spare accommodation. Ashwood Timber

5. Submitting the Application

Submissions can be made by post or hand, but for reasons of economy and sustainability, the government prefer you to do it electronically through the Planning Portal. Apart from containing a host of useful information about the planning system and making planning and building regulations' applications, this website has a number of advantages. They include:

- Only one copy needed of plans – simply convert each plan into a jpeg or pdf file, which can be done on any printer/scanner/copier.
- Draft versions can be created, allowing you to spend as much time as you need getting the application right – this is more useful than it might seem, since incorrectly completed applications can be rejected: it's been hinted this is more likely to happen if your local planning department has a heavy workload and is looking for reasons to lighten it.
- Submitted versions can be archived, providing a backup to your own files.

Details of fees in England and Wales are also available, along with the opportunity to buy an updated site plan.

6. Monitoring the Application

Tracking the progress of your application will alert you to any concerns that arise, and may enable you to address them by making minor adjustments to the design. Some planning authorities allow applications to be tracked online, but you'll gain more information by using the phone.

Planners have to complete their report and recommendations a few days before the planning committee meeting to give councillors time to consider them, and this gives you the opportunity to do the same.

If it looks like an application is heading for rejection, you can save time and money by withdrawing it and submitting a revised version. Reapplications made within 12 months of the original do not incur a further fee.

7. The Planning Committee

The meetings are public, so you're free to spend a nerve-wracking evening waiting for your proposal to be discussed. Take a notebook and/or an unobtrusive recorder.

If you're lucky, your application will simply be granted without discussion. If not, keep a record of what's said

and, if possible, who said it; it will be useful information for a revised application.

If applicants are allowed to speak, prepare your arguments carefully beforehand and rehearse them thoroughly. If public speaking terrifies you and you have an eloquent and experienced designer – delegate.

WHAT TO DO IF YOU FAIL

Galling as a rejection is, you should at least have a good idea of the changes needed to make your design acceptable. You may, of course, find those unacceptable, but that needn't be the end of your project. There are still several options left to you. You can:

- Develop a completely new design that addresses the planners' concerns but also satisfies you.
- Submit two new applications – one that precisely follows the planners' requirements but looks execrable, while the other is essentially the original design with minor amendments. By doing this you have:
  - established your determination to go ahead with the development, even if you end up with a monstrosity;
  - confined the discussion to two design alternatives, rather than the acceptance or rejection of one. Hopefully the planners will decide your original design is the lesser of two evils.
- If a fresh application looks like it's also heading for rejection, hint that you're prepared to go to appeal – making an appeal application costs you nothing, but involves the local authority in a good deal of time and expense.
- Go to appeal – a written representation is the cheapest and most common option, but be aware that only about a third of appeals are successful.
- Appoint a planning consultant – you can find one locally through the website of the Royal Town Planning Institute (see contacts). This is certainly advisable if you are planning an appeal.

OTHER PLANNING SITUATIONS AND WHAT TO DO ABOUT THEM

Bungalow Eating

This is the popular term for buying an existing property and demolishing it to provide a plot. The bungalows that gave rise to the term typically came from the 1930s and were often accompanied by huge gardens.

The trick is to buy a property in a poor state of repair at a price that reflects this. If you're lucky, it may only be marginally more expensive than a plot with planning permission in the same area. In popular spots, however, vendors of such properties are usually very aware of their potential and, if they aren't, estate agents are likely to enlighten them swiftly.

Replacements do, however, have numerous advantages, which may outweigh the extra cost. Since a house already exists on the site, planning permission is likely to be granted for a replacement. Services, such as gas, electricity, water and sewerage are already in place. Landscaping and boundary walls or fences will already be in place. The savings you make in not having to pay infrastructure charges could easily cover the cost of demolition. Even more may be recouped by selling off materials from the demolition, particularly bricks. You may also be able to live in the existing house while the build is underway, enabling you to sell your current home and avoid the need for short-term borrowing to fund your project.

As in all planning matters, nothing is entirely straightforward. Local planning policies towards replacement dwellings differ widely. Planners may insist the new property is no larger than the original or perhaps no more than 50 per cent bigger. They may also insist it sits on exactly the same footprint. Check the details with your local planning department, not just in terms of the general policy but also how it's interpreted.

One way of overcoming a restriction on size is to invoke 'permitted development rights' (PDRs). PDRs allow you to extend your property under certain restrictions but without having to seek planning permission. You can, for example, extend 4m to the rear over a single storey or 3m over two storeys, and expand your roof space by up to 50m^2. (This applies to England; the details are slightly different for Scotland, Wales and Northern Ireland.) You can build a garage with a roof height of up to 4m (or 3m if it's flat), as long as it's no closer to the highway than the house. You can also cover up to half your garden with outbuildings, such as sheds, garden offices or gyms – as long as they aren't used for sleeping accommodation.

At the time of writing, however, proposals are going forward for increasing the scope of PDRs, so do check with your local planning department. PDRs are useful in three ways. You can:

• tell the planners you intend to extend as soon as you

complete, so they might as well allow the size of the extension in the original build (if they do, they may impose a condition withdrawing any future PDRs);

• extend the existing property before you apply for a replacement (an expensive option, unless you intend to wait a few years, since it will eventually perish with the rest of the building);

• more sensibly, build an extension to the full extent of your PDRs with an outbuilding close by, then demolish the original property (carefully), leaving the extension and outbuilding intact and incorporate them into the new build.

Incidentally, once an outbuilding has been built – say, a garden office with a kitchenette and a WC – it can later be converted to sleeping accommodation under PDRs. Building regulations approval may be required, but it's handy way of acquiring a granny annexe, teenage accommodation or extra guest rooms.

If the plot is very large, you may even be required to use it more effectively by erecting two or three replacement homes. This isn't as disastrous as it sounds, since you could still obtain planning permission and then sell the spare plots to other self-builders or a developer – a handy way of subsidising your project, while retaining some control over the design of neighbouring houses.

Demolition and rebuild is generally more complicated in localities where special planning rules apply, such as conservation areas, National Parks, Areas of Outstanding Natural Beauty and Green Belt. There are likely to be very strict conditions imposed on the design and materials used.

Replacement prospects should also be habitable. If a house is derelict and has been unoccupied for many years, local planners may decide there is no longer a residential use for the property. Before buying, check its status with the local planning department.

One form of rural rebuild prospect can seem an excellent bargain, at least at first sight. That's a property subject to an agricultural tie. It's likely to be up to 50 per cent cheaper than you'd expect to pay. The reason is that it can only be occupied by someone working in agriculture, horticulture or forestry. To buy it you will need take up one of those occupations locally, and prove that you have to the satisfaction of the planners.

Alternatively, you can make a planning application to have the tie removed. To do that, you need to prove there is no longer an agricultural need. One method is to show that the property has been marketed for between

Agricultural ties can be problematic even for agricultural workers: this 1960s bungalow in an Area of Outstanding Natural Beauty was subject to an agricultural tie and failed to sell. Neighbouring farmer Michele Meyer, who wanted to replace it with a self-built eco-home, only succeeded after going to appeal, despite giving up her existing farmhouse and continuing to work her farm. Michele Meyer

Top Tips for Successful Planning Applications

If in doubt, favour the local architectural style You may have no choice if you're building in a conservation area, an Area of Outstanding Natural Beauty or a National Park, but even when you're not, creating a design that blends in with the surrounding buildings is likely to be more acceptable, and certainly to your new neighbours.

Opt for the vernacular This is particularly important in areas that have a distinctive local architecture. Like much of the British population, planners and planning committees aren't generally fans of the new and innovative, and tend to prefer the tried, tested and traditional. If your design at least nods towards the local vernacular style, it may help to tip the balance towards acceptance.

Play the green card The government has pledged that by 2016 all new homes will be 'zero carbon', i.e. the amount of carbon dioxide produced in their method of construction, the materials used and the energy consumed from living in them will be neutral. How this will be achieved is explained in a document called the Code for Sustainable Homes (see Chapter 11). The government's climate-change policies – if continued – will eventually require vast numbers of existing homes to be upgraded to zero-carbon standards. This will involve equally vast expenditure, and local authorities may well have to make a contribution. Allowing your eco-home now could well reduce the burden on the local authority's coffers. At least, that's your argument.

Offer a sacrifice Asking planners to consider a plan is, effectively, inviting them to make changes, partly to prove they've actually looked at it and also to justify their existence. Deliberately adding a feature that you know will be unacceptable can satisfy honour on both sides. But do take advice from a designer with local experience. Otherwise your sacrifice could be something you'd set your heart on, while you're stuck with an 'unacceptable' monstrosity.

Always be reasonable and workmanlike This may be the most personal project you've ever undertaken but treat your design as a business project, which you and the planners will handle as reasonable and fair-minded individuals, especially when you know in your heart that you are the only intelligent, discerning person in the room. This approach may not always get you exactly what you want, but acting otherwise will almost certainly not.

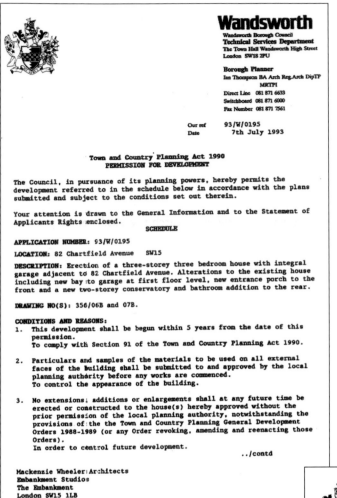

Wandsworth
Wandsworth Borough Council
Technical Services Department
The Town Hall Wandsworth High Street
London SW18 2PU

Borough Planner
Ian Thompson BA Arch Reg.Arch DipTP
MRTPI

Direct Line   081 871 6633
Switchboard 081 871 6000
Fax Number 081 871 7561

Our ref   93/W/0195
Date   7th July 1993

Town and Country Planning Act 1990
PERMISSION FOR DEVELOPMENT

The Council, in pursuance of its planning powers, hereby permits the development referred to in the schedule below in accordance with the plans submitted and subject to the conditions set out therein.

Your attention is drawn to the General Information and to the Statement of Applicants Rights enclosed.

SCHEDULE

APPLICATION NUMBER: 93/W/0195

LOCATION: 82 Chartfield Avenue   SW15

DESCRIPTION: Erection of a three-storey three bedroom house with integral garage adjacent to 82 Chartfield Avenue. Alterations to the existing house including new bay to garage at first floor level, new entrance porch to the front and a new two-storey conservatory and bathroom addition to the rear.

DRAWING NO(S): 356/06B and 07B.

CONDITIONS AND REASONS:

1. This development shall be begun within 5 years from the date of this permission.
   To comply with Section 91 of the Town and Country Planning Act 1990.

2. Particulars and samples of the materials to be used on all external faces of the building shall be submitted to and approved by the local planning authority before any works are commenced.
   To control the appearance of the building.

3. No extensions, additions or enlargements shall at any future time be erected or constructed to the house(s) hereby approved without the prior permission of the local planning authority, notwithstanding the provisions of the Town and Country Planning General Development Orders 1988-1989 (or any Order revoking, amending and reenacting those Orders).
   In order to control future development.

../contd

Mackenzie Wheeler Architects
Embankment Studios
The Embankment
London SW15 1LB

The ultimate prize: permission finally granted – with conditions.

conclude, logically but infuriatingly, that there is no longer a property to replace, therefore your application is invalid.

The Agricultural Tie

If you're serious about changing to a rural career, there is also the option of applying to build a new house. As with demolition and re-build, you'll have to prove a local need for your occupation. This will entail operating a qualifying business for at least 3 years, and achieving a profit in at least one of them. You'll also need to show it can't function without a full-time worker, and that there is no existing dwelling that you could use instead.

Building a Rural Home of 'Exceptional' Design Merit

Under the government's Planning Policy Statement 7 (PPS7), allowance is made for an isolated house of 'exceptional quality' to be built in open countryside where permission would not normally be granted. Such a property should be 'truly outstanding and ground-breaking' and reflect 'the highest standards of contemporary architecture'.

If you're lucky, or rich, enough to have such a design, and the means to build it, it could be worth a try, though only a fraction of PPS7 designs have ever been accepted.

6 and 12 months without takers. If, however, the tie has been breached for over 10 years – perhaps because non-agricultural workers have been living there – and the local authority hasn't served an Enforcement Notice, you can apply for a Certificate of Lawful Existing Use and Development, which can also remove the tie. Both approaches need the advice of an experienced planning consultant and the outcome is by no means certain.

Whatever the circumstances, however, there is one golden rule to demolition and rebuild: *never demolish before you have obtained planning permission for a replacement.* If you do, the planners may

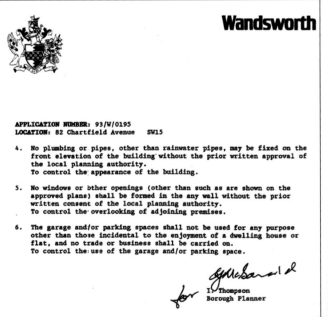

Wandsworth

APPLICATION NUMBER: 93/W/0195
LOCATION: 82 Chartfield Avenue   SW15

4. No plumbing or pipes, other than rainwater pipes, may be fixed on the front elevation of the building without the prior written approval of the local planning authority.
   To control the appearance of the building.

5. No windows or other openings (other than such as are shown on the approved plans) shall be formed in the any wall without the prior written consent of the local planning authority.
   To control the overlooking of adjoining premises.

6. The garage and/or parking spaces shall not be used for any purpose other than those incidental to the enjoyment of a dwelling house or flat, and no trade or business shall be carried on.
   To control the use of the garage and/or parking space.

I Thompson
Borough Planner

CHAPTER 11

Obtaining Building Regulations Approval

Once you've obtained planning permission you can now move on to the next stage: gaining building regulations approval. This involves another local authority department – building control. Its remit is to ensure that any substantial form of construction within its jurisdiction, including your house, will be built in accordance with the building regulations. In other words, it won't fall

down, let in the rain, catch fire easily, electrocute you or cause you any other form of harm. Neither will it waste or contaminate the mains water supply. It will also conserve fuel and power.

In England and Wales the exact requirements are set out in fourteen, legally enforceable 'approved documents' issued by the government. This is stretched to

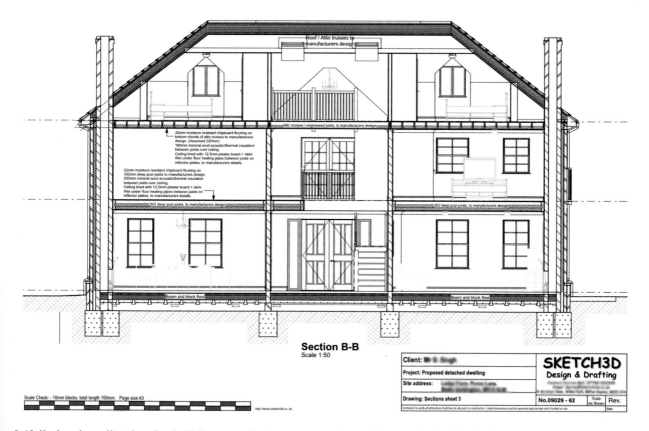

Section B-B
Scale 1:50

Scale Check: - 10mm blocks, total length 150mm.   Page size A3

Client:	**SKETCH3D**
Project: Proposed detached dwelling	Design & Drafting
Site address:	
Drawing: Sections sheet 3	No.09029 - 62	Scale As Shown	Rev.

A 'full plans' application for building regulations approval contains more detailed information than shown in a planning application, including sections through the building. Sketch3D

LEFT: The accompanying notes should provide a comprehensive summary of the materials and methods of construction. Sketch3D

BELOW: Detailed drawings are also included of critical areas of the build, in this case details of a 'warm roof' where insulation is fitted between the rafters, leaving the loft space habitable. Sketch3D

Main roof generally
- Clay roof tiles on 25x38mm treated battens on
- 25x38mm treated counter battens on
- Tyvek breather membrane on 12mm OSB sheathing on
- Attic trusses to manufacturers design (Top chords against sheathing). (70mm)
- 220mm Celotex FR4000 between top chords of trusses tight against sheathing. Fill all gaps between and around each layer of boards with canister applied expanding foam. Ensure an air tight seal.
- 50mm Celotex GA3000 below top chords of trusses. Tightly fit boards & tape joints. Fit gaps with canister applied expanding foam. Ensure air tight seal.
- Ceiling lined with 12.5mm plaster board, board joints taped and whole ceiling skimmed.

12mm plaster board + skim internal linings. Ensure all board joints are taped and filled prior skimming.

Plaster board line underside of insulation within voids.

Install access hatches were appropriate in each loft bedroom to allow storage within voids.

Deep profile skirting boards to perimeter of rooms. Allow 5mm gap below to allow movement.

Top of tuft floor 2625mm above first floor. 22mm moisture resistant flooring grade chipboard.

Install 100mm Celotex insulation from top of cavity to butt tightly against roof insulation. Seal gap with a continuous bead of canister applied expanding foam insulation to ensure an air tight seal. Continue 100mm mineral wool acoustic insulation to butt up against celotex insulation. Pack over junction to prevent any voids.

Top of attic trusses within voids lining with flooring grade chipboard.

Tyvek roof membrane raised at roof edge over a kick constructed using 12mm OSB on timber fillets fixed to the truss tails.

Build up fascia and soffit detail with timber and ply fixed back to truss tails.

Allow 98mm ventilation gap between bottom soffit member to provide continuous ventilation to void.

Seal junction between ceiling plasterboard and wall plaster before fixing cornice.

Top of wall plate 5336mm above finished ground floor level.

75 75 75 75

300

Typical eaves/roof detail Main house
Scale 1:10

Scale Check : 10mm blocks, total length 150mm. Page size A3

http://www.sketch3d.co.uk

Client: Mr S. Singh		SKETCH3D	
Project: Proposed detached dwelling		**Design & Drafting**	
Site address:			
Drawing: Eaves details Sheet 1		No.09029 - 80	Scale As Shown	Rev.

Client: Mr S. Singh		SKETCH3D	
Project: Proposed detached dwelling		**Design & Drafting**	
Site address:			
Drawing: Notes & Details		No.09029 - 100	Scale As Shown	Rev.

Scale Check : 90mm blocks, total length 150mm. Page size A3

eighteen parts in Northern Ireland, while the Scottish Building Standards manage with just seven. All cover essentially the same ground.

Applying for building 'regs' (as they're known in the trade), involves many of the same drawings you've prepared for planning, though with much more technical detail. This includes not only the method of construction and materials to be used, but also sections through the building, ground levels, floor levels, levels and routes of new drains and detailed technical drawings of any special design features.

Calculations from a qualified structural engineer may be needed, too, typically proving that load-bearing elements, such as foundations, walls, roof or any supporting beams, will be up to the job. In Scotland these calculations go into a Structural Design Certificate.

Finally, a full SAP assessment is required (*see below*). SAP stands for Standard Assessment Procedure, and two things are assessed: one is the energy efficiency of your new home; the other is the amount of carbon dioxide it emits. The calculations involved are fiendishly complicated, even for architects, and generally require specialists known as domestic energy assessors.

Many believe the figures bear only a passing reference to a home's performance in the real world, but they do result in the issuing of an Energy Performance Certificate (EPC). This is likely to be of growing interest to estate agents and future home-buyers as energy efficiency standards, and fuel bills, continue to rise.

As with planning applications, securing building regulations' approval may well involve a degree of negotiation, particularly in terms of SAP assessment. Unlike planning, however, the whole matter is handled solely by the building control department. Because the regulations are fairly clearly defined, there is much less scope for interpretation or argument. As a result, the application process is a lot speedier, typically around 5 weeks.

Even if an application is rejected, amended plans can be submitted and considered much more quickly, sometimes within days.

SITE INSPECTIONS

Gaining approval, however, is only the start of building control's interest. Once underway, your project will be inspected at key stages to ensure you're doing what you said you'd do, and to the appropriate standard. Typically, these stages are:

- Commencement of build (site clearing, demolition, setting out, etc.).
- Excavation of foundation trenches.
- Completion of foundations.
- Oversite preparation (preparation of the area beneath the ground floor).
- Walls at damp-proof course (dpc) level.
- Inspection of any structural work, e.g. steel or concrete beams.
- Drains laid.
- Drains tested.
- Completion of build.

Other significant points might be: walls at wallplate level (when they are ready to receive the roof), completion

Pouring foundations cannot take place before a building control officer has approved the trenches, one of several inspections that occur throughout the build.

of waste pipework, installation of the central heating boiler and hot-water system and measures for fire and sound insulation.

Normally, building control will only require a day's notice to make an inspection – five in the case of commencement and completion.

Incidentally, proceeding without the building inspector's approval is extremely risky. If you do, he or she can compel you to expose the work to prove it's been carried out properly and, if it hasn't, order you to re-do it to an acceptable standard. The same goes for any work that's deemed to be below the appropriate standard.

In practice, the inspector's powers are less a burden than a vital safeguard. Delaying an inspection of a buried

aspect of the building, such as a drain through foundations, only to discover a problem at a later date, can be extremely costly.

At the end of the build it's the job of building control to issue a completion certificate, confirming that the work has been carried out in accordance with the requirements of the building regulations.

ALTERNATIVES TO BUILDING CONTROL

Although most people tend to use their local authority Building Control Department, it's not obligatory. You can choose to use an approved inspector, i.e. an individual or company authorized by the Construction Industry Council. If you do so, an 'initial notice' has to be served on the relevant local authority building control department, 5 days before work starts. This gives them time to check out the inspector's credentials and insurance. Once that's done, the approved inspector takes over the usual building control duties and issues the completion certificate.

If a dispute arises between you and the approved inspector, local building control will step in to resolve it and, if necessary, enforce the correction of any defective works.

At the time of writing, there are about sixty approved inspectors in England and Wales, accounting for about 20 per cent of all building control work. Most belong to the Association of Consultant Approved Inspectors, whose website includes contact details (see Contacts). Currently there are no plans for private inspectors in Scotland.

Why Would You Choose an Approved Inspector?

If you have an unusual or innovative design, an approved inspector may be more inclined to view it sympathetically and provide certification. Local authority building control departments are, arguably, more comfortable with traditional, well-established forms of construction.

An approved inspector may also save you money – first, on fees, but also by combining the building control service with a warranty scheme. For example, the National House Building Council (NHBC) operates both a warranty scheme for self-builders, Solo for Self Build, and a building control service. Using both services will minimize costs and the number of site visits.

What's in the Building Regulations

In England and Wales, the building regulations are divided into fourteen 'approved documents' or 'parts', covering different aspects of construction. They are:

Part A: structural safety.
Part B: fire safety.
Part C: resistance to contamination and moisture.
Part D: toxic substances.
Part E: resistance to the passage of sound.
Part F: ventilation.
Part G: sanitation, hot-water safety and water efficiency.
Part H: drainage and waste disposal.
Part J: heat-producing appliances.
Part K: protection from falling (stairs, ramps, guard rails, etc.).
Part L: conservation of fuel and power.
Part M: access to and use of buildings.
Part N: glazing safety.
Part P: electrical safety.

In Scotland the regulations are covered by technical handbooks, divided into seven sections: structure, fire, environment, safety, noise, energy and sustainability.

You can download free digital versions of the English and Welsh documents at the Planning Portal website, Scottish versions from the Scottish Government website, and Northern Ireland regulations from the Northern Ireland building control website (see Contacts).

Why Would You Choose Your Local Building Control Department?

A local building inspector will have useful knowledge of local ground conditions and local building professionals. Building control officers aren't allowed to recommend or give opinions on individuals or companies, but suggesting a name and observing the inspector's reaction can sometimes provide useful clues.

Being inspected by both building control and a warranty provider will also bring two sets of expert eyes to your project, reducing the chances of a defect being overlooked.

TWO WAYS TO ACHIEVE BUILDING REGULATIONS' APPROVAL

A 'full plans' application is the most common form of submission. As well as the application form and fee, it requires revised versions of the plans previously submitted to the planning department, including much more technical detail, explanatory notes and sectional views. The latter shows a vertical slice through the building to reveal constructional details.

To the beginner, plans of this kind can seem written in a foreign language, littered with references to unexplained British Standards and obscure proprietary materials ('150mm concrete slab with A252 mesh bottom on visqueen gas barrier').

Once the build is over, it will make a lot more sense, but for the moment this is an excellent excuse to hand the whole business over to your designer. These plans aren't just to convince the building inspectors that your house won't fall down, they provide the information that enables contractors to quote for the project and actually build it. This is another good reason to go the full plans route. Working out the fine details at this stage is a lot easier and less expensive than on site. Even then, there may well be later modifications because aspects of the plans prove impractical or you decide to make minor changes. Fortunately, building control is well aware of this and solutions can usually be negotiated at the appropriate point.

There is, however, an alternative route to building regulations approval – it's known as a building notice. This involves simply submitting a form and giving building control 48 hours' notice that you are starting your build. From then on, however, you will still need to arrange for the usual stage inspections. Building notices, incidentally, don't apply in Scotland, where no start can

be made without a 'building warrant', the local equivalent of full plans approval.

In practice, a building notice is only used for minor works. Employing it for something as large and complex as a house build is extremely risky. It's only justified if your design is exceptionally conventional and preferably undertaken by a single contractor known to, and trusted by, the local building control department.

COMMON SNAGS AT BUILDING REGULATIONS' STAGE

Not all of these issues are technically part of building regulations, and they may have been picked up and dealt with at the planning stage. But, since they involve practical work on-site, they are included here.

Public and Private Sewers

In residential areas, most public sewers lie beneath the streets, linked to houses through individual drains or via a private sewer taking drains from several homes. The latter is owned jointly by the home-owners involved, who are therefore jointly responsible for repairs. If you build over a private sewer, you will need to protect it from damage to the satisfaction of building control. You should also obtain the consent of the owners.

If a public sewer happens to cross your plot, things become more complicated. Public sewers are owned by the local water company. It will need to be informed if you plan to build within 3m and you won't be allowed to go ahead without written consent. Where the sewer is below 160mm in diameter, the water company may allow your builder to divert it, or offer to do the work themselves.

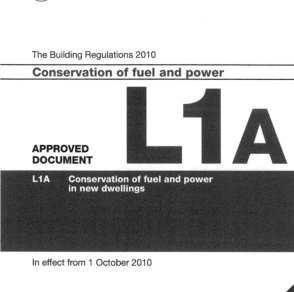

Part L1A of the building regulations deals with energy efficiency, one of the most challenging aspects of a new build.

Building within 3m or even above the sewer, will usually require a survey by closed-circuit television to check the sewer's condition. Any repairs needed will be done by the water company. After the work is finished, a follow-up survey will be carried out. Repair for any fresh damage discovered will be charged to you.

Needless to say, all this can be very expensive and result in considerable delay. In fact, water companies advise builders planning to build over or near public sewers to contact them before they apply for building regulations' approval.

All in all, it's likely to be a lot easier and cheaper to avoid the sewer and the problem, if at all possible.

Getting SAP'd

The SAP requirements are entirely laudable. No-one wants to spend more than they need on heating bills,

especially when declining resources of fossil fuel mean they can only rise. Even worthier, though arguably less practical, is the desire to reduce carbon dioxide emissions and combat global warming.

Whether or not Britain's contribution will actually make any difference on a world scale is debatable. Nevertheless, the government aims to reduce Britain's CO_2 emissions by 34 per cent of the 1990 total by 2020 and an ambitious 80 per cent by 2050. Since housing accounts for around a quarter of all our current emissions, all new houses are scheduled to be 'zero carbon' by 2016.

In broad terms, this means that the net sum of all CO_2 emissions produced by both living in, and building, the home will be zero. It's part of a strategy called the Code For Sustainable Homes, which you can read about below, and which has an increasing influence on the building regulations. For the present, however, you will need to deal with SAPs.

Perhaps the easiest way to understand them is to start with the fabric of your house. Each element – the walls, floors and roof – allows heat to pass through it at a different rate. For example, heat passes much more quickly through a single sheet of glass than it does through a sheet of polyurethane foam, which is why we use polyurethane rather than sheets of glass to insulate our homes.

A solid 225mm-thick brick wall, for example, has a U-value of around 2.00 (see Chapter 8 for a definition of 'U-value). A house built with walls like this would demand a lot of heat to make the interior comfortable. If you line the inside of the wall with around 65mm of polyurethane insulation, the U-value drops to 0.30 and the interior requires much less heat to feel comfortable. So, the lower the U-value, the more effective the insulation.

The building regulations, at the time of writing, include maximum acceptable U-values for each building element, which are: walls, 0.20; ground floors, 0.15; roofs, 0.13; windows, 1.40 and doors, 1.20.

Despite the poor thermal efficiency of brickwork on its own, achieving these values is relatively straightforward. For example, a cavity wall consisting of 100mm-thick brickwork, a cavity containing 90mm of rigid foam insulation, 100mm-thick dense blockwork and a plasterboard interior, can easily achieve the required U-value.

Meeting U-values, however, is only one aspect of an SAP assessment. The problem is that, even if your house is packed with insulation, it still won't save much heat if it has single-glazed windows, uses an elderly, inefficient boiler or is riddled with draughts. A recent German study found that, if 140mm of insulation has just a single 1mm gap in it, its efficiency drops by 40 per cent.

The SAP assessment, then, aims to overcome this by looking at the energy efficiency of the house as a whole. That includes its heating and hot-water systems, its internal and external lighting, the effect of the sun's warmth, the heat lost through gaps in the fabric and what's known as 'cold bridging'. This is where a part of the interior – such as a floor joist or a window frame – touches the uninsulated exterior, and allows heat to leak through the 'bridge' that's created.

The Code for Sustainable Homes

The code is effectively a super-SAP, an attempt to create a new standard for house building that is low-carbon and environmentally friendly in England, Wales and Northern Ireland. (Scotland currently uses an earlier standard known as Ecohomes.)

The code takes into account not only the energy consumed by a house and the amount of CO_2 it emits, but eight other factors, including the amount of water it uses, the amount of waste and pollution it produces, the materials used in its construction, the health and well-being of the occupants and the environmental impact on the site. It even reaches the level of a recommended size of bath (thus saving water), the need for bicycle storage (because car use is not encouraged) and a compost heap (to help you grow your own food).

There are six levels, each given a star rating. The starting point is the energy efficient requirements of Part L of the building regulations in 2006, when the code was first written:

Level 1 represents a 10 per cent improvement on 2006.
Level 2, 18 per cent.
Level 3, 25 per cent.
Level 4, 44 per cent.
Level 5, 100 per cent.
Level 6 represents a totally zero-carbon home.

Each level is achieved on the basis of points awarded for specified enhancements, such as installing a high-efficiency condensing boiler, fitting dual-flush toilets or using a washing machine with a maximum volume of 60ltr. Some of the requirements are mandatory but, as with SAPs, others are optional and there's room for negotiation.

At the time of writing, all new homes must receive a code rating, but there's no requirement to reach any particular level. If you don't want to carry out an assessment, you can simply opt for a 'nil rating' certificate.

So why bother?

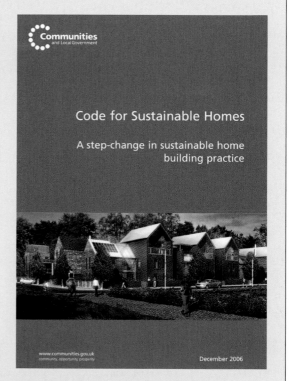

The Code for Sustainable Homes describes six levels of increasing energy efficiency and sustainability, with the highest producing a sum total of zero carbon dioxide emissions in its construction or services.

It's the government's aim to make the requirements of the building regulations move gradually closer to those of the code in order to reach its 2016 zero-carbon deadline. After that time, then, the code rating of new homes should have increasing importance, not just in terms of running costs but also in terms of marketability.

One comforting thought is that, under the code, building materials need to achieve a certain sustainability rating, as judged by a Green Guide published by the Building Research Establishment (see Contacts). Brick structures are rated A+, pretty much as high as you can get, so choosing brick should present few problems under the code.

You can check the latest version at the Communities and Local Government website (www.communities.gov.uk/thecode).

The final complication of SAP is the 'Carbon Index Rating'. This calculates the amount of CO_2 the finished house will produce. It's measured in kilograms of carbon dioxide per square metre of floor area per year.

A figure known as the 'Target Emission Rate', or TER, is reached by working out the rating of a hypothetical house of the same size and type. When your build is finished, another calculation is made, based on the actual CO_2 emissions of the house. It takes account of any changes made from the plans and the result of an air-tightness test, which essentially measures how leaky the house is. A large fan is attached to the front door, air is extracted and a reading taken of the rate at which it is replaced.

The result of the fresh calculation is known as the 'Dwelling Emission Rate' or DER. If your DER is the same or lower than your TER, you've passed. If not, you'll need to make adjustments.

Complicated though the SAP calculations are, they do have one major advantage, which is that, within their limits, they are negotiable. A designer is allowed to 'trade off' certain factors against others. For example, fitting solar heating panels or a whole-house ventilation system could enable you to apply the rules less stringently elsewhere, perhaps by using slimmer insulation in the walls in order to save a few valuable centimetres on a tight plot.

Gaining Access

If you're physically able and don't live with very young children or elderly relatives, Part M, the part of the building regulations that deals with accessibility, can seem an unnecessary complication. But with a steadily ageing population, which will eventually include yourself, most of the requirements aren't too onerous. They include, for example, positioning power sockets no lower than 450mm above the floor and light switches no higher than 1,200mm – ideal for a wheelchair user.

There must also be a WC on the ground floor or entrance storey. It doesn't need to be large enough to accommodate a wheelchair, but the door should open outwards and the doorway wide enough to allow a wheelchair-user access. For the same reason, the hand-basin shouldn't obstruct the entrance.

Halls, passageways and doorways on the ground floor should be wide enough for a wheelchair. Generally speaking, the narrower the doorway, the wider the passageway needs to be, depending on whether the doorway is approached head-on or from the side. For example, the minimum width for a passageway leading directly to a 750mm-wide doorway is 900mm. If the doorway is to one side, so that a wheelchair has to turn to enter it, the passageway's minimum width rises to 1,200mm. Entrance doorways, meanwhile, should be at least 775mm wide, though they needn't be the front door, merely the one designated as the accessible entrance.

It's outside, however, where things get trickier. Before Part M, there was no specific requirement covering external access. On a sloping site any number of steps could lead up to the front door. Now Part M requires 'reasonable provision' for disabled access. Where the ground leading to the front door has a slope no steeper than 1 in 15, it recommends building shallow ramps. Where the slope is steeper, steps are

The Building Regulations 2010

Access to and use of buildings

M

APPROVED DOCUMENT

M1   Access and use
M2   Access to extensions to buildings other than dwellings
M3   Sanitary conveniences in extensions to buildings other than dwellings
M4   Sanitary conveniences in dwellings

2004 edition incorporating 2010 amendments

Part M of the building regulations has made a significant difference to the way main entrances and corridors are designed, and even the positions of light switches.

permitted, but they should be at least 900mm wide and no step should be higher than 150mm. If there are three or more flights, a handrail needs to be provided.

Given the huge variety of possible sites, it's reasonable to expect a degree of flexibility from building control, but that still leaves the front door sill. Traditionally, it's been a brick or two higher than the damp-proof course, simply to keep the rain out. Part M requires that the threshold be 'accessible'. Here, that means level and flush with the floor, both inside and out. In practice, it allows a threshold no higher than 15mm, not a huge obstacle to a sudden downpour. The answer is an external drain running the width of the sill, which can be bought or fashioned on-site. There also needs to be some very careful detailing with the damp-proof membrane beneath the threshold and where it protects the floor slab and the floor finish on top of it.

If all this seems a pain, bear in mind it's exactly the same method used to install folding, sliding doors between a ground-floor room and a patio or terrace outside, creating an instant 'room in the garden' – currently one of the most popular design features for extensions, as well as new builds.

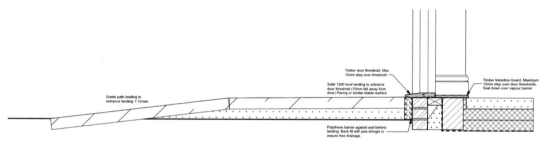

Ramped access entrance door threhold detail
Scale 1:10

The thresholds of main entrances can now be no higher than 15mm to allow for wheelchair access; ensuring that no water enters demands careful detailing.

CHAPTER 12

Hiring a Main Contractor

If you feel you lack the experience or confidence to project manage your own build, or you're unable or unwilling to devote the time and effort it requires, hiring a main contractor is a happy compromise. A single professional takes over the burden of realizing your design. As a result, you have only one individual to deal with and the arrangement is governed by a contract that you both sign, giving a fixed price for the build and an agreed date for the completion.

The only obvious catch is choosing the right contractor. If you take the traditional route of having your build managed by an architect or other building professional, they can put the building work out to tender to contractors they know to be competent and reliable. Based on the prices quoted, and each contractor's response, they will then recommend the most suitable. You will be charged for this service but, once the contractor is

hired, you're not obliged to continue using the architect or other professional, as a project manager, unless, of course, you want to.

If you'd rather opt out of choosing altogether, you can also use one of the few design and build package companies who specialize in brick and block. They will either build your house for you or recommend a contractor. Removing the element of competition, however, isn't likely to encourage keen pricing or leave you much room for negotiation.

FINDING YOUR OWN MAIN CONTRACTOR

The best advertisements for builders are personal recommendations and their own work. If neighbours, friends or relatives have been impressed by a contractor, get their details. Or if you've seen a new build you've admired, trace the contractor responsible via the phone book, internet, planning and building regulations' applications at the local planning department, or simply ask on-site. Often this is the only way to find good, local builders who survive happily on word-of-mouth alone.

If none have made it into your design file, there are a number of organizations that list tradesmen and offer a degree of reassurance, either in terms of a warranty scheme or ratings by previous clients.

Trustmark (see Contacts), for example, is a non-profit, government-sponsored scheme whose members have signed up to a code of good practice. They also provide insurance-backed warranties, including protection for deposits if a firm goes bankrupt. Trustmark works in conjunction with the Federation of Master Builders (FMB), which represents small and medium-sized building firms. The FMB has lists of vetted contractors, as

Hiring a project manager, who can advise you on the choice of a main contractor as well taking care of the day to day running of your build, can reduce a large amount of stress.

well as its own building insurance scheme, Build Assure. Both of these organizations can be accessed online. A number of websites offer find-a-tradesmen services – some provide their own vetting, while others operate more like an online 'word-of-mouth' service, allowing previous customers to rate their members.

Wherever you look, opting for local contractors has the advantage of a builder who is likely to be familiar with local conditions and local officialdom. It should also be easier to visit the builder and previous clients.

NARROWING THE FIELD

Once you're satisfied with your list of candidates, now's the time to get in touch and discover whether they are willing to quote. You can download a standard query letter for free from the website of the Joint Contracts Tribunal (see Contacts), an independent body, which is the leading provider of standard building contracts. Telephoning or meeting in person is an opportunity to gain first impressions.

Expertise on a building site doesn't always go with advanced social skills, but if a builder is particularly elusive or persistently neglects to return calls, it's reasonable to assume your work isn't that important to him.

Most reliable builders will be happy to talk about previous jobs and give you contact numbers of former clients. Do follow these up. The chances that a cowboy builder has been astute enough to organize friends or relatives as satisfied 'customers' may seem remote – and unlikely to remain undetected after a few minutes' conversation – but the information you gain will be invaluable.

Key questions might be:

- Did the builder complete the project within budget, within schedule and to your satisfaction and, if not, why not?
- How communicative was he? Was he easy to contact, did he keep you informed about progress or warn you of possible delays or problems in advance?
- Was any extra work charged for fairly?
- Was the site kept tidy and all rubbish removed at the end?
- Did the builder and his workforce behave reasonably throughout; for example, without constant swearing or loud music, showing politeness to both yourself and neighbours, and respect for your property?

The Architect's Edge

There's another good reason to choose an architect to source a main contractor. Architects are not only familiar with reliable local builders, and so well-placed to make recommendations, contractors are more likely to respond to an architect's invitation to quote than from a stranger, i.e. you. The reason is simple: local architects provide a regular source of work, you don't; or at least on nothing like the same scale.

If it's a choice between spending a day or two quoting from a familiar architect's detailed tender document (see below) or spending time on a single client's tender, which may not be so detailed or so professionally presented, chances are the architect will get their attention. This is particularly relevant with smaller builders who don't have the time or resources to devote to quotes they might regard as more speculative.

- What was the worst crisis in your project and how was it solved?
- Was the builder open to suggestion regarding building techniques or materials?

The last query will vary in importance according to your aims and the depth of your research. Some self-builders will know more about the latest building methods than many builders, who are too busy or insufficiently interested, to keep up to date. In this case, an open-minded, adaptable and resourceful builder will be a valuable asset.

FINAL CHECKS

Insurance

Your main contractor should have public liability insurance to a minimum of £1 million. This covers them against claims as a result of injury or death from third parties – including passers by, neighbours and trespassers on your site – as well as damage to property. If they don't, or it has lapsed, you could find yourself liable.

Check also that they have contract works or 'all-risks' insurance. This provides cover against all manner of perils, from fire, flood and storm damage to theft. If your contractor doesn't have it, and your half-completed building burns down, all that time, effort and expense could go to waste.

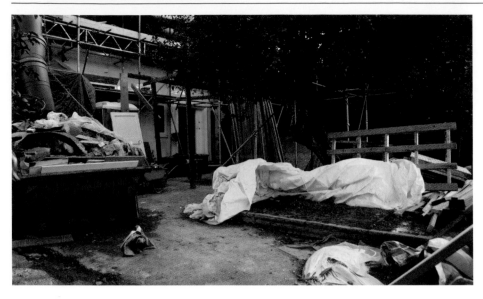

Try to visit a potential main contractor's current site; its state can be an indication of their organizational and general abilities.

Membership of Professional Bodies

This is most important in terms of warranty providers. In practice, lenders will insist your main contractor is, for example, registered with the National House Building Council (NHBC) and their membership is current, before releasing funds. If you are providing your own finance, you will need to check this yourself before signing a contract.

The UK's largest building trade association is the Federation of Master Builders, whose membership is vetted and includes general builders, as well as specialist tradespeople. The FMB operates a 'find a builder' and dispute resolution services, trade certification schemes and even lists builders falsely claiming membership. Its website (see Contacts) is a mine of information.

More prestigious is the Chartered Institute of Building. Though you can telephone the CIOB to verify a membership, it is otherwise not consumer-orientated.

Site Visit

If possible, pay a visit to a builder's current project. If it's neat and well-organized, this is generally a good sign. If it's a mess with materials piled haphazardly and left open to the weather, mud covering the pavement and street, and rubbish blowing about, think again.

HOW TO INVITE QUOTES

It might seem that all the detail shown in your build-

ing control-approved plans should be enough for a builder to go on, together with a covering letter listing any additional requirements and a thorough discussion on site. Some contractors will be happy to proceed on this basis – for the simple reason that you are handing the bulk of the decision-making to them. That greatly simplifies their lives and their ability to ensure a decent profit through the prudent use of materials, design details and, to a degree, standards of workmanship.

This isn't to suggest that builders will automatically rook you, given the chance. Like everyone else, they have to make a living and, if a client seems unfussed by the use of 'trade' bathroom or kitchen fittings, or bog-standard skirting and architraves, and this shaves a few hundred pounds off the builder's costs, where's the harm?

Most people, however, self-build because they want something more individual and of a higher standard. And, for that, you will need to be much more specific in your directions to your builder.

So how much information should you provide?

The easy answer is: as much as possible, but in a structured way. The ideal is to produce 'like-for-like' quotes, where each element of the build is listed with a space left for pricing. This will allow you to compare and contrast each quote in detail, and perhaps use the differences as a basis for negotiation.

Architects call this process 'tendering', and the basis of it is a detailed specification: a precise description of every aspect of your design.

WRITING A SPECIFICATION

If you've done your design work thoroughly, you'll have a good idea of how many items in a house need to be specified. Few complete beginners appreciate the complexity of a full technical specification – it can easily run to more than twenty pages.

You can, of course, write your own, ensuring it includes all the elements that are most important to you. Beyond that, you will have to rely on the judgment of your contractor, and trust that any variations or corrections will be covered by your contingency fund.

You can also buy a specification online from the NBS, an offshoot of RIBA, based on JCT contracts. Or you could take the easier, faster and arguably much safer route of handing the task over to your designer. He, or she, after all, is the expert on your design.

HOW A SPECIFICATION IS SET OUT

A specification of the sort used for a major construction project has a standard layout. A house build won't need to be so comprehensive, but many of the essential points are the same. Typically, there are four sections: preliminaries and general conditions; the specification itself; a summary and form of tender; and appendices.

Preliminaries

These are all the details that cover the way work is to be conducted on site. It includes hours of working, arrangements for providing temporary power and water supplies, storage of materials, rubbish removal, parking arrangements, preferred means of access, security fencing, toilet facilities, any restriction on loud music. Anything, in fact, that you can think of to make the site operate smoothly.

It should also include the form of contract you would like to use; there are more details about this below.

The Specification Itself

The aspects to be covered include the following:

- External works (clearing the plot, tree removal, etc.).
- Excavations and foundations.
- Brick and blockwork (types of brick and block specified, colour of mortar, type of joints, form of damp-

Domestic Specification

Specification template for small residential building projects

PROJECT: _____

CUSTOMER: _____

CONSULTANT: _____

CONTRACTOR: _____

DATE: _____

A specification, based on JCT contracts, can be bought online from the NBS, an offshoot of the Royal Institute of British Architects.

proof course, depth of cavity wall, depth of insulation, form of wall ties, positions of air vents, type of cavity trays, etc.).
- Ground floor (form of construction).
- Scaffolding.
- Roof structure (form of construction, covering, insulation, etc.).
- Rainwater goods.
- External windows and doors.
- External drainage.
- External paving.
- Internal walls, upper floors and door frames.
- Internal doors and ironmongery.
- Kitchen units and fittings.
- Staircase.
- Plasterboard, plastering and coving.

- Plumbing, heating and sanitary fittings.
- Electrical installation and fittings.
- Floors and finishes.
- Wall tiling.
- Internal decorations.

Summary

Here, the total sums for each of the categories above are brought together and a grand total reached.

Form of Tender

This confirms the final price, states how long the work will take and the date on which the contractor can start. It should also confirm that the tender will remain valid for 3 months.

Appendices

These include the plans approved by building control, together with any drawings of key details of the design and any structural engineer's drawings and calculations. These should all be clearly numbered. If you intend to use products or materials from specific manufacturers, technical and other details, including catalogue numbers, could also go here.

How Do You Guarantee the Quality of Work?

If your building experience is limited or non-existent and you don't have an architect or other professional supervising your build, this can be a major worry. It's easy enough to spot if brickwork isn't plumb or if cables or pipes are left hanging from the wall, but what about the parts you can't see? How do you know if the wiring has been done correctly or if the flooring has the appropriate grade of chipboard?

Regular inspections by the building inspector provide a good safeguard, but only up to a point. His, or her, job is to ensure that the work accords with the requirements of the building regulations, which can be surprisingly forgiving. The quality of workmanship is only of concern if it causes a violation of those regulations.

The building inspector isn't around all the time, either, allowing plenty of opportunity for a hard-pressed or lazy contractor to cover up poor work. It's only if an inspector has good reason to believe that hidden work isn't up to the regulations that he, or she, can demand that it be exposed and inspected.

Inspections by warranty providers are marginally more rigorous, but again their site visits are infrequent.

One basic safeguard, of course, is the plans, which have gained building regulations' approval. They will have numerous references to various British Standards, which govern the quality of workmanship.

For building sites, the relevant British Standard is BS:8000. It has fifteen parts, each establishing a code of practice for everything from excavation and filling (part 1) to hot and cold water services (part 15). In between, there's masonry, glazing, plastering and even painting and decorative wall surfaces. There's also a British Standard for tolerances – BS: 5606 – covering the acceptable variations in size, flatness, moisture content and so on from the ideal.

Writing these standards into your specification and your contract gives them legal force. That doesn't mean, of course, that your contractor will be thoroughly conversant with them or even have heard of them. If a dispute arises over workmanship, an adjudicator, who should be a qualified building professional – probably a surveyor – will know them, and be able to use them as a basis for his or her judgment.

Professional bodies also provide safeguards of their own. Electrical installations, for example, should be installed in accordance with the Institute of Electrical Engineers (IEE) wiring regulations. Gas appliances and related pipework should be installed, commissioned and certified by operatives registered with the Gas Safe Register (the successor to CORGI).

Heating and hot-water installations should be provided with a benchmark certificate, demonstrating the competence of the installer. There are similar schemes for oil appliances and tanks (through OFTEC), solid-fuel appliances (HETAS) and double-glazing (FENSA). (See Contacts for details.)

Again, all these can be written into a specification, though, in practice, any competent contractor will abide by them automatically.

For ultimate peace of mind you can always hire a building surveyor to check the standard of workmanship either at the end of the build, before completion is agreed or at any point when you need reassurance. There are also specialist snagging services that will to go over your completed house and compile a list of defects.

One ingenious self-builder I knew used to pay tradesmen a percentage of their daily rate to visit his site after hours and check the work of their co-professionals. This not only allowed him to correct defects on a regular basis but to create a largely spurious reputation as an experienced developer with an eagle eye for poor workmanship.

WHAT A SPECIFICATION – AND A TENDER – CANNOT TELL YOU

However comprehensive or detailed a specification is, there are aspects of a build that won't be included, either through choice or their own nature. Top of the list is foundations. Even after a thorough soil survey, no-one can predict exactly what soil conditions are like until the ground is dug. Sod's law dictates that the one piece of land that isn't surveyed turns out to be made-up ground or the site of a forgotten well.

Some contractors will only provide an estimate – not a fixed quote – for work of this kind, where its full extent isn't yet clear. This is known as a 'provisional sum'. In this case it's likely to be based on standard, metre-deep concrete foundations but, if the ground proves unsuitable, more elaborate and expensive options may be needed, which will have to be priced accordingly.

There are also items that you could have included in the specification but choose to leave until later. Kitchen and bathroom fittings are typical examples, for the understandable reason that you're unwilling to make a decision until you see where they're going. Here, a 'prime cost' or PC sum is quoted, which effectively states a maximum price for each item. You don't have to stick with this, of course, though going well beyond it may mean busting your budget and risks the possibility of the item being unavailable or not deliverable within your build schedule.

Alternatively, if you have decided early on about specific items that you plan to supply yourself, the specification can state 'fitting only'. Potentially, this can be a tricky point. If you simply specify a particular item and leave it to the contractor to supply, he's likely to obtain it at a trade price but charge you the listed price. It's effectively a fee for supplying exactly what you want, though a well-established one. This practice, however, has been undermined to an extent by the growth of the internet, which makes it much easier for non-professionals to buy at trade prices or even lower. Your contractor may bow to the inevitable on this, or not. For an item you're very keen on, it should be discussed before you buy.

The same goes for products, materials or services that the contractor may not be familiar with, such as underfloor heating, rainwater harvesting or home-automation systems. These often depend on specialists with whom you will make separate agreements. Some manufacturers will offer training schemes – sometimes free – to bring your contractor up to speed. Again, you should let contractors know so that this can be included in the specification.

SENDING OUT TENDERS

The ideal number of quotes is three. Any more and you're making work for yourself; any less and it's hard to make a judgment.

To achieve this may well mean sending out four or five tenders. Even though your candidates may have agreed to quote, their circumstances could have changed or the sight of your incredibly detailed specification could deter them.

The tender should be accompanied by a covering letter and, by way of gentle encouragement, a stamped addressed envelope, though using email will, hopefully, speed up the process.

Allow up to four weeks for replies, during which time you can expect candidates to visit your plot. This is an opportunity to talk through the specification, answer queries and clear up any ambiguities or uncertainties. A follow-up phone call will maintain contact and help to provide mutual reassurance.

MAKING YOUR CHOICE

Comparing quotes usually provides an interesting tutorial in the imprecision of language. What may be perfectly obvious to one contractor, clearly confuses another, while a third appears to ignore whole sections of the specification. This, of course, may be as much a reflection of the specification and the way it's written, as it is of those reading it.

That said, your immediate concern is going to be the grand total. Three broadly similar prices are usually an indication that the specification was probably accurate. More common is two broadly comparable and a third markedly lower or higher.

A low price suggests that the contractor has miscalculated, either through error or inexperience, or perhaps an intention to make up the deficit with over-priced extras. An ability to start immediately also implies a degree of desperation,

A much higher price suggests a contractor is only willing to take on the work if he can guarantee a comfortable profit, either because he can afford to pick and choose or there's an aspect of the build that he's not confident about pricing accurately – perhaps something innovative or unfamiliar in the design. A start date some months away would tend to support this.

On the other hand, an excellent builder may have just had a job cancelled and is keen to keep his workers employed, even at a reduced profit. Or the highly priced contractor may have realized something significant about your design, or your plot, which hasn't occurred to his rivals. The only way to find out, of course, is to talk to the contractors.

The advantage of an itemized specification is that rivals' pricing can be compared easily. Asking one contractor why certain of his prices are significantly different to another's can be highly illuminating. It's not, incidentally, rude or provocative to be nit-picking at this stage. You are paying an awful lot of money and you've every right to safeguard your interests. A good contractor will respect that. If a builder is clearly uncomfortable with close questioning or imprecise in his answers, this is not a good sign.

In fact, the relationship you establish – or don't – will be key to your final choice. Do you, on balance, have confidence in this individual and, equally important, feel comfortable with them? You're going to have a great deal of contact over many months. Beyond costs, recommendations or any other objective criteria, gut feel is invariably the decider.

WHAT IF ALL THE QUOTES ARE TOO HIGH?

This can be a shock, but not as disastrous as it seems. If you've been doing your own specification, it's a sharp lesson in house-building realities. If you've been relying on the opinion of your architect or designer, it's a reminder that many designers are best at designing.

So what do you do?

First, check that the prices are accurate and identify the high-cost items. Is it the hand-made bricks, the designer bathroom or the innovative multi-fuel under-floor central heating system? Ask yourself how important these budget-busting items really are.

Second, talk over with your preferred contractor how costs can be reduced. Don't be embarrassed about this. Contractors do this all the time and may have cost-cutting suggestions that haven't occurred to you.

If, after this, you are still beyond your budget, you have two choices. You can re-tender – you may simply have picked three contractors who are unable to meet your budgetary needs. Your conversations with them

may give a clue to this, but also take the advice of your designer. Alternatively, carry out your own cost-reduction review. Again, your designer can contribute.

One approach is to use cheaper items and materials in areas that can be easily upgraded later. For example, vinyl flooring in kitchens and bathrooms instead of tiling, gravel for the front drive instead of paving and grass seed for the garden in place of extensive landscaping.

Another approach is to check how many specialist sub-contractors your main contractor has included in his pricing. He will usually have added his own mark-up, so savings might be made by employing them directly, perhaps after the main contractor's work is finished. This is difficult with plumbers, electricians and plasterers who are so integral to the building structure, but easier with flooring, kitchen and bathroom fitters.

Sourcing more of your own materials, perhaps through the internet, could also produce savings.

You might also fit pipework, wiring and other ancillary parts for systems and services you can't immediately afford. Examples are a two- or three-coil hot-water cylinder with pipework for multiple sources of heating, or ducting for a whole-house mechanical ventilation system or central vacuuming. This may seem an indulgence, but it will minimize expensive disruption later and, as part of the initial build, be VAT-free.

Finally, there are the nuclear options. One is simply to dispense with a main contractor altogether and project manage your own build.

Another is to go for a shell build. Here, your contractor merely provides a basic, weather-proof structure, leaving you to complete the interior as and when you can afford to. But don't expect your lender to take this option well.

AGREEING A CONTRACT

However precise your specification, or fervent your builder's insistence that he'll follow it to the letter, there's a degree of reassurance – on both sides – in making your agreement legally binding. House-building is a complicated business and, despite the best intentions, things can go wrong. The existence of a contract not only provides immediate peace of mind, but also a basis for negotiation if disputes arise.

Your architect or designer may prepare a contract, your contractor may present you with one or you can write or adapt your own.

Helpfully, there are a number of off-the-shelf contracts for building works, which you can buy or even download for free. The Joint Contracts Tribunal (JCT) publishes the best known. It comes in two forms: the building contract for the home-owner/occupier who has not appointed a consultant to oversee the work; and a version for those using an architect, surveyor or other project manager.

An alternative is the Plain English Domestic Building Contract from the Federation of Master Builders (FMB), which is available free on the FMB's website. Both this and the JCT contract come with guidance notes and both are noted for their clarity and lack of jargon.

In Scotland, either a Design and Build or a Standard Building Contract can be bought from the Scottish Building Contracts Committee (see Contacts).

WHAT THE CONTRACT SHOULD INCLUDE

Names Full names of you, your contractor and any professional, such as an architect, managing the contract on your behalf.

The work required A brief description of the project, the contractor's quote, the detailed specification, including any agreed changes and relevant drawings. Each party should initial each page of the documents – so there's no doubt everyone has read them – while you keep the originals and the contractor a full set of copies.

The price The accepted quote, which can be revised up or down, if there are agreed changes to the specification.

Duration of the project The start date and the time within which it will be completed. Completion should be when both parties agree the main work has been done.

Payment When and how payment should be made; for example, at the end of every month or on completion of agreed stages of the build. If your lender is making part payments on this latter basis, it should be made clear that the work needs to be inspected and approved by the lender's surveyor before payment is made.

Retention Typically, this involves withholding between 2½ to 5 per cent of the price for 3 to 6 months after completion. It's to encourage the builder to remedy any 'snags' – minor adjustments or defects – that have become apparent during the build, or appear during

A building contract can be downloaded free from the website of the Federation of Master Builders.

the retention period. Incidentally, though retentions are common practice, they can't be presumed or imposed, unless they're agreed in advance. Any contractor who is faced with one without warning is not going to take it well.

Insurance The contractor should confirm that he has sufficient and current public liability and all risks cover.

Penalties If the work over-runs significantly due to 'unwarranted delays', i.e. not involving the weather, acts of God or any other matter the contractor couldn't reasonably have foreseen, this allows you to claim compensation (the official term is 'liquidated damages'), usually at an agreed sum for every week's delay. This only has real force if you risk a direct loss as a result of a delay and can prove it. In reality, all builds over-run and the fact that it's inconvenient shouldn't trigger a penalty payment – unless, of course, the delay becomes so extended there's genuine doubt that the work will ever be finished. In which case, you will find yourself in dispute.

Dispute resolution An agreed procedure to follow if either of the parties decides to start proceedings against the other. Typically, you both agree to appoint an adjudicator whose costs will become part of the contract. The adjudicator should be an individual or a body with construction expertise, such as a surveyor or a trade association.

WHAT IF YOU AND YOUR CONTRACTOR FALL OUT?

First, at some point, you will. With an enterprise this complicated, this prolonged and with so much riding on it, it's inevitable; and normal.

In fact, most relationships with contractors follow a well-established pattern: initial euphoria, dawning realization that your builder is fallible, returning respect (hopefully mutual), euphoria (tempered with exhaustion and relief).

Second, few contractor–client relationships break down completely. This is because the contractor knows that if that happens he'll almost certainly never see his money, or only after expensive legal wrangling and a lot of time.

The client, on the other hand, will have to put the build on hold while he, or she, finds a replacement. Builders, however, are generally reluctant to take over others' jobs, largely because they are wary of assuming responsibility for work they haven't done and there's a good chance that it's of poor quality. They may well insist on starting over again.

In other words, it's in everyone's interest to reach an agreement, however unsatisfactory or galling it may feel in the short term.

If the prospect of this sort of situation fills you with dread, you may feel easier using your architect, designer or project manager as an intermediary in the event of a dispute. This should be written into the contract you agree with them.

SO WHAT CAN GO WRONG?

The most common situations are:

- **The disappearing act** The contractor starts well, then the numbers on site begin to fall and the work rate slows. Eventually the contractor vanishes completely for long periods. Likely cause – a problem site elsewhere, taking on too much work, cashflow problems.
- **Poor workmanship** Even an amateur can see walls aren't plumb, brickwork is messy, pipework is left disconnected. Likely cause – promised quality workers or sub-contractors are either not available, or have been moved to other sites where their skills are urgently needed, or another client is complaining more loudly than you about poor workmanship.
- **Health and safety and environmental issues** A messy site where holes are left unguarded, materials uncovered and noxious chemicals leak. Likely cause – all of the above and/or you've mistakenly hired a not very competent contractor.
- **Insolvency** Most builders juggle two or more jobs to maintain their cash flow and keep their workforce fully occupied. But a run of bad luck – poor weather, a problem site, one or more clients refusing to pay – and the most competent and experienced can come unstuck. The clients, however, may not know about it until the contractor's credit runs out and they receive urgent requests for advance payments.

WHAT CAN YOU DO?

The first step is always to talk to your contractor. He may be genuinely unaware of the problem or too distracted by other matters to have noticed, but it should be a clear warning to him to up his game.

If nothing changes, or the situation improves but then deteriorates, you may have to move to step two, which should be part of your contract. This is to issue a written warning, stating the reasons for your dissatisfaction and giving your contractor 7 days to remedy matters or otherwise resolve the situation.

If nothing happens by that time, or nothing that reassures you, you can legally terminate your contract, again in writing. You'll still have to pay, however, for work properly carried out and for materials on-site.

Step number three is to resort to an adjudicator, though at any point both parties can decide to settle the matter between themselves.

The one event likely to scotch this is the contractor becoming insolvent. If he is registered with NHBC, or you have a building warranty with another provider, there will be a provision to cover the cost of the completion of your build.

CHAPTER 13

Hiring Sub-Contractors

Even if you've opted for a 'turn key' operation, you'll almost certainly have some dealings with sub-contractors, otherwise known as 'subbies'. If you project manage your own build, you'll be dealing with them almost exclusively. This can be a daunting prospect for those with little experience of building or staff management. Most of us have mixed experiences of tradespeople.

Assembling your own team of sub-contractors is very much like engaging a main contractor, only writ small. Things become generally less formal, payments smaller and more regular, and relationships rather more important.

WHO ARE THE 'SUBBIES' AND WHAT DO THEY DO?

Sub-contractors are the sharp end of the building business, the workers who make sense of the plans. Most are specialist tradespeople, who often pick up related skills. Most are self-employed but are usually linked informally to larger groups, which come together on an ad hoc basis.

Skill levels can range from the extraordinary to the barely competent, which is one reason why personal reputations and relationships are so important. Essentially, subbies reflect the fragmentary, intermittent and largely unregulated nature of the industry. Sub-contractors also include specialist companies.

Groundworkers

They do pretty much everything up to ground-floor level. That means clearing and levelling the site, excavating the foundation trenches, pouring the concrete for the foundations, building the footings and completing the foundations to ground floor level.

Groundworkers also excavate trenches for soakaways and drains, which they also lay. They build manholes, driveways, pathways, patios and can tackle other aspects of hard and soft landscaping.

They can work as individuals, small gangs or be provided by specialist companies.

Groundworkers do everything up to ground-floor level, from clearing the site and laying drains to foundations.

Piled foundations require specialist equipment from specialist companies.

Bricklayers

'Brickies' or 'trowels' also lay blocks. They build the inner blockwork wall and the outer wall of brickwork, installing cavity insulation and forming openings for windows and doors as they go. They also build the gable ends – the triangular brickwork at each end of the roof – plus the chimney and any internal brick features. Sometimes, bricklayers, rather than groundworkers, will build the footings, too.

Bricklayers often work as a pair sharing a labourer/ hod carrier who keeps them fuelled with bricks, blocks and freshly mixed mortar. Although they can be supplied by specialist companies, the most skilled are in such demand they are usually self-employed.

Carpenters

'Chippies' tackle all the timber work of the build, from cutting and laying the floor joists and floors to erecting the roof. Along the way, they build the studwork for internal walls, assemble and install the staircase, fit the door linings, doors, architraves and skirting,

Scaffolders work in gangs, returning at intervals to install a new 'lift' or level of scaffolding, as required.

Carpenters handle all the timber work of the build, though some specialize in roofing or first or second fixing.

and complete any boxing-in. Some specialize in certain aspects, such as roofing, first and second fixing.

Scaffolders

Scaffolding is needed as the bricklayers complete the walls to first-floor height. It's installed by a gang, often provided by a specialist company. Scaffolders work quickly and then disappear until another 'lift' – another level of working platforms – is required.

Roofers

Roofers provide the covering for the assembled roof, secure waterproof underlay over the rafters, fix battens to which the tiles or slates are attached and complete the roof details, such as sealing the joins between the roof covering and brickwork and where slopes of the roof meet. Roofers work in gangs and are often supplied by a specialist company.

Plasterers and Dry-Liners

They 'spread' plaster masonry walls, laying a render coat first then a top or skim coat for maximum smoothness. Dry-liners tack plasterboard to the ceilings and interior studwork, and tape the joins, making it ready for decorating, or finishing with a skim coat.

Plasterers can also lay floor screeds, creating a level surface for tiles or timber flooring. They usually work alone, or with a labourer, or are provided by a specialist firm.

Plumbers and Heating Engineers

They install and commission the central heating system, including the boiler, hot-water cylinder, radiators and associated pipework for both water and gas supplies. They also fit the sanitary ware, sinks, basins, baths, showers, waste pipes, guttering and downpipes and install a standpipe to provide a mains water supply for the site at the beginning of the build.

Plumbers usually work on their own or with a mate. They can also be provided by a specialist firm.

At the completion of the job, heating engineers will issue a certificate certifying that the equipment complies with current building regulations. To do this they must be registered with a government-approved self-certification scheme, such as those operated by the Association of Plumbing and Heating Contractors or the Gas Safe Register.

Electricians

'Sparks' install all the wiring necessary for the house, fit the consumer unit, all lighting and power points, switches, cooker, cooker hood, extractor fans and central heating controls and make and test all the connections. They also set up a temporary consumer unit for builders' use at the start of the build.

Electricians usually work alone or with a mate and can be supplied by a specialist firm. Once the job is done, they will issue an electrical safety certificate. To do this they must be registered with a government-approved self-certification scheme, such as those operated by the National Inspection Council for Electrical Installation Contracting (NICEIC), ELECSA or the National Association for Professional Inspectors and Testers (NAPIT).

Painters and Decorators

These are jobs many self-builders do for themselves, largely because most of us have personal experience of them. You may hire professionals because you don't have the time or skills for DIY, or you are looking for the best possible finish. Both these trades work

Roofers are responsible for covering the assembled roof and ensuring it is fully waterproof; they usually work in gangs, often supplied by a specialist company. Michele Meyer

Dry-liners nail or screw plasterboard to ceilings and studwork walls and tape the joins ready for decoration or skim plastering.

individually or with mates, and can be provided by specialist companies.

Ceramic Tilers

Like the above, a job for individuals or specialist companies.

Labourers

Most labourers will come as part of a gang of specialized tradespeople. The most important on a traditional build is the bricklayer's labourer or hod carrier. An experienced individual who anticipates the needs of the bricklayers can have a major impact on the speed and efficiency of the bricklaying. General labourers will do a range of jobs from moving materials around the site to tidying up.

Other Trades

These tend to be specialist companies supplying and installing items such as custom-made double or triple-glazed windows, fitted kitchens, fitted flooring, home-automation systems, basements, photovoltaic and solar heating panels for the roof, and so on.

HOW DO YOU FIND SUB-CONTRACTORS?

The easy answer is: much as you find a main contractor, i.e. by seeing and admiring their work, by personal recommendation (from acquaintances, other tradespeople or online) or by approaching representative trade organizations.

Many of the trades mentioned above have them (see Contacts) and their websites provide lists of members, usually traceable by speciality and location. All have codes of practice, many offer complaints procedures and some have insurance-backed warranties to cover work that doesn't meet the building regulations and offer redress if a member goes bust.

Impressively, one, the National Inspection Council for Electrical Installation Contracting (NICEIC), includes a Wall of Shame on its website, naming contractors who have falsely advertised themselves as being members. Excellent PR as this is, it also indicates that membership is commercially worthwhile.

Asking for recommendations from others in the trade can also be useful. Builders' merchants, plumbers' merchants, electrical factors, decorators' merchants and tool-hire shops all have daily contact with tradesmen and should have an idea of who is in constant demand.

Your architect or designer may have some suggestions. You can also approach tradespeople directly on other sites.

In practice, however, it's often the sub-contractors on your site who are the most reliable source of other trades. They may well recommend individuals they get on well with, but they are also likely to be competent and dependable, since no one wants to work with someone who isn't. This should also help to create a happy site – another plus; a miserable or stressed workplace won't attract or retain workers, or encourage them to excel. Remember: your build may be a major event in your life, but to your subbies, it's just another job.

Incidentally, if you do follow up a personal recommendation, always let the sub-contractor know who recommended them. The loosely structured nature of the building industry means that it depends heavily on personal contacts. Showing you're part of it, however marginally, helps to establish your credibility.

WHAT TO LOOK FOR IN A BRICKLAYER

A bricklayer doesn't simply lay neat, clean, regular courses of brickwork. He (and, currently, it's predominantly 'he') will calculate the runs of brick so as to avoid awkward cuts at the ends of walls. He will also set out the facing brickwork on the ground before any of it is laid, working out the positions of external doors and windows, and the brickwork needed to create the reveals surrounding these openings. For this he will need to be able to read plans and drawings.

This is a good reason to involve your master bricklayer as early as possible, ideally at the design stage. Architects don't always take runs of brick into account, with unhappy results if this is only discovered on-site. A good bricklayer should be able to point out any flaws or potential problems from the plans.

Early involvement is also important to be sure of booking the bricklayer of your choice. A master bricklayer will have work lined up months in advance. The wait will be even longer if you want special skills in such things as traditional bonds, decorative patterning or using special mortars, such as lime.

In your first discussions, the bricklayer will want to know details of the bricks, blocks, mortar, lime, plasticizers and, especially, sand to be used. He's likely to have preferences or suggestions of his own. Assuming they don't alter your design unacceptably, these should be taken seriously. He'll almost certainly know a lot more about brickwork than your designer.

Demonstrating adaptability and a capacity to work well with others, as well as knowledge of the building and safety regulations, are all good signs.

One of the best indications of expertise, however, can be age. Bricklaying may seem an occupation for the young and fit, but a mature bricklayer who has been 'on the tools' for several decades can more than make up for any reduction in energy or stamina, with accumulated skills, breadth of knowledge and consequent efficiency.

Needless to say, of all tradespeople on a brick and block build, it's essential to see examples of his work. He should be happy to let you view previous jobs and talk to clients; he may also have a portfolio to show.

HOW TO RECOGNIZE GOOD BRICKWORK

Good brickwork is usually immediately obvious to most of us. It's where it seems lacking in some indefinable way that makes it hard to judge. Here are a few pointers to pinpoint problems:

Banding and patches Brickwork usually has a predominant colour, or pattern of colours, which should be largely uniform. To achieve this effect, bricks from different batches should be blended before they are laid. If they're not, bands or patches with a slightly different colour or shading may form at random across a wall. Up close, they may not be obvious, but, when you stand back, they shout.

Smudges and stains Brickwork should be clean. Smudges of mortar not only look messy, they're a sign of carelessness in the bricklayers. Another indication is rain stains. It shows that the scaffold boards have not been turned up at the end of the day to protect the fresh brickwork from splashing.

Vertical joints Each of the vertical joints – the perpends – should be plumb and follow a neat line up the building.

Hatching and smiling The horizontal joints should be fully filled and level so that the lower edge of each brick lies flush with the course below. Bricks laid unevenly produce an ugly effect known as 'hatching

and smiling'. It becomes particularly obvious when sunlight strikes the wall at an angle.

Bowing Unless checked early on, a gentle bulge, either vertical or horizontal, can sometimes go undetected until a large area has been completed.

Laying 'smile up' Moulded bricks, particularly hand-made, often sag in the mould, creating a curving crease known as a 'smile'. These bricks should be laid 'smile up'.

The 'perpends' – the vertical joints between bricks – should be plumb and follow a neat line up the building. Given these two examples, which bricklayer would you hire?

Some bricks have a curving crease known as a 'smile' and should be laid, as here, 'smile up'.

A check for competent bricklaying: look into the cavity in external walls and check there are no 'snots', excess mortar left on wall ties, insulation or at the bottom of the cavity; it can lead to damp bridging the wall.

Pointing Neat, even pointing is a sign of good craftsmanship. This is especially so where the bricks have uneven surfaces or irregular shapes – as many handmade and reclaimed examples do. Producing the best effects with bricks of this kind takes great skill.

Checking for 'snots' If you visit a bricklayer on-site, take the opportunity to look down inside the wall cavities. It should be clear of excess mortar, known, unappealingly, as 'snots'. Snots can build up on the cavity insulation, the ties that span the cavity or at the base of the wall. Left in place, they can form bridges, which allow moisture to cross and create damp patches on the inner wall.

HOW DO YOU HIRE SUB-CONTRACTORS?

This depends to an extent on the job. Sub-contractors on the heavy side of building – groundworkers, bricklayers, carpenters, labourers – generally work as individuals or small gangs under a foreman with whom personal agreements are made. They are also likely to be 'labour only'; in other words, they bring themselves and their tools to the job, while you provide their materials and other equipment.

Ideally, you should give a prospective subbie a copy of your building regulations' approved plans to explain the job, agree a quote and terms of payment and have it confirmed in writing.

Written quotes, however, may only be cursory and, in practice, only come from you – that is, a letter confirming what you want done and the sub-contractor's verbal quote. They should contain:

- Full details of the work, including reference to plans, which should be numbered to avoid any confusion.
- The agreed quote.
- Payment arrangements.

Any attempt to impose the conditions found in a main contractor's contract, such as penalty clauses and dispute procedures, is likely to provoke alarm and will almost certainly be ignored. More importantly, from your point of view, they will be virtually unenforceable.

As with a main contractor, you should also check references, view examples of previous work and confirm up to date membership of any trade association, especially if it offers a warranty scheme. In practice, unless you are prepared to commit a great deal of time

Trade Associations

Groundworkers:
- Chartered Institute of Building
- Federation of Master Builders

Bricklayers:
- Association of Brickwork Contractors
- Federation of Master Builders
- Guild of Bricklayers

Carpenters:
- Institute of Carpenters
- Timber Research and Development Association (TRADA)

Scaffolders:
- National Access and Scaffolding Confederation

Roofers:
- Confederation of Roofing Contractors
- National Federation of Roofing Contractors (NFRC)

Plasterers and dryliners:
- Federation of Plastering and Drywall Contractors

Decorators/tilers:
- Painting and Decorating Association
- The Tile Association

Plumbers and heating engineers:
- Building and Engineering Services Association
- Chartered Institute of Plumbing and Heating Engineering (CIPHE)

- Gas Safe Register
- National Association for Professional Inspectors and Testers (NAPIT)

Electricians:
- British Standard Institute's Kitemark
- Electrical Contractors Association
- National Association for Professional Inspectors and Testers (NAPIT)
- National Inspection Council for Electrical Installation Contracting (NICEIC)

Window and door installers:
- British Standard Institute's Kitemark
- National Federation of Glaziers
- Fenestration Self-Assessment Scheme (FENSA)
- Glass and Glazing Federation
- Plastics Window Federation
- Steel Window Association

Landscapers:
- British Association of Landscape Industries

Basement specialists:
- Basement Information Centre
- British Structural Waterproofing Association

Renewable energy:
- ELECSA
- HETAS
- Microgeneration Certification Scheme

and effort, you are only likely to do this with the most important tradesmen, which, in a traditional build, will be the bricklayer.

Hiring sub-contractors, especially those on the heavy building side, really is a matter of mutual trust, depending on good communication and adequate supervision. It pays, then, to keep arrangements as simple and straightforward as possible – worryingly casual as that sounds.

This is less of a concern with the succeeding trades – electricians, plumbers, roofers, etc. – for two main reasons. First, they are more likely to be small firms or well-established one-man bands. Second, they will almost certainly be 'supply and fix'. In other words, they

bring both labour and materials to the job. As a result, it's much easier to get a written quote out of them and even a contract, though they will probably have written it themselves. There will also be a fixed price for the work. Fixed prices make it much easier to keep control of the budget, enabling you to see at glance how much each job will cost and arrange stage payments accordingly.

The main disadvantage of supply and fix is the increased cost. Sub-contractors will expect to make a profit on the materials supplied – typically, the difference between the list price and the trade price they negotiate with trade suppliers. Small firms will also have overheads – transport, yards, offices, staff costs – which they will have to cover.

Heavy side workers are less likely to have these costs, and therefore more likely to favour 'day work', labour charged by the day or hour. This is less attractive to clients who aren't familiar with local rates of pay or how much a sub-contractor can reasonably be expected to do in a day.

The alternative is to charge by a 'measured rate'. For a bricklayer, plasterer or tiler, this might be a price for every square metre; for a groundworker laying drains, a price per metre run. Widely used on commercial sites, this depends on having a pretty clear idea of the work involved and full agreement on what's actually been done. For example, bricklayers are wont to include door and window openings as part of the total square metreage of bricks laid. This is known as 'measuring through' and makes up for all the awkward extra work around openings.

In practice, both measured and day rates only make sense to inexperienced self-builders for work not covered by the fixed price quote, either because of a change of mind or because a particular aspect proves more time-consuming than either side foresaw. Then it becomes a matter for negotiation. By that point, however, you should have a much clearer idea of what your sub-contractors can do and in what time, and, hopefully, more confidence that they won't take advantage.

Labour-only workers working on either day or measured rates will normally expect to be paid at the end of each week's work. Be very wary, however, if a sub-contractor requests payment up front. Labour-only subbies will usually have materials and equipment provided by you. Unless you have specifically requested them to provide certain materials, there should be no need for advance payment. A possible exception may be where the foreman of a gang wants to ensure he can pay his workers at the end of the week. Whether you agree to this or not is really a matter of personal judgement, and how keen you are to keep these particular workers on-site.

Supply and fix workers will have bought their own materials, but 30-day payment is normal for trade account holders, plenty of time for the sub-contractor to show he is competent and reliable before favours like this are asked.

Finally, in discussing your requirements for the job, make sure you discuss the tradespeople's needs, too. For labour-only sub-contractors, especially, ask about the materials and pieces of equipment they will want on-site. If they have made incorrect assumptions about what you will provide, the morning they start on-site isn't a good time to find out.

How to Get Rid of a Sub-Contractor

If a sub-contractor's work proves unsatisfactory, or they persistently fail to turn up, have a quiet word to find out why. Tea breaks, especially if you provide the tea, are useful for chats of this kind.

If the situation doesn't improve, or the subbie takes it amiss, it's important for the good of the project, and your own peace of mind, to act quickly. Subbies aren't fired; they are 'finished'. This should happen immediately, with work paid up to date – either for the day, the week or the agreed payment stage (unless it's only just started) – and preferably in cash, so there's no uncertainty about cheques being honoured.

The sub-contractor concerned should then leave the site with any tools or equipment belonging to him.

Why?

You really don't want to risk a disgruntled ex-employee returning and spreading disaffection or, worse, carrying out sabotage. It's not unknown for drains to block mysteriously after an aggrieved groundworker has returned after working hours. Some pieces of ingenious mischief may take months, or even years, to reveal themselves.

The prospect of finishing a burly sub-contractor isn't a particularly pleasant one, but if it's done quickly and fairly, and without losing your temper, it's only going to enhance your reputation as a competent manager.

On the other hand, if you and sub-contractor have a serious falling out – and it's not mended quickly – chances are they will simply fail to turn up the next day.

In practice, the main issue in 'finishing' a sub-contractor is finding a replacement. Sub-contractors are generally reluctant to take over someone else's work because they assume it's been unsatisfactory, which means they will probably have to spend time correcting it and they may still get blamed for their predecessor's mistakes. Or they suspect the first subbie may have discovered a problem, which they've neglected to mention to you.

CHAPTER 14

Managing Your Build

A house build entails dozens of separate tasks, some running successively, others simultaneously, each demanding specific tradesmen, materials and services. At the same time, close control of the finances is needed to ensure cash flow is maintained and bills are paid on time. For the build to run smoothly, all these aspects need to be carefully co-ordinated, otherwise you risk delays, tradesmen being left idle and disappearing to other sites, and interest on loans piling up unnecessarily.

Using professional project management will, of course, remove much of this burden, especially on a day-to-day basis. But the reality is that, whoever supervises your build, all the decisions are ultimately down to you – which is as it should be.

Having an overview of your project, then, is essential for its success, whoever happens to be giving the orders on-site. You don't have to be an 8 – you're surrounded by them, after all – but you should be aware of what should happen and when.

WHAT HAPPENS AND WHEN

A large detached brick and block house of around 200m^2 – not untypical for a self-builder – and of a reasonably conventional design, should take around eight months to build. That assumes there are no major hiccups along the way, which, of course, can never be assumed.

The build stages are, broadly, as follows:

- **First month** Clear and level site; set out the layout of the external and internal load-bearing walls; excavate foundations and service trenches; build the 'footings' (blockwork or brickwork to ground-floor level); install the damp-proof course; complete the ground floor.

- **Second month** Raise ground-floor walls to first-floor level, including openings for doors and windows; construct first floor.
- **Third month** Build upper-storey walls to wallplate height (point on which the roof timbers rest); start construction of roof.
- **Fourth month** Complete roof structure; install roof covering, fascias, guttering and downpipes; start internal carpentry (assemble and install staircase, door linings, window boards, etc.); erect internal studwork walls.
- **Fifth month** Install 'first fix' electrics (i.e. lay wiring runs); install 'first fix' plumbing (i.e. pipework runs) for hot and cold water and heating; start plastering/ drylining and floor screeding.
- **Sixth month** Complete plastering/screeding; start 'second fix' internal carpentry (hang internal and external doors, fit skirtings, architraves, decorative mouldings, finish staircase, etc.); lay and connect drains.
- **Seventh month** Complete 'second fix' carpentry; start 'second fix' plumbing (connect pipework to boiler, radiators, hot-water cylinder, sanitaryware, etc.); start 'second fix' electrics (connect wiring to lighting pendants, switches, power points, etc.); start kitchen installation; start decoration; start external works (driveway, pathway, patio, landscaping).
- **Eighth month** Finish plumbing, wiring, kitchen, external works, decoration; snagging; completion.

Even the best-run build won't necessarily follow this pattern precisely. You could, for example, leave much of the decoration until the building has dried out completely, which may take several weeks. Or, if digging the service trenches early on causes access problems, this could be postponed until excavations are made for the drains much later in the schedule.

THINKING LIKE A PROJECT MANAGER

There are a few points it might be useful to bear in mind before your project management role goes 'live'.

Confidence

First, huge numbers of self-builders have been this way before. Many will have started out knowing much less than you, but the great majority completed their projects successfully. That may be, of course, because self-builders are an usually hardy and tenacious breed. But it undoubtedly helps that house-building is a long-established activity, supported by a substantial industry and an army of professionals whose livelihood depends on a degree of success. Making a complete hash of it, then, takes rather more ineptitude and ill fortune than most of us will ever aspire to.

Second, house construction is, nevertheless, an immensely complex business, involving so many skills and areas of expertise, that no-one can know it all. You, then, will make mistakes. If you think you haven't, you just haven't noticed them yet. Treat them as part of an essential learning process. Don't beat yourself up about them, and don't blame anyone else if you know it's down to you. Just get on and do what you can to put them right.

In fact, few blunders in building cannot be corrected – especially with a system as modular and flexible as brick and block – and ingenious solutions to sudden disasters will often result in improvements that might otherwise never have occurred to you.

On-Site Relationships

If you are project managing your own site, you may be technically an employer, but all your 'employees' are freelances. Your relationship to them is more, then, of a team-leader than a long-term boss.

As with most skilled individuals, communication is the key to using their skills most effectively. If you show a genuine interest in, and respect for, their work, most are happy to share their knowledge and much more inclined to offer helpful suggestions. That doesn't mean, of course, you have to accept everything they say.

If you use a main contractor, your main relationship is with them or their representative on site. Any changes to the specification should be agreed only with them. Instructing one of the contractor's employees or sub-contractors directly is likely to create confusion and

lead to mistakes. Your contractor won't be too pleased, either.

Keeping In Touch

If you don't live on site, try to visit at the beginning of the day, perhaps on your way to work. Building sites usually operate from 8am to 5pm. In the morning there's still the best part of a day to correct any problems that arise. By late afternoon, everyone's focus is shifting to food or the pub. If daily visits aren't possible, keep in touch by phone. This is easier with a single, main contractor who is used to spending a large part of his day on a mobile.

If you are managing your own sub-contractors, you may be able to appoint one as a foreman. He can act in a supervisory capacity on site and take your calls. On a brick and block build this is a typically a master bricklayer who will, in any case, need to co-ordinate his work with that of other trades. You'll need to agree extra payment to cover the additional responsibility.

Try to organize weekly site meetings to check progress, deal with problems and flag up future requirements. If an architect or other professional is project managing, this should be part of their contract. If you're on your own, you may need to be insistent. Successful builders are likely to be frantically busy and hard to pin down. Most sub-contractors prefer to do rather than discuss.

Off-Site Relationships

A common tale in the self-build world is of the couple who turn up at a self-build show full of enthusiasm for their project, which is either underway or due to start soon. A year or two later one of the pair is back, with a new partner in tow. The self-build, it turns out, was a resounding success. It was the relationship that failed.

Self-build is tough on close relationships, especially if one or both of you have full-time jobs. Even the best planned and most efficient build imposes a huge burden on spare time and peace of mind. Two things, however, can ease that burden.

First, decide who is boss on-site. In other words, who is the point of contact for the main contractor or sub-contractors. It should really be the person who is there most often. If two clients are operating independently, it's a recipe for disaster, both on site and off.

Second, schedule in a break. The temptation is always to press on whenever there's a spare moment. Who knows what delays lie ahead? Actually, your chances of making an horrendous blunder are hugely improved by mental and physical fatigue.

Aim to take a day off a week, and be grateful if you achieve a morning or afternoon. You'll need it – both of you.

Neighbours

Being a good neighbour, especially to those on either side, always pays dividends, even if they don't immediately reciprocate. You may need them for such things as: clearing their vehicles from the road when heavy deliveries are due, signing for urgent deliveries when the site is unoccupied and allowing scaffolding to be erected on their property where there isn't enough room on your plot.

Neighbours aren't obliged to allow you access for new build – only for necessary repairs to existing property. They may have no objection or an excellent reason for doing so. This needn't be a disaster; scaffolding can be erected internally, if necessary. This is something to check out as early as possible. The same applies where on-site storage is limited but a neighbour has space they can allow you to use. Not unreasonably, they may request payment or some other form of compensation.

Even if they think you're a delightful addition to the community and your project is hugely exciting, several months of constant noise, dust, muddy pavements and large delivery vehicles regularly blocking the road will soon blunt their enthusiasm. So keep them informed, especially when things are due to get exceptionally messy or noisy, be sympathetic to their complaints and bite your tongue. As soon as you've built enough to show what the finished house will look like, give them a tour. Even if they loathe you they won't be able to resist, and a stunning new addition to the street might well cause them to revise their opinions.

Even the best run building site can't avoid noise, dust and mess, so be prepared for your local popularity to decline during busy periods of your build.

Heavy deliveries can become a bone of contention with neighbours, who may have to move vehicles to allow access; do your best to give them adequate notice.

PLANNING YOUR SITE

Setting out your site in a logical way can make an enormous difference to the efficiency of your build, saving you time and money, as well as improving safety. Essentially you need to assemble a jigsaw with half a dozen separate pieces. On a tight site, some of these may need to double up, forcing you to make use of the road or neighbouring land, if only temporarily. The pieces are:

The footprint of the house It will need a minimum space of about one and a half metres all the way round to allow room for the scaffolding.

An access area to receive deliveries It should be close to the road, as level as possible and large enough and firm enough to take a fully-loaded truck. To achieve this you may need to lay hardcore, though this can later be incorporated into a driveway.

A heavy storage area Adjacent to both the build and the access area, of which it might be part. It mini-mizes the distance needed to carry heavy loads by hand (which may also add to labour costs). Material stored here should rest on plastic sheeting and a further base, such as pallets, to prevent it becoming waterlogged or sinking into the mud after heavy rain.

A secure storage area For items that are vulnerable either to the weather, such as timber or plasterboard, or to theft, such as tools. Lockable containers can be hired or bought second-hand. If you're planning a detached garage, it may be possible to build this first and use it for storage.

On-site accommodation Including a portable WC. Living on-site is usually easier if a caravan or mobile home can be positioned a little distance from the build, though it should still have a clear view of the access area, so deliveries are not missed. Consider resting it on a hardcore base, which might serve for a future shed, greenhouse or garden office. A hardcore path from the road – perhaps a future garden path – will also make life a little less messy.

Service trenches For gas, electricity and water supplies, drains and cabling for television/telephone/internet. They can be dug by the mechanical excavator used for the foundations. If the necessary ducting and drains are not laid immediately and the trenches backfilled, they will need to be boarded over and clearly marked to avoid accidents or vehicles crossing, causing the walls to collapse. Otherwise, the line of the trenches will need to be marked and kept clear until they are dug.

An area for rubbish A good place is the edge of the access area to make removal easy. Hiring a skip is the simplest, most efficient way to deal with it.

Boundary security Hopefully, on buying your plot, you will have ensured it was fenced off and protected from trespassers. Once your build is underway, however, you're likely to need sturdier defences against thieves. Two-metre-high, steel mesh security fencing comes in interlocking panels, which can be erected in minutes. Heras is the best known and can be hired, though over several months it may be cheaper to buy and sell on when it's no longer needed. E-Bay is a good source of second-hand examples. On a small site, or one with narrow access, it may be simpler and cheaper to use fence posts and hoarding made from plywood, or doors from a nearby skip.

ABOVE: **If you have no room for a skip on site, you will need a permit to leave it on the pavement or road, as well as providing it with warning cones and amber flashing marker lights at night.**

RIGHT: **Once plant and equipment are on site, security becomes an issue; both steel mesh fencing and a lockable container, for tools and materials vulnerable to the weather, can be hired.**

CHAPTER 15

Last-Minute Preparations

Before work starts on-site there can be periods when time seems to crawl and you begin to doubt that the ground will ever be broken. Then, everything begins to firm up, a start date is fixed and suddenly an awful lot needs to happen at once. To avoid that eventuality here is a handy checklist.

If you are using a main contractor, many, if not most, of these points will be handled by them.

TWO MONTHS BEFORE BUILD START

This is the time for confirming start dates and prices for a main contractor, sub-contractors, suppliers and utilities.

Water supply Confirm that the local water company will provide a new mains connection by the start of the build.

Electricity Confirm that the local electricity supplier will provide a new mains connection by build start.

Gas Confirm that a mains connection will be made in time for second fix plumbing.

Sewerage If you are planning to connect your drains to a main sewer in the adjacent roadway, contact the local water company and your local building control department, both of whom who will need to inspect the connection. If the roadway is a public highway, you will also need to contact the local authority's highway department for a Street Works Licence, a permit for road-opening.

Main contractor/sub-contractors Re-confirm start dates for groundworkers, bricklayers, carpenters.

Long delivery items Check that items with lengthy delivery periods are on course for agreed arrival dates. They include windows, doors and especially hand-made bricks and brick 'specials', which bricklayers will need within the first couple of weeks.

Temporary accommodation If you plan to move into rented accommodation, try to make the move around now. This will give you a month to settle in and establish a routine before the build takes all your attention. If you plan to live on site, investigate hire or purchase of a caravan or mobile home. If you have not already done so, however, check, whether planning permission is required.

ONE MONTH BEFORE BUILD START

Trade accounts Visit local builders' merchants, set up accounts and take advantage of estimating services.

Warranty provider Inform them of build start.

Setting-out professional Confirm that a site engineer, surveyor or other suitable professional to set out your site will be available at the agreed time.

Equipment hire Arrange hire of mechanical excavator and driver plus tipper lorry and driver for removing spoil (if not arranged by groundworkers). Alternatively, for a smaller site, arrange the hire of a skip for spoil.

Soil disposal If spoil disposal isn't being handled by groundworkers, find the location of the nearest licensed tip to avoid delays when work starts. There, soil disposal will be subject to Landfill Tax (charged at £2.50 per tonne at the time of writing).

Plan the site layout (see Chapter 15)

On-site storage Investigate hire or purchase of a lockable container for storing building materials, tools and equipment.

Follow up other sub-contractors Confirm that a plumber will be available to install a temporary

---

Using Waste Oil On-Site

Avoid paying Landfill Tax by agreeing with your main contractor or groundworkers that excavated soil will be spread across the garden and compacted or used to level uneven ground.

(Note: most excavated material is subsoil, which won't support plant growth; it will need to be covered with a layer of topsoil.)

Plywood entrance gates, made up on-site, can be a cost-effective alternative to purpose-built security fencing, especially on a narrow site.

standpipe for the new water mains connection, and that an electrician will install a temporary consumer unit. Keep roofers, plumbers, electricians, etc. informed of progress and confirm their availability.

ONE WEEK BEFORE BUILD START

Building control Inform the local authority building control department of your build start date.

Insurance Ensure you have contract or 'all risks' and personal accident cover. If you are project managing your own build, add employers' liability insurance.

Consents If there isn't sufficient space on-site for materials' storage and/or parts of the scaffolding and you need to use the roadway, local authority permits will be required. They normally require a week's notice and there will be a charge.

Photography Photograph the site, adjoining road(s) and boundaries (as a personal record and a precaution against potential damage claims).

Most builders' merchants will have stocks of blocks, cement, builders' sand and hardcore available at short notice.

Neighbours Inform your immediate neighbours that work is about to begin on-site.

Hardcore Order hardcore for the drive/delivery area/on-site accommodation. This is ordered in tonne loads and it's usually safer to over, rather than under, order as any surplus can be put aside for pathways and patios.

Early call for groundworkers They may be needed to lay hardcore for the delivery area/on-site caravan or mobile home. Also to dig trenches for services to on-site accommodation – water, electricity and drainage.

Order blocks, builder's sand and cement for footings Normally available at short notice from local builders' merchants.

Arrange hire of concrete mixer For mixing the mortar for both bricks and blocks. For a small plot on good, load-bearing ground, you may get away with using it for the foundation concrete.

Foundations concrete Alert your supplier of ready mixed concrete, ensuring it can be delivered as soon as the foundations are excavated. Deliveries are normally made through a 3m long chute. If the delivery vehicle can't reverse to within 2 or 3m of where the concrete is needed, consider using a pump, which can reach to around 9m. This, however, needs to be ordered well in advance and will add to costs. Alternatively, use wheel barrows.

Security fencing Arrange for delivery and erection.

Portable toilet If not supplied by a main contractor, and there's no practical alternative, hiring a chemical

Safety On Site

Health and safety issues on building sites are governed by the Construction (Design and Management) or CDM Regulations, and very comprehensive they are, covering every aspect of construction from design to washing, dining and toilet facilities on-site.

They don't, however, apply for construction work being carried out for a client who either lives on the premises, or will do so once it's finished – with one exception. That is where you act as your own project manager and the number of sub-contractors on site at one time exceeds five. Realistically, though, the likelihood of a health and safety officer dropping by on those occasions is vanishingly small.

That doesn't mean, of course, that health and safety can be overlooked, not least because the most likely accident victims are you and members of your family. Helpfully, the Health and Safety Executive website includes a couple of free downloadable guides, the most digestible of which is 'The absolutely essential health and safety toolkit for the smaller construction contractor', which is well worth a look.

As an indicator of the likely perils, here are the most common self-build injuries, and ways to avoid them:

Head and Foot Wounds
Caused by objects dropping from heights, walking into head-height scaffolding, stepping onto nails, screws or splinters left upright in timber, dropping bricks, blocks or timber onto feet.

Remedies Always wear a hard hat on-site, and encourage subbies to do the same; wear thick-soled, steel-toed boots or shoes; ensure that head-height lengths of scaffolding are sleeved with yellow scaffold tube padding; check that piles of bricks, blocks and timber are stable; keep the site tidy and remove waste timber with nails, screws or jagged splinters showing as soon as they're spotted; encourage a main contractor to do the same.

Groin Injuries
Caused by slipping on exposed joists.

Remedies Ensure the joists are properly secured before walking on them (and suitably braced if they are I-beams); check that scaffolding boards or flooring panels are secured.

Concrete and Mortar Burns
Caused by wet concrete or mortar staying in contact with the skin for more than a few moments, or cement dust blowing into eyes.

Remedies For any prolonged contact with wet concrete, wear waterproof gloves, Wellingtons, safety goggles and clothing that does not leave skin exposed; watch that concrete or mortar doesn't fall into boots – if it does, clear them immediately; cement dust in eyes should be flushed out with lots of clean water; do the same for any skin touched by wet concrete or mortar, even through clothing that has become saturated.

Broken Limbs
Caused by falls on uneven ground, into unguarded trenches or pits, stepping on unstable materials, falling down stairwells, from ladders, scaffolding and roofs.

Remedies Mark and fence off open trenches or holes; don't climb on stored materials; ask the carpenter to install a temporary balustrade on open stairs; ensure ladders are secured top and bottom and extend at least a metre beyond the landing point; ensure scaffolding is correctly erected and maintained with guard rails, toe boards (to stop items falling off the edges) and fully supported scaffolding boards; don't go onto any part of the roof without scaffolding a short distance below.

Back Strain
Caused by lifting inappropriate weights.

Remedies Test the weight of anything that looks as if it might be beyond your limits before committing. Unless you're extremely fit, it probably is.

Electrocution
Caused by cutting through or tripping over electric cables, touching cables that have frayed, leaving wires exposed.

Remedies Use cordless power tools and plant, or invest in a transformer and choose 110V tools and plant rather than the more dangerous 240V. If 240V equipment is unavoidable, run the cabling through a Residual Current Device (RCD), which will cut the power instantly if the cable is earthed.

Children's Injuries
All of the above.

Remedies Keep children well away. If you are living on-site, fence off your living accommodation. This should work for toddlers. After that, you only have persuasion and carefully supervised visits, wearing suitable attire, which can be presented as treats for good behaviour.

toilet will save a lot of time. It should be sited on firm, level ground, close to the site entrance, so emptying will be easy. Connecting to an electricity supply will allow it to provide hot water for washing.

Health and Safety

If you are using a main contractor, they will be expected to follow the appropriate health and safety regulations, but for your own health and safety you should be aware of them. This goes double if you are acting as project manager. In either case, the following are advisable:

- Buy a comprehensive first-aid kit. Check the website of the Health and Safety Executive for recommendations on its contents, or choose a kit that complies with HSE guidelines.
- Buy a fire extinguisher. Let your main contractor or sub-contractors know where it, and the first-aid kit, are kept on site.
- Buy hard hats, steel-toed boots, safety goggles, face masks and protective clothing. If you are likely to be inspecting the site after work, consider keeping a boiler suit on site, or in the boot of your car, to pull over work clothes, saving time and cleaning bills.
- Erect safety signs at the site entrance, particularly 'Danger: Keep Out' and 'Safety helmets must be worn in this area'. A main contractor should do it, anyway but, if you are your own project manager, it's up to you, and will improve your case if an accident occurs and an insurance claim is made.

A portable chemical toilet should be sited on a firm, level ground, close to the entrance for easy emptying.

Safety signs are a requirement of health and safety regulations, and an eminently sensible precaution.

CHAPTER 16

Groundworks

A ground-breaking time – literally. The culmination of months, if not years, of preparation, worry and effort, which are finally paying off. Enjoy the moment, because the real work now begins.

DAY ONE TO TWO OF BUILD: STRIPPING THE SITE

Who Needs to Be There
- Main contractor (if you have one, his presence or that of a representative is now presumed at all stages).
- Architect/designer/project manager/site engineer/surveyor (if required).
- Groundworkers/mechanical excavator driver.

Equipment
- Mechanical excavator (JCB).
- Tip-up truck/skip.
- Wheelbarrows.
- Spades, pickaxes, cutting equipment.
- Hammers, nails.

Materials
- Hardcore.
- Fence posts.
- Hoarding.
- Security fencing.

Any tree subject to a Tree Preservation Order should be fenced off before the site is cleared to avoid damage.

Activities

Tree Preservation Order (TPO)
Mark any trees subject to a TPO and fence off if necessary to avoid damage.

Mechanical excavators, used to clear and level sites, are generally hired with a driver and, often, a lorry to dispose of the spoil.

is necessary for establishing such things as the depth of the foundation trenches, the height of the damp-proof course above the ground and the fall of the drains.

The datum can be an existing point, such as a manhole cover, a kerbstone or a wooden peg knocked into the ground or set in concrete – as long as it's unlikely to move during the course of the build. It's often helpful to make the top of the datum the same level as the top of the structural ground floor (i.e. the floor minus the finishing screed).

Site Stripping and Levelling

Use a mechanical excavator (otherwise known as a 'JCB' after the leading manufacturer) to remove vegetation and at least 150mm of topsoil to clear most roots.

Soil Storage

Set aside the topsoil for your new garden. Create a spoil heap where it won't obstruct building activities, but piled no higher than 1m, otherwise, the soil will become impacted and de-oxygenated, rendering it useless for plant growth.

Area to be Stripped

Confirm from the plans the position of the house and the area of topsoil to be stripped. If you don't have a main contractor to do this, consider enlisting the help of your designer or other professional.

Typically, topsoil is removed from the footprint of the house plus 1½m all the way round to allow room for scaffolding. Stripping the area between the roadway and the build avoids churned up topsoil impeding vehicles and spreading mud. It also exposes the area where service trenches will be dug from the boundary to the house.

If the site is heavily overgrown, or you have specific plans for the garden, you may choose to strip the entire site.

Establish a Datum Point

The datum is a point on the ground marking a level from which all other levels on the build can be measured. This

---

The Issue of Address

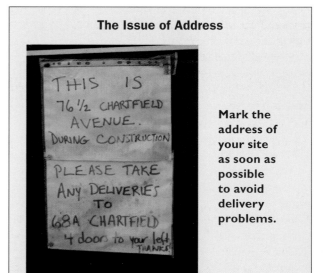

Mark the address of your site as soon as possible to avoid delivery problems.

Don't forget to mark the address of your site prominently on the fencing/hoarding facing the road. You may be the only building site in miles and assume any delivery driver will easily spot you, but it's surprising how easily sites can be missed.

You will also need to agree the number of the house with the local authority.

Soil Disposal

Any subsoil you can't dispose of on site will need to be loaded onto a truck and delivered to a licensed tip.

Access and Materials' Storage

Lay hardcore between the site entrance and the build to create a space for a large delivery vehicle and a firm base on which to store materials.

Security

Erect temporary security fencing and/or fence posts and hinged hoarding to act as a securable entrance gate.

DAY TWO TO THREE: SETTING OUT

Today is when you, or your main contractor/architect/project manager/site engineer, mark out the foundation trenches on the cleared site – in other words, the footprint of your house.

Accuracy is essential, not just to ensure that the walls follow the plans so that all the different elements fit together, but also to make sure the house is where it should be. Generally, a few centimetres either way may not be too important, but on a tight site, especially when building up to a boundary or when planning permission has been very specific about positioning, this becomes critical. If the local authority decides you have built in the wrong place, it can insist you demolish and rebuild.

Who Needs to Be There

As day one.

Equipment

- As day one, plus surveying instruments (e.g. theodolite, laser level, Cowley level or Dumpy level and levelling staff) or builder's square, plumb bob and water-level. These are all for accurately measuring distances and levels.
- 30m tape measure.
- Long spirit level.
- Metre lengths of board.
- Lengths of 50mm × 50mm timber.
- Saw.
- White string.
- Hosepipe.
- Lime powder, sand or spray paint.

Planning Ahead

Notify the building inspector that you will be setting out in the next couple of days. Building control normally requires 2 days' notice for this inspection. Depending on the site, however, it may be combined with the inspection of the excavated foundations.

Notify the warranty provider.

Activities

A builder's square, one of the oldest and most reliable tools for setting out buildings.

Setting Out

One corner of the house is found by using the distances shown on your plans from fixed points, such as a boundary wall or the pavement. It can be marked with a wooden peg with a nail in the top.

The distance to the next corner is found by using a tape measure, surveying equipment, a builder's square or Pythagoras' theorem. A second peg and nail can mark it.

Once all the corners are marked, lengths of white string, drawn tight from nail to nail, will outline the footprint of the house.

All the distances and angles should then be checked against the plans. Are opposite sides parallel? Are the diagonals the same distance? Are the sides at the marked distances from other fixed points as shown on the plans? After a double check, any necessary adjustments can be made.

How to Check Right Angles

A simple way to check that the corners of the house are square is to use Pythagoras' theorem (the square on the long side of a right-angled triangle is equal to the sum of the squares on the other two sides).

Measure 4m along the line of wall from a corner peg, knock another peg into the ground and fix a nail in the top. Now measure 3m from the corner peg along the wall at right angles to the original and knock in a second peg and nail. Next, draw a string between the two nails.

If the corner is square, the string should be 5m long.

Profiles

Strings strung between profiles are used to establish the positions of the foundation trenches, external walls, any load-bearing internal walls and fireplaces (which will need to take the weight of the chimney).

The lines of the trenches on the ground are marked with lime powder, sand or spray paint. The strings can then be removed.

Service Trenches

The positions of service trenches should be marked from the boundary to entry points on the house. They will usually be 450mm wide, the size of a small bucket on a JCB. This will act as a guide for the mechanical excavator driver if you plan to dig the trenches at the same time as the foundations, or an indication to leave the area clear for digging later in the build.

What is a Profile?

A profile is a length of board (floorboards will do) about a metre long, fixed upright and level in the ground by timber stakes at either end. Four nails are then fixed in the top of the board.

The outermost nails should be about 600mm apart – the width of a JCB's bucket and so the width of a foundation trench. (A 450mm bucket can also be used, but leaves less margin for error.) The two inner nails should indicate the width of the wall that will sit on the foundations: in other words, the width, including the facing brick, an inner block and the cavity between them.

A profile is set into the ground at each corner of the house, parallel with the wall it faces. It should be far enough away from the position of the trenches to allow a JCB to operate.

A string is then run from a nail on the profile to the equivalent nail on the profile at the opposite end of the wall. The outer and inner strings follow the outlines of the foundation trench to be dug. Sometimes a central line is also made as a guide for the JCB driver.

Once the lines of the foundations have been marked on the ground, the strings can be removed, leaving the profile boards in place. After the foundations are poured, the inner strings can be replaced as a guide for those building the footings.

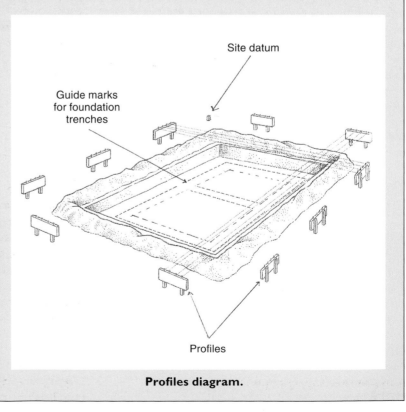

Profiles diagram.

Drains

The positions of the drains (*see below*) should be marked according to the plans. They will generally be about 600mm deep and the same width as service trenches. Deeper trenches will need temporary support for the side walls.

Bringing in the Services

The services and drains run in trenches from connection points at or just beyond the boundary. Each has a slightly different requirement.

Mains Water

It comes from a meter at the edge of the roadway in a blue plastic MDPE (medium density polyethylene) pipe. It needs to be buried at least 750mm to avoid freezing. If you plan to have several bathrooms, or an unvented, high-pressure water system, use a 25mm diameter pipe rather than the cheaper 20mm.

To minimize leaks, the pipe should be continuous. Excess lengths can be left at either end of the trench to make the necessary connections. The house end

Black protective ducting needs to put in place before an electricity cable can pulled through and connected to the street supply.

will need to pass through openings in the footings and ground floor.

The ends of the pipe should be taped up to keep the interior clean.

Gas

It comes in yellow polyethylene pipe, buried at about 400mm. Again, excess lengths, ready for connection, can be left at either end of the trench. Unlike the mains pipe, however, the connection is made externally to a white plastic meter box which will need to be fitted to the outside wall.

Electricity

The supply cable runs at a similar depth through ducting, normally coloured black, and also enters the house via a meter box. The cabling is pulled through the ducting when the connections are made.

Ducting is also used for cable television and telephone wiring. A temporary pull cord – run through the ducting before it is laid – will make installation a lot quicker and easier.

Water, gas and electricity providers will need to inspect the trenches before they can be backfilled. They may also have additional requirements, such as insisting on a separate trench for their own service.

All this can cause a certain amount of confusion, if not frustration, even when carefully co-ordinated, which is why service trenches are often left for a less hectic time.

Laying the Drains

Digging drainage trenches at the same time as the foundations can potentially save money – largely by

A main water supply requires a blue plastic MDPE pipe.

foregoing the need to recall a mechanical excavator later. But the decision will depend on your site, build schedule and the positions of the drains. If they have to run through the foundations, for example, it may be advisable to sort them out as early as possible.

The drainage layout will be shown on your plans. Choosing the components will be down to your main contractor, designer, groundworker or yourself. Catalogues and technical advice are available from manufacturers.

If there is an existing drain serving one or more neighbours, connecting to it is usually the simplest and cheapest option, though you will need to obtain permission first from the drain's owners. These may be your neighbours or the local water company. Unless your site is particularly isolated, however, the more likely scenario is that you will have to make a new connection to the nearest public sewer.

Your home's drains carry two varieties of waste: 'foulwater' and rainwater. Foulwater can be further divided into 'black water' (from the WCs) and 'grey water' (from washing and cooking). In some areas both can be discharged into the nearest main drains; in others rainwater goes to a separate surface-water sewer. Increasingly, however, rainwater is piped into a 'soakaway' on your property. This is simply a 1m-deep hole sited at least 5m from the nearest building and filled with rubble, allowing the water to soak away into the surrounding soil. As well as reducing pressure on the public sewage system, it has the additional advantage of a slightly lower water bill.

Most foulwater discharges into the same point: a single vertical 110mm-diameter pipe, known as the 'soil vent pipe' or 'stack'. This is usually sited inside the house. The top extends above the roof and is left open to equalize the pressure in the system when toilets flush. The bottom end connects to the main drains. This is why positioning bathrooms above kitchens minimizes pipe runs to the stack, saving money and making maintenance easier. Where foulwater is drained separately – perhaps from a downstairs WC – it will need its own manhole outside before joining the discharge from the stack at a further manhole.

Foulwater drains operate on a few simple principles. They should run in straight lines. Wherever a corner or bend is unavoidable there should be either a manhole or a rodding point (a pipe to the surface angled up at 45 degrees) to allow access for inspection and clearing blockages. Wherever pipe runs join there should also be a manhole.

The most common 100mm-diameter drain needs to drop at a gradient of about 1 in 80 (larger pipes can be shallower). Anything steeper may cause the liquid to out-run the solids, causing blockages.

If the main drains are markedly lower than the house, an especially deep backdrop manhole, sited near the boundary, can accommodate a steep drop.

Where the main drains are markedly higher, a pumped sewage system will be needed. This is usually easier and cheaper than installing a private drainage system, such as a septic tank, mini-treatment plant, cesspool or reed bed (see Chapter 5 for details).

Plastic pipes are most commonly used for drains. Coloured the terracotta of their clay predecessors, they are lightweight, use integral push-fit connections and come with ready-made manholes in a wide variety of sizes. They are laid on 100mm of fine gravel, known as pea shingle, which is then packed round the pipe. A further 100mm is added before the trench is backfilled with rubble-free soil.

Where there's a risk of a pipe being deformed, perhaps by pressure from a driveway or the roots of nearby trees, it must be encased in concrete. The same applies if it runs within a metre of a load-bearing wall.

Drains need to be inspected by building control before they can be backfilled (1 day's notice is required).

Rainwater Harvesting

Rainwater from the roof can also be collected in a rainwater harvesting system and used for toilet flushing and in washing machines. After filtering, it's fed into a large tank, usually buried in the back garden, though specially strengthened tanks can be installed beneath driveways.

From there, the water is either pumped directly to the points of use or to a secondary storage tank in the attic, from which it flows by gravity to where it's needed. Both kinds of supply are topped up by the mains supply via flow switches, which operate when the water level reaches a low level.

Rainwater used in this way can only be used through a separate system of pipework, which has no connection with the mains supply. It will, however, cut water bills and, in hard water areas, reduce limescale damage to washing machines and improve their efficiency.

Drainage Layout Abbreviations

These are used on the building regulations approved version of your plans:

RWP – rainwater pipe.
SVP – soil vent pipe.
G – gully.
RWG – rainwater gully.
RWG/TG – rainwater gully that discharges directly onto the ground.
S/A – soakaway.
IL – invert level. This is the depth of the lowest point on the interior of a drainage system, as measured from the site's datum point. The IL figures shown at various points along the line of a drain enable you to calculate its gradient.
CL – cover level. This is the highest point of the cover of a manhole measured against the datum point.

They also need to be tested for watertightness, which is best done at this stage, though it can be left until connection is made to the main drains.

DAY FOUR TO FIVE: DIGGING THE FOUNDATIONS

Who Needs to Be There
As day one, plus building inspector.

Equipment
As day one, plus boning rods (*see below*).

Materials
• Timber.
• Sheets of plywood (perhaps hoarding left over from constructing the entrance gate).
• If laying drains and service trenches, ducting and drainage components (pea shingle, pipe, manholes, gullies, lubricant).

Activities
This is the day when you find out what the ground under your new home is really like. Trial holes may have indicated good soil conditions, perfect for standard, metre-deep foundations. But the foundation trenches may reveal patches of made-up ground, less stable subsoil or perhaps a large root from a nearby or recently removed tree. None of these need be disastrous – soft patches

The water level: a cheap and reliable method of transferring levels accurately, even around corners.

What Sort of Foundations Do I Need and Why?

Foundation types are normally decided by your designer in conjunction with building control and, if ground conditions are difficult, a structural engineer. If you're lucky, conventional foundations will be fine. They come in two varieties:

- **Strip foundations** – these consist of a layer of concrete laid at least 150mm deep on the bottom of the trench. The footings are then built off this to the level of the damp-proof course. Typically, they are two walls of blockwork, backfilled to ground level

with lean-mix concrete for additional strength. They can also be built with dense engineering bricks or 'trench blocks', large lightweight blocks which are twice the size of the usual variety and span the width of the wall.

- **Trenchfill foundations** – as the name suggests, the entire trench is simply filled with concrete, usually to within two brick courses of ground level. It uses a lot more concrete, but it's quicker and less labour-intensive.

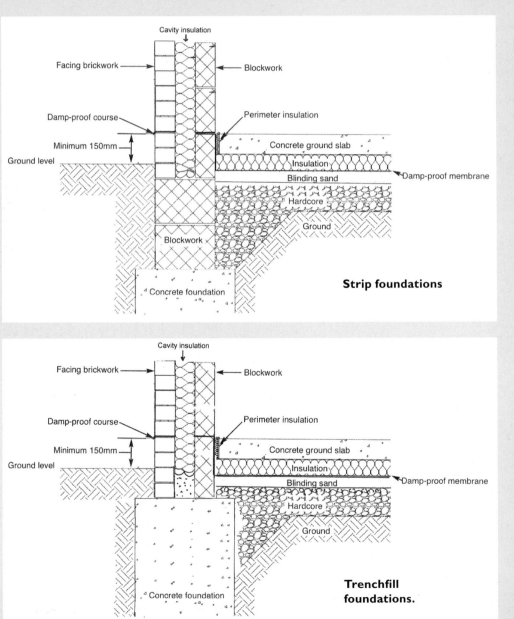

Strip foundations

Trenchfill foundations.

Both types of foundations will normally be around a metre deep. This is to reach a level that's unaffected by ground movement. Clay soils, for example, are notorious for expanding and shrinking with the seasons. They can be dealt with by sheathing foundations in material that's either compressible or collapses under pressure, leaving a void.

If good load-bearing ground isn't found within a couple of metres, it's usually cheaper and easier to look at alternatives, such as the following:

Raft Foundation
Here, a steel-reinforced concrete raft is cast on a hard-core base across the entire footprint of the house. It combines the foundations and the slab of a solid ground floor and spreads the weight of the house evenly over areas of good and bad ground. The edges are made extra deep to support the walls and prevent any sideways movement.

Piled Foundations

These are used where load-bearing ground is particularly deep, or non-existent. They consist of steel-reinforced concrete columns sunk into the ground at intervals around the footprint of the house. The steel rods are tied together at ground level and cast in a concrete ring beam, on which the house is built.

Piles can be pre-cast and mechanically hammered into the ground – never a popular option with neighbours. Or they can be cast *in situ* after a mechanical augur has excavated a shaft of the appropriate depth.

Piles work either by resting on solid ground or by the combined lateral pressure of the surrounding soil over their entire length. They are increasingly popular, thanks to new developments like mini-piles and screwpiles.

The latter resemble very broad augurs which are simply screwed into the ground until they can be screwed no further, then left in place. Other time-saving systems combine the piles with complete, damp-proofed and insulated ground floors.

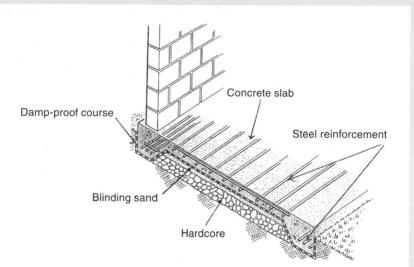

Damp-proof course

Concrete slab

Steel reinforcement

Blinding sand

Hardcore

Steel reinforcement rods are inserted into the shaft before it is filled with fresh concrete; the rods are then tied together at ground level and cast in a concrete ring beam, which supports the buildings.

A mechanical augur excavating a shaft for piled foundations.

can usually be bridged or filled with deeper foundations – but they will add to costs. The building inspector will decide what is needed.

Excavation
Use the JCB to dig the foundations to the depth shown on the plans.

Clean Cuts
The sides of the trenches need to be vertical and the bottom as level and smooth as possible. Depending on soil conditions, trenches will usually be stable to about a metre. Any areas that appear unstable should be shored with timber.

Depth Checking
The depth of the trenches is measured with 'boning rods', wooden T-shapes with vertical lengths about a metre longer than the intended depth of the trench. One rod is fixed at the desired depth at one end of a trench, a second at the opposite end. Once both are level and plumb, the top of the second rod can be lined up with the top of the first. A third rod is used to set out the bottom of the trench by lining up its top with the tops of the other two.

Levels can be checked against the datum, using surveying instruments or, more simply, a water-level.

The distance between the top of the foundation concrete and the level of the damp-proof course should

Roger Bullivant's SystemFirst foundations combine mini-piled foundations with a an insulation-filled steel framework, over which a concrete ground slab is cast; the result is a virtually 'instant' ground floor, ready for the bricklayers to start work.

> **Using a Water-Level**
>
> This is a length of transparent hose with an identical, transparent open-ended tube at either end. Each tube is graduated at 50mm intervals over the same 10cm length.
>
> One tube is attached to a vertical stake at the site datum; the other is taken to another vertical stake at the point where a level needs to be gauged.
>
> When the hose is filled with water, and both tubes are plumb, the second tube can be adjusted until its water level matches that in the datum tube.
>
> The advantage of the device is that levels can be transferred easily and accurately over any distance determined by the length of the hose. It can also work around corners, which will be increasingly useful as the walls rise.

be decided in courses of brickwork or blockwork, depending on which is used. That way the footings can be built in complete bricks or blocks.

The proposed top level of the concrete can be marked with a wooden peg every 2 or 3m.

Making Allowance for Services and Drains
Where these pass through the foundations, ducting or a void is required.

Building Control
The excavated trenches have to be approved before concrete can be poured. Building control need 1 day's notice for an inspection.

Typical demands are for an increase in depth to overcome patches of 'bad' or suspect ground, or shoring of the trenches to guard against collapse.

DAY FIVE TO SIX: POURING THE FOUNDATIONS

This should be done as quickly as possible after the foundation trenches have been dug and approved. Any delay risks either rain, which could flood the trenches, causing them to collapse or, in winter, a drop in temperature, which makes concrete pouring impossible.

Foundations' concrete is typically supplied ready mixed for speed and convenience. It should be poured as continuously as possible. Concrete is workable for up to 2 hours, but if one batch starts to set – or 'cure'

Self-Compacting Concrete

Opt for self-compacting concrete, which flows under its own weight and is self-levelling. It will cost around 10 per cent more but saves time and effort.

After the foundations have been poured, the concrete normally needs between 2 and 3 days to cure, depending on weather conditions.

– before the next, a weak point can form at the join, threatening the integrity of the foundations.

Who Needs to Be There
As day one, plus building inspector.

Equipment
- Ready-mixed delivery lorry.
- Concrete pump (if ready mixed concrete lorry can't back up close enough to trenches).
- Wheelbarrows.
- Spades.
- Concrete rakes.
- Tamping boards.

Materials
As day four.

Activities

Pouring and Levelling
A job for all hands on-site. Fresh concrete should have the consistency of thick custard. Shovels and concrete rakes are used to ease it along the trenches, working it into the edges and corners, and smoothing it to create a level surface at the marked depth.

Allow two to three days for the concrete to cure. If the temperature is likely to drop significantly, the concrete should be covered up with hessian or other breathable fabric.

Building Control
The building inspector will need to approve the foundations after concreting; 1-day's notice is required.

WEEK TWO: BUILDING TO DAMP-PROOF LEVEL

Who Needs to Be There
As day one, plus bricklayers.

Concrete Facts

The standard mix for foundations is 1 volume of Ordinary Portland Cement (OPC) to 3 of sand and 6 of gravel (written 1:3:6). This is known as a GEN 1 (for 'general application') mix. Other mixes include RC, for reinforced concrete, and FND, for soils containing sulphates, which attack ordinary concrete.

Ready-mixed concrete is ordered in cubic metres and a full lorry load is around six. To guard against under-estimates, it's safer to over-order and request full loads. If possible, any extra quantities can be used as foundations for a detached garage or hard standing for on-site accommodation.

Equipment
- Concrete mixer.
- Spot boards.

Materials
- Blocks or engineering bricks.
- Cement.
- Builder's sand.
- Plasticizer.
- Facing bricks.
- Airbricks (for a suspended ground floor).
- Concrete lintels.
- Damp-proof course.
- Insulating foam or flexible pipe surround.

Planning Ahead
- Give the building inspector 1-day's notice that the damp-proof course is ready for inspection.
- Alert warranty provider's surveyor of the same.
- Order lintels (see Chapter 18) for window and door openings.

Activities

Setting Out Facework
Together with the designer and any main contractor, the master bricklayer uses the profiles to mark the position of the walls and corners on the foundations. He also sets out the facing brickwork in dry bricks along the ground. This is to ensure it has a balanced appearance over the length of a wall. Gaps for the window and door openings are left in the positions marked on the plans. The arrangement of the bricks to be used for the sides, or 'reveals', of these openings is also worked out to produce a balanced appearance.

Ideally, the lengths of the walls and the reveals should all be multiples of a brick stretcher (using its 'co-ordinating size', which includes the mortar joints). Sometimes, however, this isn't possible. If the mismatch is relatively small, allowance can be made by adjusting the width of the joints, either by 'tightening' or 'opening' them; over the length of a wall this can be undetectable.

Where the mismatch is too large for this, or the expanse of brickwork too small, the answer is to create a 'broken bond'. This is a column of bricks cut to make up the shortfall. To make it less obvious, it's often positioned in the middle of a window opening.

An alternative is to use a 'reverse bond', which is essentially leaving the brickwork to be asymmetrical either at the ends of a wall or on either side of openings.

All of these adjustments should be agreed with the designer.

Building Footings
Blocks or engineering bricks are used for the inner wall, or 'leaf', of the footings; facing bricks for the outer leaf. Both can be laid either by groundworkers or bricklayers. To guarantee greater accuracy, it's usually wiser to use bricklayers.

The master bricklayer starts laying at the corners with what are known as the 'quoin' blocks or bricks. The first to be laid is checked against the site datum, which typically marks the level of the damp-proof course. This enables the bricklayer to work out the depth of the first layer of mortar, so that the damp-proof course is reached in complete blocks or bricks.

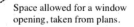

Space allowed for a door opening

Space allowed for a window opening, taken from plans.

To ensure the brickwork will have a balanced appearance over the length of each wall, facing bricks are set out 'dry' along the ground, leaving gaps for door and window openings.

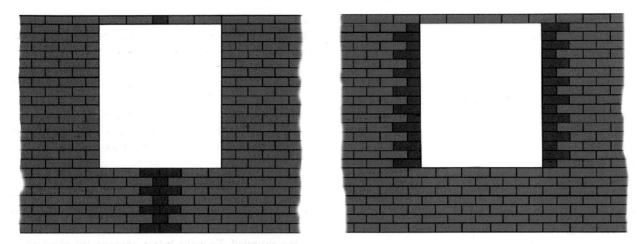

Two ways of dealing with a wall whose length isn't a multiple of a brick stretcher: 'broken bond' hides the use of headers in the middle of a window opening; 'reverse bond' uses window reveals to do the same.

Typically, the datum level is transferred – perhaps by a water-level – to a peg knocked into the ground close enough to the corner for a spirit level to be used.

Following the lines marked by the profiles, a second quoin block or brick is laid at the opposite end of the wall. A taut line is then stretched from quoin to quoin as a guide for the first course to be laid.

What is a Spot Board?

This is a flat surface, usually about 600mm^2, on which mortar is placed, ready for the trowel. Typically, it's made on site from plywood by the bricklayers, and they may ask for the materials to be available. For convenience, it's often placed on a collapsible stand.

Metre-square, plastic versions, usually octagonal in shape with a raised rim, can be bought. They are used for larger quantities of mortar or concrete.

As soon as it's complete, the corners are built up and the courses in-between filled in, each one guided by a line running between successive quoin bricks – a process known as 'laying to the line'.

Constant checks should be made that the brickwork and blockwork are lined up vertically and plumb, and that the mortar joints are even. For this, a 'gauge rod' is used (see Chapter 18 for details). The walls should also be checked diagonally to ensure they are square.

Installing Breaks in the Footings

Where service ducting and drainage pipes pass through the footings, openings are created with concrete lintels. At least 50mm should be left around pipes to allow for movement. The gaps are then sealed to prevent vermin entering.

Where the ground floor is suspended from the footings, the void underneath needs to be ventilated to avoid condensation and any build-up of stagnant air or dangerous gases.

Fitting an airbrick every couple of metres creates a through draught. It should be above ground level at

The same setting out procedure used for an unbroken wall: either a 'broken bond' is made centrally, or a 'reverse bond' is made at both ends.

about the level of the damp-proof course. Where the void is lower, telescopic airbricks can cope with a drop of up to five courses between inner and outer leafs of a cavity wall.

Filling the Cavity

On a strip foundation, the cavity wall is strengthened below ground by filling the cavity with a weak concrete mix. The top of the concrete, which is just below ground level, is angled to deflect moisture towards the external leaf.

Damp-Proof Course (dpc)

A dpc is a roll of thick, black polythene, which prevents moisture rising any higher in both walls of the cavity. It's laid on fresh mortar and covers the final course of the footings. It should be at least 150mm above the existing or planned ground level.

On the external wall the dpc should extend a few millimetres, so that a thin black line is visible.

On the internal leaf, at least 50mm should overlap the edge so that a continuous layer can be formed with any damp-proof membrane beneath the floor. On the sides facing into the cavity, the dpc should be flush with the wall.

Building Control

The dpc will need to be inspected and approved before it can be covered by the next course of bricks or blocks.

To ensure courses remain level, bricks and blocks are 'laid to the line'; this is a length of cotton, hemp or nylon, held to the wall by the tension between two wooden corner blocks, which are used to avoid the line touching and damaging the fresh mortar.

CHAPTER 17

Ground Floor

Once the dpc is in position, you're entitled to breathe a sigh of relief. What is potentially the most problematic stage is now over. What happens next depends on your choice of ground floor.

TYPES OF GROUND FLOOR

These fall into two main categories: solid concrete slabs, which rest on the ground, and suspended floors, made from concrete or timber, which rest on the footings, leaving a void beneath.

Why leave a void?

You may have a sloping site, which requires a large volume of hardcore to create a level base. Or there may be patches of bad ground within the 'oversite', the area of ground covering the footprint of the house.

Increasingly, however, it's a matter of choice. Suspended floors are generally simpler, easier and faster to construct.

All ground floors, however, need to include insulation – it can be placed above, below or within the structure itself. For details of what type to use and ways to calculate the amount see later in this chapter.

SOLID SLAB

How Is It Made?

At least 100mm of concrete is laid over a thick polythene damp-proof membrane (dpm), which is laid over binding sand, which is laid over compacted hardcore.

The final layer – the floor itself – is either a smooth, top-screed or tongued and grooved chipboard panels, which simply rest or 'float' on top of the slab or the insulation above it. Often an additional dpm is placed beneath the final layer to ensure that it dries quickly or remains dry.

Insulation

This can be placed either beneath the slab (but over the dpm), or above the slab (but under the finishing screed or flooring). You can also use chipboard panels backed with rigid insulation.

Pros

Solid slab is the cheapest for materials. It provides a stable surface for floor tiles or stone flags and makes it easy to build a waterproof, centrally draining floor for a wet room.

It's also best for underfloor heating systems.

Cons

It's the most labour-intensive method and on a sloping site could be very time-consuming. Deep hardcore will also need to be thoroughly compacted to avoid any risk of the slab becoming undermined and cracking. This is why the NHBC – Britain's best-known warranty provider – insists on a suspended floor, if more than a 600mm depth of infill is required.

The finishing screed must also dry out thoroughly before wooden flooring or carpeting can be fitted, which may take some time.

PRECAST CONCRETE

How Is It Made?

In two forms: 'beam and block' and 'hollowcore'. In the former, the beams are typically 150mm deep, shaped like an inverted 'T' and rest on the damp-proof course of the inner leaf. They are spaced just far enough apart for standard concrete blocks to slot in between and create the floor. Where an internal wall is planned, beams are usually doubled up.

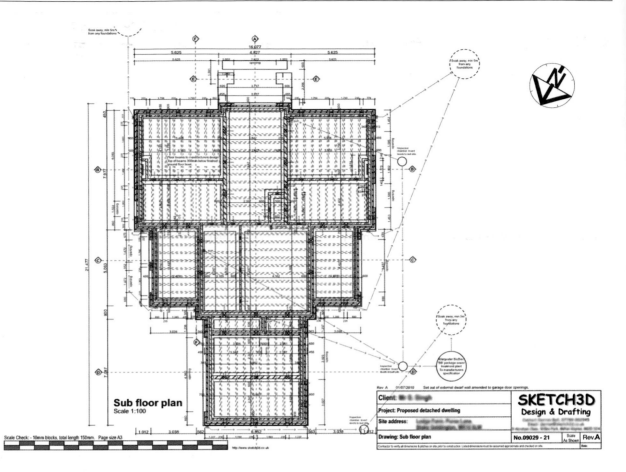

Sub floor plan
Scale 1:100

The layout of a ground floor to be built using block and beam. Note that the points where the drainage system penetrates both the floor and the footings are carefully marked. Sketch3D

Beam and block floors use standard concrete blocks laid between precast concrete beams in the shape of an inverted 'T'. Hanson

Beams are usually doubled up beneath internal walls.

Hollowcore precast concrete panels are simply slotted together to create a floor, but require a crane to lift into position, adding to costs.
Basement Information Centre

Hollowcore consists of prefabricated panels, typically 1.2m wide, with a series of hollow, tubular cores running their length. As with beam and block, they are supported by the inner blockwork and simply butted together.

With both precast systems, all the joints are sealed with a grouting mix of sand and cement.

Insulation

This is placed on top, then covered with a sand and cement screed, a 'floating' floor or conventional floorboards fixed to battens.

Superinsulated Beam and Block

Instead of concrete blocks, Hanson's Jetfloor system uses blocks of expanded polystyrene, combining both support and excellent insulation. Hanson

Beam and block floors can also be constructed with blocks made from rigid, expanded polystyrene (EPS) instead of concrete. These are much more thermally efficient and no more insulation is necessary, though they need to be covered with a protective reinforced screed.

Pros

A fast, easy way to create a rigid, stable, fireproof floor that doesn't need to dry out. Hollowcore has superior sound-proofing qualities and can provide very long spans on which masonry internal walls can be built without further support.

Hollowcore floors can provide very long spans without extra support, ideal for large, open plan layouts.
Basement Information Centre

Unlike hollowcore, where openings for services need to be built in at the production stage, the blocks in beam and block floors can simply be cut down or drilled on site.

Cons

Single spans of beam and block are limited to around 5.5m, though they can be extended by resting a second beam on an internal 'sleeper wall', which needs its own foundation.

Hollowcore panels need to be craned into position, which adds to costs.

Because they are precast concrete, holes for services need to be built in at the production stage.

Precast is more expensive than a ground-bearing slab. Suppliers compile orders from approved plans and delivery can take up to 2 months.

Timber joists are now routinely supported by galvanized metal joist hangers, which slot between the joints of the inner blockwork walls.

SUSPENDED TIMBER

How Is It Made?

Timber joists span the inner blockwork on which they either rest or sit in metal joist hangers set into the blockwork. Tongued and grooved chipboard or plywood panels, or traditional floor boards, are then nailed or screwed and glued on top.

The joists can be solid timber or 'I-beams. Solid joists are usually 200mm deep × 50mm wide softwood, spaced 400mm, 450mm or 650mm apart (depending on your plans).

I-beams are made from two timber battens joined by either a strip of engineered wood or an open, metal web. They exploit the fact that a joist's strength lies mainly in its top and bottom edges; the timber in between simply keeps the two apart.

I-beams' main advantages are: they're strong but very light, easily handled by one person; they can span much greater widths than a conventional timber joist; they accommodate wiring and pipework easily; and they don't shrink, warp or creak like conventional timber. They are, however, more expensive.

Insulation

The depth of the joists leaves plenty of room for rigid insulation to rest on battens, or for mineral wool to lie on plastic netting or chicken wire strung between the sides.

Pros

Timber copes well with a sloping site, as no deep hardcore is required. It also provides an instant dry floor, ready for covering. Using timber with the Forest Stewardship Council (FSC) trademark is also sustainable, good for an eco-home.

Cons

Timber can rot and suffer from fungal or insect attack. Protective chemicals are extremely toxic. The void beneath needs to be well ventilated and the ground covered with a concrete slab over polythene to prevent damp or the growth of vegetation.

Once in place, a timber floor needs to be well-protected to avoid being damaged as the build progresses.

WEEK THREE: COMPLETING THE GROUND FLOOR

Who Needs to Be There
- Groundworkers.
- Bricklayers.
- Building inspector.

Equipment
- Concrete mixer.
- Plate compactor (for compacting hardcore).
- Crane (if using hollowcore flooring or concrete beams).

Materials
- Hardcore.
- Ready-mixed concrete.
- Cement, sand, mortar mix.
- Damp-proof membrane.
- Blocks.
- Precast beams/hollowcore panels/timber joists/I-beams (as specified).
- Floor-grade chipboard panels.
- Insulation (rigid panels/rolls of mineral wool, as specified).

Planning Ahead
- Confirm delivery of facing bricks.
- Confirm availability of scaffolding for first lift.
- Order trussed rafters/attic trusses/prefabricated panels for the roof structure (see Chapter 20 for details).

I-beams provide the strength of solid timber joists but with the ability to span much greater distances and incorporate pipework and wiring much more easily.

Activities

Concrete Ground Slab

Hardcore is simply tipped onto the cleared soil and compacted with a plate compactor, more commonly known as a 'Wacker'. The depth will be specified in the plans. A layer of blinding sand is then applied to protect the damp-proof membrane. This typically consists of sheets of heavy, 1,200-gauge polythene, which overlap where they join. The outer edges are turned up over the damp-proof course of the inner brickwork to create a continuous damp-proof barrier. It's only broken where openings are made to allow service pipes or drains to pass through, and these will need to be sleeved with polythene and gaps sealed to prevent vermin entering.

The building inspector will now need to inspect and approve the base and the damp-proof membrane. One day's notice is usually required.

Where openings for services are made in the external walls, pipework should be sleeved and any remaining gaps sealed to prevent vermin entering.

Next, either a rigid layer of insulation is laid over the dpm and the concrete for the slab poured over it, or the concrete is poured and the insulation added later. In both cases, strips of insulation should be set upright around the edges of the concrete to make a continuous thermal barrier.

Ready-mixed concrete is typically used for the slab, poured in bays created by the internal walls. This allows time for the concrete to be levelled and tamped down. To avoid any damage from the rigours of the building process, finishing off to the specified floor level with a screed is usually left until the plastering stage.

Beam and Block/Hollowcore

The cleared ground between the footings is first covered with thick polythene weighed down with sand or a weak concrete mix. The underfloor void needs to be a minimum depth of 150mm. It also needs to be ventilated via airbricks in opposite external walls to create a through draught.

The beams are laid to follow the supplier's layout plan and can be filled with blocks immediately. Where drains or service ducting comes through the ground floor, blocks or sections of block can be omitted. The ends of the beams will need to be filled in with blocks cut to fit or specially shaped blocks provided by the supplier.

Ground-Floor Insulation and How to Calculate It

The ground swallows between 10 and 15 per cent of the heat from a house, a lot less than goes through the roof or walls. If you've trodden barefoot on a cold tile or stone floor, or even draughty floorboards, you'll appreciate the value of ground-floor insulation.

With a timber floor, the insulation simply rests between the joists, so you can use the same type as in the cavity or the roof, which can provide savings through bulk buying.

With a solid slab or suspended precast floor, the insulation also has to support the weight of the floor above – that rules out loose fill or quilt insulation. The main alternatives are rigid foam boards, which are not only stronger but are unaffected by contact with wet concrete. They are, in order of increasing thermal efficiency:

- **Expanded polystyrene (EPS)** – this is roughly equivalent to mineral wool and fibreglass insulation, though the latest varieties claim increased thermal efficiency by including graphite particles, which reflect back heat.
- **Extruded polystyrene** – a physically stronger and more thermally efficient form because its cells are filled with gas rather than the air of EPS.
- **Polyurethane (PUR), polyisiocyanurate (PIR) and phenolic** – these are the most thermally efficient foams, around twice as effective as conventional mineral wool. Usually backed with aluminium foil, they are also around three times as expensive but are valued for their space saving qualities.

Calculating the thickness of ground-floor insulation isn't as straightforward as with the walls and roof, largely because heat rises. As a result, most of the heat loss occurs through cold bridging around the edges of a house.

Currently, the building regulations require you to achieve a maximum U-value of 0.25 for the ground floor (*see* Chapter 8 for a definition of U-value). To discover the depth of insulation you'll need to meet that, you first need to work out the uninsulated U-value of your ground floor. You do that by calculating the ratio between the perimeter of the house – measured in metres – to the ground floor area, measured in square metres.

On a house with a ground floor measuring, say, 10×6m, the area would be 60m² and the internal perimeter 32m. The P/A (perimeter/area) ratio would, therefore, be: 60 divided by 32, which gives 0.53.

Insulation manufacturers provide tables enabling you to read off the required depth and type of insulation using this figure.

The joints between the blocks are then sealed with grouting. Normally, the insulation and a finishing screed are left till later.

Hollowcore panels can be installed even more quickly than beam and block. Beforehand, however, check that any openings for service ducting or drains will be in the right positions. Openings need to be built into the panels by the manufacturer.

Because both hollowcore and beams are made of pre-stressed concrete, they can't be cut or drilled on-site without risking their structural integrity. If you need to do so, consult the manufacturer first.

Incidentally, if you plan a floating chipboard floor or conventional floorboarding, you'll still need to lay a screed to achieve a level floor surface. Both types of precast flooring have a gentle camber on their upper surface – another consequence of pre-stressing.

Timber

The ground beneath has to be thoroughly sealed with both heavy polythene sheeting and a layer of concrete, 70mm to 100mm thick. Airbricks should provide cross-ventilation every 2m. As with a suspended concrete floor, there needs to be a minimum of 150mm between the underside of the joists and the top of the ground cover.

Timber for the joists and floor boarding material comes from a local timber or builders' merchant. I-beam joists may have to be sourced from specialist suppliers, who will normally provide layouts based on your plans. Some also provide a fixing service. Both types of joists can be attached to the inner blockwork with metal joist hangers built into the wall.

Where standard timber joists are longer than 2.5m, they need be cross-braced for rigidity. This can done with off-cuts known as 'noggins' or steel straps spanning the joists in a herringbone pattern.

Being lighter and flimsier, I-beams will need temporary bracing until the flooring is glued and screwed into place and the floor achieves maximum rigidity.

As soon as the floor is completed, the surface should be protected against physical damage and damp until the superstructure of the house is complete.

Buying Timber Joists

Under the building regulations, timber used for structural purposes has to meet certain requirements. It's important to check that the timber you use does so.

One requirement is strength and the timber industry provides grades. The most common are C16 and the stronger C24 (formerly SC3 and SC4), and timber is marked accordingly.

The second requirement concerns moisture content. Structural timber should have a maximum of 20 per cent. Above 25 per cent it becomes vulnerable to decay and insect attack. It can also twist and warp as it dries out in a heated home, where the average moisture content of timber is around 12 per cent.

Dry-graded timber, then, should be used for the joists. It's helpfully marked as either 'DRY', showing the timber has been dried naturally, or 'KD' for kiln dried.

Kiln drying takes place in a controlled environment and produces a lighter, stronger timber, which is more stable dimensionally and has a smoother finish when machined.

Any timber with more than 20 per cent moisture content is marked 'WET' and shouldn't be used structurally.

Your local building control department may also require you to use timber treated with preservative, especially in areas subject to certain types of insect attack. This is most easily done by your timber supplier using a pressure treatment and should be specified with your order.

Finally, don't rely on grade marks to guarantee the suitability of any timber. Check deliveries for bent or warped lengths and defects such as knots (which can work loose), 'shakes' (cracks along the grain) or 'splits' (cracks extending through the timber). These should be returned and replaced.

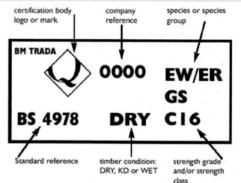

All structural timber should have grade marks indicating its strength and moisture content, as well as showing the quality assurance scheme used to make the grading; here, it is the Q-Mark from **BM TRADA Certification.** TRADA

CHAPTER 18

Walls

With the ground floor in place, work can now begin on the shell of the house, and the building will speed up considerably. A bricklaying team – two brickies and a labourer – can lay up to 1,000 bricks a day, or 30 to 40m² of blocks.

For cavity walls, brick and blocklaying are done together: the blockwork first with the brickwork following. At the same time, steel or plastic wall ties, designed to stabilize the twin walls, are fitted between them and insulation is inserted into the cavity.

Meanwhile, openings are created for doors, windows and bays. This will involve installing lintels or beams to support the wall above, along with cavity trays and vertical damp-proof courses to prevent damp from crossing the cavity.

The bricklayers can then either build and fit templates for the openings, install 'cavity closers' (*see below* for details), which perform the same function, or fit the door and window frames, though this is usually left to carpenters at a later stage.

Internal masonry walls and brickwork for chimneys are built at the same time. Once first-storey height is reached, work begins on the first floor with the close involvement of the carpenters.

WEEK FOUR: BUILDING THE FIRST STOREY

Who Needs to Be There
- Bricklayers and labourer.
- Carpenters.
- Scaffolders.

Equipment
- Scaffolding.
- Scaffolding boards.
- Building ladders.
- Wheelbarrows.
- Concrete mixer.

Materials
- Facing bricks.
- Blocks.
- Cement, sand, mortar mix.
- Lime, plasticizer, accelerator, retardant.
- Insulation.
- Cavity wall ties.
- Lintels/beams.
- Cavity trays.
- Cavity closers.

Activities
Buying Bricks
Facing bricks from the major manufacturers are normally only sold through a builders' merchant or brick factor. The system is commission-based, so, if you're quoted a price for a particular brick, merchants will want to register your details with the manufacturer. This may seem reasonable, until you discover that every other supplier of the same brick subsequently quotes the same price. It's advisable, then, to be sparing with your details.

Direct sales are usually only available from smaller, specialist brick-makers. That said, I know of one master bricklayer who ran short close to a major manufacturer's plant, called in to ask for help and was immediately sold a pack of bricks that were delivered the next day. As in most aspects of construction, it often pays to be a bit cheeky.

Other important factors in a purchase are delivery times and the cost of delivery. Bricks are usually sold

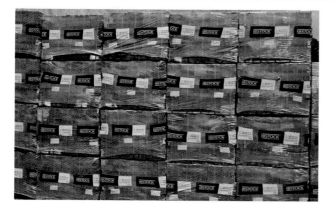

Bricks are typically sold by the thousand but delivered in pallet loads of between 300 and 500.

by the 1,000 and delivered in pallet loads of between 300 to 500 bricks. Delivery costs will depend on the distance travelled.

How Many Bricks and Blocks Will I Need?
You can, of course, leave this to a builders' merchant offering an estimating service, your main contractor or, for maximum accuracy, a quantity surveyor. There are also brickwork calculators online. As a double check, it's useful to know how it's done.

Start by working out from your plans the areas of brickwork in square metres. For rectangular or square walls, simply multiply length by height. Triangular gable ends will involve a reacquaintance with Pythagoras's theorem, or simply divide the gable end vertically in two, square off each half and divide the result by two.

Now calculate the areas of doors and windows and subtract them from the total.

For the standard stretcher bond used typically for a cavity wall, a rough rule of thumb is sixty bricks for every square metre.

For blockwork, which also uses the stretcher bond, it's ten blocks per square metre for the standard-sized block. On top of this figure, add between 5 and 7 per cent for wastage and breakages.

For more accuracy, use the standard dimensions of a brick face – 215mm long × 65mm deep, known as the 'work size'. Now add 10mm, both vertically and horizontally, for the mortar. Known as the 'co-ordinating size', this also allows for slight variations in brick dimensions, and gives a figure of 225mm × 75mm, or 0.01688m².

Some of the most attractive bricks – those hand-made – are not always entirely symmetrical, which is, of course, a major part of their appeal. Allowance can be made for this in the mortar joints, but, for safety's sake, it's wise to discuss your choice of brick with your bricklayer before committing to an order.

The standard size of concrete blocks is 440mm long × 215mm wide × 100mm deep. Adding mortar takes them to 450mm × 225mm and a face area of 0.10125m².

How Much Mortar Will I Need?
This depends on the thickness of the wall, the type of bricks and how they're laid. Solid bricks, quite reasonably, have the smallest surface and require the least mortar. Perforated bricks and bricks with deep frogs laid frog up take more.

For example, for each 1,000 bricks of a 102.5mm-thick cavity wall, you will need the following quantities of mortar, measured in cubic metres: solid brick – 0.30m³; perforated wirecut – 0.32m³; shallow frog – 0.37m³; deep frog down – 0.50m³; deep frog up – 0.39m³.

To build a wall measuring 6 × 5m (or 30m²), then, you would need 1,800 bricks (30 × 60, assuming sixty bricks per square metre). If you used solid bricks, 1.8 × 0.30m³ = 0.54m³ of mortar would be required.

This is useful information because the constituents of mortar – cement, sand, water and additives – are mixed by volume. What is less useful is the fact that these materials are sold by weight; cement typically comes in 25kg bags.

One way round this is to assume that the volume of 25kg of cement is 0.0175m³, which for most purposes it is. A 'gauge box', equal in volume to a bag of cement, can then be built on-site for mixing the mortar. Made from timber, and without a fixed bottom, it is used to measure corresponding volumes of other constituents.

Alternatively, mortar can be purchased pre-mixed in dry form, or delivered ready mixed (*see below*).

Mixing Mortar
The mortar used for brickwork, known as 'muck' in the trade, contains the same Ordinary Portland Cement and fine 'builder's sand' used to make concrete, but without the gravel. A typical mix is 1:6 (one part of cement to six of sand). Plasticizer, which traps tiny air bubbles within the mix, is usually added to improve workability.

In cold weather, accelerators can be added to speed up the setting time and reduce the risk of frost damage.

The mortar used for brickwork – known as 'muck' in the trade – typically consists of one part cement to six of sand; plasticizer is usually added to increase workability.

In hot weather, adding retarders will prevent the mortar setting before it's gained full strength.

Mortar should be 'fatty', i.e. spread easily without being sticky. A stronger mix (1:3 or 1:4) is normally used for work below ground, where damp obviates the need for plasticizer.

Laying Bricks and Blocks
Blocks are laid by the same method as bricks, usually using a simple stretcher bond.

Blending
Bricks can vary in colour, shade and pattern, depending on where in the kiln they are fired. With stocks and handmade bricks especially, the variations can be large. To create a uniform look, bricks should be blended from at least three different packs – and up to six. They should also be taken from down the pack rather than across, to allow for variations in temperature at different heights in the kiln.

Building Thin and Fast

The 'thin joint' system uses extra-large aircrete blocks (up to 675mm long × 375mm wide × 100mm deep). They are laid using a thin layer of quick-drying cement-based glue, rather than mortar. This can double the normal speed of laying, allowing entire storeys to go up in a day.

In fact, all the inner blockwork walls can be completed before starting the external brickwork. This allows the insulation to be installed much more easily and accurately. Thermal efficiency is also improved by the narrower joints – less than 3mm rather than the usual 10mm.

Because the glue used is stronger than mortar, however, the joints need to be reinforced at certain points with steel or fibreglass mesh. Accuracy is also important for the foundation course; the shallow joints leave little room for correction during building, though the shape of blocks can be adjusted by hand saw or rasp with relative ease.

The 'thin joint' system uses a cement-based glue rather than mortar to lay aircrete blocks, greatly increasing the speed of construction.
Hanson

Gauging the Mortar

Accurate 'gauging' or measurement of the constituents is essential not just to ensure a consistent strength and durability, but also a consistent colour. If colour pigment is being added, achieving a consistent colour is much easier using premixed mortar. This can be delivered dry in bags, or wet and ready to use in tubs. Retardants are typically added to the latter, making the mortar workable for up to 36 hours.

Ensuring that the mortar joints are even – known as 'keeping the gauge' – is managed with a 'gauge rod'; seen here on the right, it's a length of timber marked with the depth of each block or brick, plus the correct depth of mortar.

Keeping Level, Plumb and Flush

A long spirit level is used to keep the brickwork level and flush and check that the perpends are vertical and in line. Brick should always be laid to the line. This is a length of cotton, hemp or nylon drawn taut and level across the brickwork to act as a guide for each successive course.

Keeping the Gauge

Ensuring that the mortar joints are even – otherwise known as 'keeping the gauge' – is done with a 'gauge rod'. This is a length of timber, typically 50mm × 25mm, with lines drawn across it at right angles every 300mm, which is the equivalent of four courses of standard-size brickwork, including the mortar joints. Each 300mm division is then sub-divided into 75mm sections: the depth of a brick plus 10mm of mortar.

A bricklayer can 'keep the gauge' simply by holding the rod upright against the brickwork. It rests on a nail or a wooden batten that is fixed at the damp-proof course.

A storey-high gauge rod, known unsurprisingly as a 'storey rod', enables bricklayers to 'work in' the brickwork, so that it meets the positions of window and door frames without the need for odd sizes of brick. Typically, the frames will be built and placed in position as early as practicable to make this easier.

Jointing-Up and Pointing

Smoothing the mortar and making it flush with the brickwork is known as 'jointing-up'. It not only creates a tidy look, it compacts the mortar, making it more waterproof. It should be done when the mortar is soft enough to leave a finger mark without leaving mortar on the finger. On a hot summer's day that might be

every three or four courses. In winter, it might be left until the brickwork is storey high. If left too late, the mortar becomes crumbly. If done too early, wet mortar can smudge the brickwork.

If you plan to use specific kinds of pointing in your brickwork (see Chapter 7 for the options), the joints need to be raked back 12mm to 15mm on the day the bricks are laid. The pointing is then done at another time, sometimes with a different colour mortar to achieve a particular look.

Good pointing can look spectacular. It can also make a major improvement to poor or indifferent brickwork.

Mortar Dos and Don'ts

- Don't add water to mortar to keep it workable once it has started to set. Discard it and mix a fresh batch.
- Don't use washing-up liquid as a cheaper or more convenient alternative to plasticizer. The air bubbles it creates are too large and will weaken the mix. Whole estates have had to be re-built because of its use.
- Do order building sand from the same supplier to maintain a consistent colour.
- Do use clean water for mixing. Water butts on-site can often become contaminated because they are used for cleaning tools.
- Do use the same labourer to mix all the mortar. The mix is much more likely to remain consistent.
- Do protect freshly mixed mortar from the elements.

Inserting Wall Ties

Wall ties are thin strips of steel or plastic linking the walls of the cavity and serving to stabilize and strengthen them. They can also double up as fixings to hold insulation in place (*see below*).

Wall ties are typically a figure-of-eight shape with the broad ends buried at least 50mm inside opposing joints of brickwork and blockwork. The narrowest part is left in the middle of the cavity. It's designed either to shed any drops of moisture that fall or condense on it, or to divert them towards the external wall. For this reason wall ties should be angled slightly downwards towards the outside.

The type, length and positioning of wall ties will be specified in the plans. For a typical cavity wall, however, they are usually spaced at maximum distances of 900mm horizontally and 450mm vertically. The spacing is tighter around the 'jambs' – the vertical sides of door and window openings. There, they should be placed at every course of blockwork and every fourth course of brickwork within 225mm of the jambs.

Wall ties are particularly vulnerable to mortar droppings or 'snots', which need to be wiped off as the walls rise, otherwise they can set and conduct moisture across the cavity, eventually creating damp patches on the inner wall, which can be particularly difficult to remove.

Inserting Insulation

Cavity insulation needs to be beefier than that used in the ground floor, largely because about a third of all heat lost from a house goes through the walls. Under the building regulations, at the time of writing, that means the walls have to achieve a maximum U-value of 0.20 (*see* Chapter 8 for details of U-values). You can achieve this in one, or more, of four ways: by adding insulation to the cavity, by using thermally efficient aircrete blockwork or by insulating the internal or external wall surface.

As with the ground floor, you can use rigid foam boards, loose fill or quilt insulation, though in slightly different forms to cope with the location. You can also choose whether to fill the cavity completely or only partially. Each of these methods has its pros and cons.

AIRCRETE BLOCKWORK

Pros More thermally efficient than conventional block-work. As a result, it allows more flexibility in the width of the cavity and the thickness of insulation fitted in it to meet the requirements of the building regulations.

Cons Special fixings are needed to take heavy weights. Aircrete blocks are subject to shrinkage, which can cause cracking in plaster, and need to have expansion and contraction joints built into the blockwork.

MINERAL WOOL AND GLASSFIBRE INSULATION

Pros The cheapest forms of insulation. Mineral wool is especially fire-resistant.

Mineral-wool insulation needs to be stiffened, or 'wick'd', to use in partial or, as here, full-fill cavity insulation; note how wall ties are used to secure it against the inner blockwork. Knauf

Cons For partially filled cavities, they need to be in the more expensive form of stiffened, or 'wicked' (pronounced 'wick'd') batts. Achieving the required U-values will demand a thickness of up to 150mm and an appropriately wide cavity.

RIGID FOAM BOARDS

Pros Highly efficient insulators, so save space. The aluminium foil with which they are usually backed acts a vapour barrier, providing further protection against damp penetration.

Cons Expensive. Unless they are fitted tightly together, even small gaps can dramatically reduce their effectiveness.

FULL-FILL CAVITY

Pros Maximum use is made of the cavity.

Cons Moisture penetrating from outside finds it harder to drain away. This is less of a problem with rigid foam insulation, whose closed-cell structure doesn't allow moisture to enter. But mineral wool and glassfibre insulation depends on the moisture running down its stiffened, outer surface. If mortar droppings or poor installation causes the material to bunch up, moisture can collect and may eventually bridge the cavity.

Full-fill is not recommended in areas subject to severe, driving rain and is not permitted at all in Scotland.

PARTIAL-FILL CAVITY

Pros A minimum of 25mm between the insulation and outer wall allows penetrating moisture to drain or evaporate away. The NHBC requires a minimum of 50mm – 75mm in areas of severe exposure.

Cons Depending on the insulation used, a very wide cavity may be needed, reducing internal space. Extra-long wall ties are also required.

INTERNAL WALL INSULATION

Pros Plasterboard sheets backed with rigid foam insulation are fixed to the inside wall with either adhesive (known as 'dot and dab') or screwed to wooden or steel battens. Once the joints are taped and filled, the wall can be decorated immediately.

Cons Unless insulation backed with aluminium foil is used, the wall needs to be covered with a polythene vapour barrier before the plasterboard is fitted. Otherwise, damp may be trapped behind it. Mould may still form in voids left between the securing adhesive. Cold bridges can be created where internal walls meet the external walls. Internal space is reduced.

EXTERNAL INSULATION

Pros The most effective form of insulation as it encloses the entire house, eliminating cold bridges.

Cons Normally used only for single-leaf new builds, which are usually built with aircrete blockwork. However, brick slips – brick faces only a few millimetres thick – can be attached externally, giving the appearance of conventional brickwork.

RETROFITTED INSULATION

Pros Bricklayers can concentrate on keeping the cavity clear. Build time is also saved. Installation is left to specialist companies who drill holes in the internal blockwork. They then either blow loose fibres of mineral wool or fibreglass into the cavity or inject polystyrene beads or granules. The work is guaranteed.

Cons The disadvantages of full-fill insulation, especially with loose fibres that can sink down the cavity if they become wet. Polystyrene beads can escape if the cavity is breached, e.g. for repairs or extensions. Some lenders or warranty providers may not approve retrofitting for new build.

Inserting Lintels, Beams and Cavity Trays

The walls above doors, windows and bays need to be supported with lengths of either steel, reinforced concrete, stone or heavy timber. Lintels should generally project a minimum of 100mm onto the supporting walls on either side.

Wider beams – such as for a bay or the door to an integral garage – may need the extra support of specially strengthened blocks, known as 'padstones'. These can be precast reinforced concrete blocks, dense concrete blocks or engineering bricks. The sizes and specifications form part of the approved plans. They should be followed precisely and will be checked by the building inspector.

Typically, steel lintels are used in external walls. A lip on either side is designed to slip between the joints of both blockwork and brickwork, holding the lintel in position and rendering it invisible from the outside.

Because it bridges the cavity, a lintel is usually combined with a cavity tray. This is a lip of steel along the top of the lintel, which is angled up to meet the inner blockwork. Any moisture dropping down the cavity is directed towards the external wall, where 'weep holes' – small gaps between the bricks – allow it to escape. Cavity trays should also be fitted with 'stop ends' – vertical barriers – at either end to prevent moisture dropping off into the cavity.

To avoid the cold-bridging effect of the steel, insulation can be incorporated into the cavity tray. Cavity trays and weep holes are also needed below the sills at the bottom of windows and doors.

A wide range of lintels and cavity trays is available from specialist builders' merchants and manufacturers, covering virtually every size and use.

Cavity closers are slotted into the cavity either side of door and window openings as the walls rise, preventing moisture from entering; some also contain insulation to avoid cold bridging.

Inserting Vertical Damp-Proof Courses
Moisture can also penetrate the sides, or reveals, of door and window openings, while the door or window frame can act as a cold bridge. To prevent this, 'cavity closers' – usually made from PVC with insulation incorporated – are slotted into the cavity either side. Some versions are sturdy enough to take the place of temporary forms, allowing windows and doors to be simply clipped in position.

Erecting Scaffolding
A bricklayer's limit for comfortable working is a point between shoulder and face height. It's advisable, then,

The bricklayers should be consulted about the timing and height of the first level – or 'lift' – of scaffolding. On a large house, like this, four lifts will be needed to complete the build.

Scaffolding Dos and Don'ts

- Do use an approved scaffolding company with public liability insurance. Other good signs are participation in the Construction Industries Training Board (CITB) scheme and membership of the National Access and Scaffolding Federation.
- Do ensure that safety rails and building ladders are included.
- Do ensure the scaffolders hold a licence from the local authority if the scaffolding extends on to the public highway.
- Do ensure the boards nearest the wall are turned up every night. Otherwise, rain hitting damp mortar lying on the board may be splashed up onto the brickwork, staining it.
- Don't forget to clear the scaffolding of materials, tools, rubbish, etc. before a new lift is made. Otherwise, you may be charged waiting time while this is done.
- Don't allow other trades to change or adjust scaffolding. This will invalidate the scaffolding company's insurance cover and make you liable for any accidents or damage.

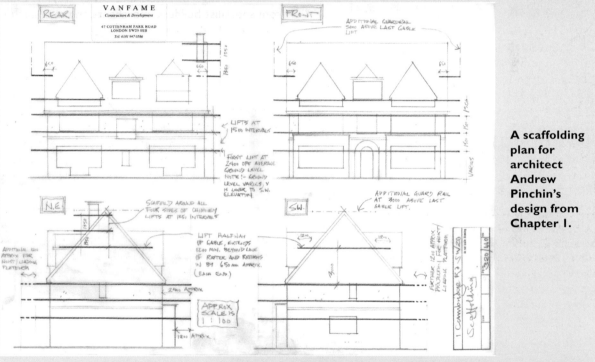

A scaffolding plan for architect Andrew Pinchin's design from Chapter 1.

Do ensure scaffolding is erected by an approved contractor with public insurance, and that guard rails and 'toe boards' – vertical boards lining the edges of the scaffold – are fitted.

to consult the bricklayers about the timing and requirements for the first level – or 'lift – of scaffolding. This will also allow you to give the scaffolders sufficient notice, ensuring there are no unnecessary delays.

Normally, each lift is 2m, though, depending on the ground level, the first can be as high as 2.7m. A typical two-storey build will need two lifts to reach the level of the wallplate – on which the roof will sit – a third to construct the roof and perhaps a fourth for the gables.

Traditional scaffolding – known as 'tube and fittings' – is usually charged per metre run per lift. Hire periods are generally for 8 or 10 week periods with additional weeks charged at a percentage of the total price. Scaffolding companies can quote from a copy of the plans and elevations

Building Internal Walls

Internal walls are either load-bearing – supporting floor joists and upper storey walls – or non-load-bearing, where they simply divide up the floor space.

Load-Bearing Walls

These need their own foundations and damp-proof course and are raised with the external walls. In a brick and block house they are usually masonry – typically 100mm-thick dense or load-bearing aircrete blockwork.

They also need to be tied into the external walls to stabilize themselves and the house structure as a whole. Blockwork can either be mortared into gaps left in alternate courses of the inner leaf, or attached with strips of galvanized steel mesh, which sit between the mortar joints of each wall.

Tying in Internal Walls

As an alternative to restraint straps, galvanized or stainless steel profiles. These are vertical metal strips screwed into the inner leaf blockwork. They are attached to the internal walls with loose-fit connector ties mortared into each course of blockwork. Quick and easy to fit, they allow for movement produced by drying out and temperature changes and reduce cold-bridging between internal and external walls.

Stainless steel profiles like these can be used to tie in internal masonry walls swiftly and easily to external walls; they also allow for movement as the walls dry out.

Door openings in internal masonry walls will need steel or concrete lintels to support the weight of the wall above.

Non-Load-Bearing Walls

Because they only need to support their own weight and that of lintels above door openings, non-load-bearing walls can be made from a variety of materials, including masonry.

The choice of construction will depend on:

* acoustic and fire-resistance needs;
* the support required for wall fixings;
* ease of maintenance and repair; and
* the type of wall surface you prefer.

Options include:

BLOCKWORK

Pros Reassuring solidity, good acoustic insulation and fire-resistance, good for fixing heavy objects (wall units, TVs, shelving, etc.). Blockwork takes plaster well, creating a smooth, hard-wearing surface that's easy to decorate and also covers any deficiencies in block laying.

Channels for suitably sheathed cabling and pipework can be cut, or 'chased', and easily filled and re-plastered, making alterations and repairs straightforward.

Cons Removing a masonry wall is highly disruptive.

Plaster will need to dry thoroughly before wallpaper can be applied.

BRICKWORK
Pros Exposed brickwork can make an interesting design feature.

Cons Bricklaying and pointing need to be high quality, unless the wall is painted.

Pipework and cabling for lighting and power are hard to accommodate.

TIMBER STUDWORK
Pros At around half the weight of masonry, timber studwork is often used for upper storeys to reduce the load on the walls below. The hollow interior is good for concealing pipework and cabling. Non-load-bearing walls can be removed relatively easily.

Cons Poor sound insulation, unless insulation is inserted between the studwork and sound-resistant plasterboard is used.

Only lightweight items can be attached directly to plasterboard and special fixings are needed. Heavier items require either 'noggins' – additional timber supports fixed in the desired positions before the plasterboard is fitted – or the use of stronger, but more expensive, gypsum fibreboard

Gaining access to pipework or cabling usually means removing, and replacing, a section of plasterboard spanning the studwork.

Damp areas require moisture-resistant plasterboard, or waterproof, cement-based board.

Alternatives
Glass blocks can be used as feature walls, room dividers, shower cubicles or inserts within other forms of partition, bringing additional light into a room or passageway.

Exposed brickwork can create an interesting design feature, but the laying and the pointing will need to be of high quality. Taylor Furniture

Glass blocks cannot be load-bearing, but can create interesting feature walls or, as here, an insert within a sturdier partition, bringing additional light through the house.

Hollow clay blocks, popular in continental Europe for external walls, make lightweight masonry partitions, which are then plastered or plasterboarded; they have good thermal and acoustic properties.

Most ground-floor internal walls can, of course, be eliminated by opting for an open-plan layout. This is easy to achieve with a precast, hollowcore, upper floor, which can span large distances unsupported and still carry upper storey walls.

Reinforced steel joists (RSJs) can also perform the function of a load-bearing wall. They will need to be supported on padstones in external walls and load-bearing internal walls, or by vertical steel beams or masonry columns built off suitable foundations. Precise details will need to be calculated by a structural engineer.

WEEK FIVE: BUILDING THE FIRST FLOOR

Who Needs to Be There
As week four.

Equipment
As week four.

Materials
As week four.

Activities
Any form of suspended flooring used for the ground floor (see Chapter 17 for details) can be used for the first, though timber is often preferred for reasons given below.

A precast floor can be laid either by bricklayers or returning groundworkers.

Timber floor joists will be cut and fitted by carpenters with the help of the bricklayers.

Which type of floor should you choose?

Beam and Block and Hollowcore
Pros Best for sound-proofing. The floor surface is immediately rigid and stable. Hollowcore provides the widest spans – ideal for open-plan designs. It also allows upper-floor internal walls to be placed wherever required without further support.

Cons A solid floor restricts the space for underfloor services, which are numerous in first floors. They will either have to run within a surface screed, be surface

A beam and block upper floor provides instant rigidity, as well as excellent sound-proofing, but cabling or pipework may need to be run above, or within a false ceiling.

mounted, concealed within a false ceiling or possibly a mix of all three.

Hollowcore cannot be cut or drilled without affecting its integrity, so openings for services, staircases and chimney flues will need to be designed in when the floor is ordered.

Both hollowcore and beam and block have to be screeded to provide a level final surface.

Timber
Pros Space between the joists is ample for services, especially if I-beams (see Chapter 17) are used.

Care should be taken in drilling, or notching, solid timber joists to accommodate services; too many will weaken the structure.

Cons Hollow timber floors are noisy, though insulation can be fitted easily between the joists. Strutting between the joists is also needed to avoid them twisting or vibrating.

Solid timber joists shrink and warp as they dry out, causing floors to creak (though much less so with I-beams).

Drilling or notching a solid timber beam to accommodate services can weaken it structurally.

Tying-In

Like internal walls, floors need to be tied into the structure. With a timber floor, the joists typically rest in metal joist hangers, which are set between the joints of the inner blockwork.

They are also tied in laterally with 30mm-wide restraint straps of galvanized or stainless steel. These are nailed or screwed across the joists, then bent through 90 degrees and mortared into the inner leaf blockwork. Lengths of wood – 'noggins' – fixed between the joists provide extra fixing points.

Restraint straps are placed no more than 2m apart and on either side of door or window openings.

Internal walls are tied into the first floor joists in a similar way.

Strutting

Timber joists spanning over 2.5m should be stiffened with strutting. The struts are made either of solid

In this beam and block build the opening for the stairwell is created by four concrete beams running between steel joists.

Timber joists over 2.5m long should be stiffened with struts, either made of galvanized steel in a herringbone pattern or solid wood, as here.

blocks of timber at least 38mm thick and no more than three quarters the depth of the joist, timber lengths at least 38mm × 38mm arranged in a herringbone pattern or strips of galvanized steel arranged in the same way.

Trimming

To make room for a staircase or a chimney flue, the joists need to be cut away and an opening formed with supportive timbers or 'trimmers'. They are the same depth as the joists but usually about 25mm wider.

WEEK SIX TO SEVEN: BUILDING TO THE WALL PLATE

Who Needs to Be There

As week four, plus the building inspector and the warranty provider's surveyor.

Equipment

As week four.

Materials

As week four.

Activities

The wall plate is a length of timber that sits on top of the inner wall of blockwork. It provides a fixing point for the roof and the ceiling joists of the upper storey. Reaching this level marks the end of another major stage of the build. As such, it prompts a visit from the building inspector, as well as your warranty provider's surveyor.

Building the walls of the upper storey is effectively a repetition of the first, but with the opportunity for some distinctive brickwork detailing, such as corbels (*see* Chapter 8 for details) on either side of the gables; they can also be fitted beneath the eaves, the verges or form the sills of windows.

As the walls rise, so does the chimney, which is usually completed before work starts on the roof.

Building the Fireplace and Chimney Breast

These are typically built with brick, medium-density block or a combination of the two, which is why the chimney requires its own foundation and damp-proof course.

As the focus for the main living area, brick-built fireplaces and chimney breasts provide a good opportunity for bricklayers to show off their skills.

Choices to make are:

- Size – from wall-spanning inglenook to a discreet, perhaps raised opening, flush with the wall.
- Position – in an internal wall (which helps to retain the fire's warmth within the house; it also allows the fireplace to be double-sided, shared with an adjoining room); in an outside wall (which enables the chimney to rise externally, freeing up floor space); corner-sited; or freestanding (as in an open plan design).
- Type – unless you have a specific appliance in mind, installing a chimney that can accommodate all types of fire maximizes your options and your home's appeal to later buyers. Choose, then a Class 1 flue, which has a minimum internal diameter of 178mm.
- Extras – building in a mantelpiece or side compartments creates space for display, fireplace furniture and storing logs.

Hearths should made of stone, brick or concrete at least 125mm thick, extend at least 150mm either side of the fireplace opening and 500mm in front, though not necessarily remain on the floor.
Limestone Gallery

A functioning fireplace and chimney have to be built according to Part J of the building regulations, which your designer should follow in the plans. The regulations determine the size of flue appropriate to the fireplace opening, the type of heating appliance used and the amount of heat it can produce.

Three areas are key:

- The hearth – this should be a slab of brick, concrete or stone at least 125mm thick. It should extend at least 500mm beyond the front of the fireplace opening and a minimum of 150mm on either side.
- The fireplace opening – the brickwork and flue liners above are supported by a special reinforced concrete lintel with a sloping back, which directs flue gases upward. The back and sides of the fireplace are lined with a prefabricated fire-proof 'fireback'. The internal brickwork above is brought inwards to restrict the size of the flue – forcing the rising gases to move faster – and to provide support for the liner.
- The flue – flue-liners protect the chimney from the corrosive effects of combustion gases and ease their passage skyward. The easiest way to install them is by using ready-made concrete, clay or pumice sleeves which slot together. They are raised with the bricks or blocks of the chimney, but jointed with fire-proof cement. The gap between flue liner and masonry is filled with a weak concrete mix containing vermiculite or perlite. These naturally occurring fire-resistant minerals expand when heated, making them good insulators.

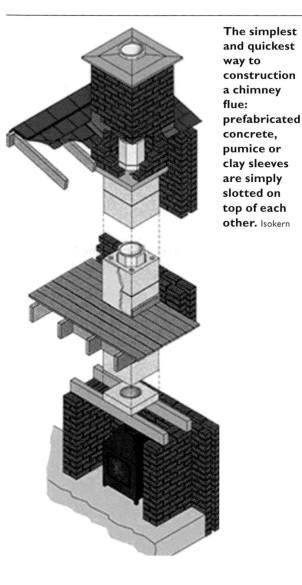

The simplest and quickest way to construction a chimney flue: prefabricated concrete, pumice or clay sleeves are simply slotted on top of each other. Isokern

Chimney Design

Tudor chimneys, like these examples from Hampton Court, display an inspired use of brickwork, but similar designs would run foul of modern fire safety regulations.

Why Do You Need to Insulate a Chimney?
A well-insulated flue keeps the combustion gases hot. As a result they rise faster, creating a better 'draw' for the fire and allowing less corrosive fluid to condense out on the sides. Any moisture that does collect, or falls from above, also evaporates more swiftly.

Pre-Cast Throating Units

For greater speed and convenience, use a pre-cast concrete 'throating unit', which combines the lintel and flue liner support.

In the past, chimney stacks have provided bricklayers with ample opportunity to demonstrate their skills, particularly in the tall, ornate spirals of Tudor times. Current building regulations make those virtually impossible to reproduce as functioning chimneys, but there is plenty of scope for varying the conventional square or rectangular stack. Circular chimneys, for example, are relatively rare but perfectly feasible.

Modern chimney pots, too, are often perfunctory, sometimes simple continuations of the flue liner. In Victoria times, however, ornamental designs were used widely, both to increase the efficiency of the chimneys and to add a personal touch. Many of those designs are still available. Before buying, though, it's important to check with the manufacturers that your choice meets the requirements of the appliance you plan to use.

Careful lead flashing ensures that no water penetrates where the chimney stack meets the roof. Hanson

Building the Chimney Stack

The position of the stack and its size are subject to a range of building regulations. They cover such things as the maximum height – no more than 4.5 times the width of the chimney, where it penetrates the roof surface – and its minimum distance from windows and the main roof ridge.

Just as important, however, is keeping the stack free of rainwater penetration. This involves:

• fitting and mortaring lead flashing into the chimney brickwork, where it meets the roof;

• inserting a specialized damp-proof tray in the brickwork above the flashing and joining it into both flashing and flue liner (in exposed conditions, another tray can be added under the top brick courses of the stack);

• building the topmost brick courses out at least 30mm on every side, so that rainwater is thrown aside;

• ensuring that the 'flaunching' – the mortar that holds the chimney pot in position – slopes downwards.

Adding the Wall Plate

The wall plate – typically 100m × 50mm timber – is usually bedded into a layer of mortar on top of the inner blockwork wall to ensure that it's level. Individual lengths need to be joined together securely with an overlapping or 'scarfing' joint.

Once the mortar has set, the wall plate can be screwed in position and secured with L-shaped galvanized steel restraint straps fixed into the blockwork every couple of metres.

Building Inspector and Warranty Provider

Inform both that the next stage of the build is ready for inspection.

Chimney Dos and Don't's

• Do keep the flue vertical for maximum draw; if that's impossible, offset it by no more than 30 degrees.

• Do ensure that the bottom of each flue liner sits inside the one below, and not the reverse; otherwise, rising moisture can work its way into the joint and eventually into the surrounding chimney.

• Do check out any similar working chimneys in the locality; their owners may have tips on the most effective positioning.

• Don't put any combustible material closer than 200mm to the flue or 40mm from the outside of the chimney.

• Don't forget to allow for adequate ventilation; depending on your appliance, you may need to fit a permanent vent in an outside wall of the room where the fireplace sits.

CHAPTER 19

The Roof

The great majority of roofs are double-pitched in order to shed rain and snow easily and to deflect wind. As long as they also support their own weight and any additional loads imposed by the elements, remain stable and prevent sufficient heat from escaping to comply with the building regulations, the method of construction is up to you.

In practice, most are made from timber rafters covered with waterproof underlay, which is in turn covered with tiles, slates or, less commonly, thatch, copper or zinc. The precise details depend on your design, how you plan to use the attic space and, as always, your budget.

There are four main options for the structure.

TRUSSED RAFTERS

A trussed or 'Fink' rafter (named after its inventor) is a triangular frame consisting of two rafter, which support the roof cover, and a bottom chord, which holds the rafters together and doubles up as a ceiling joist for the storey below. Two further triangular members stiffen the frame. A row of trussed rafters can create a roof structure virtually on its own.

Trussed rafters are prefabricated by specialist manufacturers, based on your plans.

Pros The cheapest and most popular form of roof construction, they are lightweight, easy to handle and can be assembled quickly by the semi-skilled, saving time and labour costs. They can also span up to 16m without additional support, leaving you to free to place upper storey internal walls where you like.

Cons Because they are so slim, trussed rafters need to be carefully braced, including diagonally. This effectively fills the loft space, leaving little room for more than a

Prefabricated 'trussed' rafters are the quickest and cheapest form of roof construction, but they are best suited to simple roof designs while the internal support they require makes the loft space virtually unusable.

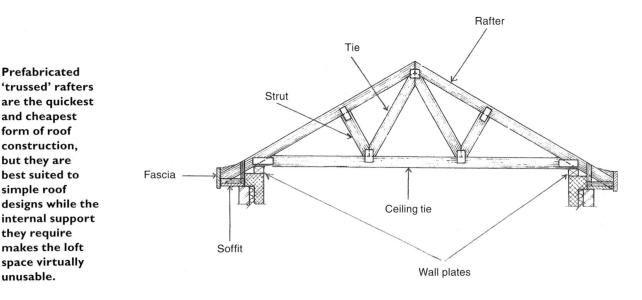

The traditional 'cut' roof is made on site, allowing maximum design flexibility, but the heavier timbers used mean that wide spans often need the support of an internal load-bearing wall.

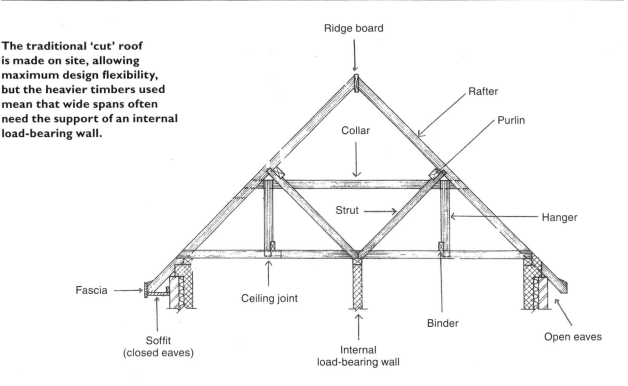

Ridge board

Rafter

Purlin

Collar

Strut

Hanger

Fascia

Ceiling joint

Binder

Open eaves

Soffit
(closed eaves)

Internal
load-bearing wall

water tank. Trussed rafters best suit simple, rectangular or square roofs with gables at either end. Though they are capable of more complex designs, this may not be cost effective. Converting the loft to create habitable space at a later date will also require major structural work.

TRADITIONAL 'CUT' OR PURLIN ROOF

This is how roofs were built before trussed rafters arrived in the 1960s. It is, in effect, a custom job, constructed on-site by the carpenter.

A cut roof consists of pairs of rafters, joined at the apex by a ridgeboard. They are braced at each mid point by a length of timber, known as a purlin, which runs from gable to gable at right angles to the rafters. The purlins rest on struts, which meet at the ceiling joists above a load-bearing internal wall. The ceiling joists are generally nailed to the wall plate and the ends of the rafters.

Pros A cut roof gives maximum design freedom, only limited by your designer's imagination, your carpenter's

skills and your budget. The loft space is left relatively free and available for storage. If there is sufficient head height, and the ceiling joists are made large enough to support a floor, later conversion to habitable accommodation is usually straightforward.

Cons Cut roofs are labour-intensive, heavily dependent on the carpenter's skills and usually the most expensive building method. Because they use sturdier timbers, which are heavier than those used for trussed rafters, they can't span such large distances. As a result, they may need the additional support of load-bearing internal walls or beams.

How to Eliminate Struts in a Cut Roof

To avoid cluttering the floor space of a cut roof with struts, use a steel or structural timber beam to support the purlin, or a ply box beam, which can be built on site.

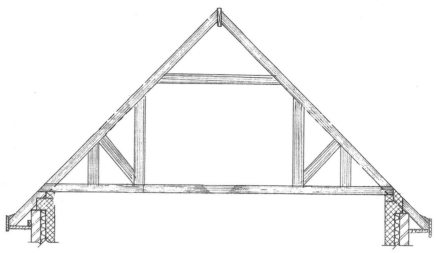

Like trussed rafters, 'attic' trusses are prefabricated, but are built sturdily enough to incorporate a habitable loft space; their weight, however, requires installation by crane.

ATTIC TRUSSES

These combine the speed, convenience and capability of trussed rafters with an open loft space, which can easily be turned into extra living space, either immediately or in the future. The pairs of rafters are braced by sturdy, upright hangers and a collar – a horizontal cross-piece close to the ridgeboard – leaving a room-sized space in the middle. Effectively it provides a pre-converted loft. Like trussed rafters, attic trusses are prefabricated by specialists.

Pros It allows you to add up to 30 per cent extra floor space for relatively little additional expense.

Cons Attic trusses are around double the cost of trussed rafters. Their weight and bulk may require installation by crane, adding to costs. If you plan to use the loft as third-storey living space, building regulations will insist that all doors opening on to the staircase be fire doors. Mains powered, interlinked smoke alarms will also be needed on the stairwell at each level.

PANELIZED ROOFS

These latest developments in roof construction take prefabrication to another level and offer a completely open loft space. Typically, they consist of either timber cassettes – box sections filled with insulation – or structural insulated panels (SIPs). A SIP is a panel made from two sheets, usually oriented strand board (OSB), sandwiching a core of rigid foam insulation.

The panels simply stretch from ridge to eaves, generally needing only a set of purlins for fixing and support. Some come with plasterboard or a finished surface already attached. Panels combine structural strength with integral insulation, providing the closest we currently have to an 'instant' roof.

Panelized roofs, like this timber cassette example, come prefabricated, complete with insulation, service void and even plasterboard on the internal side. Excel Industries

Designing Your Roof

Long, steep roofs based on the proportions of the 'golden ratio' were a characteristic of the Arts and Crafts movement, launched with the building of William Morris's Red House in 1860.

Even more than the brickwork, the roof is arguably the single most conspicuous aspect of a house. As with all design, proportion is key. The Georgians, for example, concentrated on elegant, beautifully proportioned facades, leaving the roofs low-pitched and relatively modest. The Victorians, and particularly designers of the Arts and Crafts Movement, preferred much taller, steeper, more imposing roofs.

Both made use of the so-called 'golden ratio', otherwise known as 'phi'. Essentially, if the short side of a rectangle is in the ratio of 1 to 1.618 to the long side, the resulting shape is hugely satisfying to the human eye.

This works for triangles, too. A 'golden triangle' is an isosceles triangle in which the smaller side is in a phi ratio to its two equal longer sides. A steep version provided the inspiration for tall Arts and Crafts roofs. A shallow version can be seen in Georgian buildings and, incidentally, the Parthenon. Phi doesn't have to be followed slavishly to have an effect, but it's worth bearing in mind and discussing with your designer at an early stage.

In practice, other factors, such as local planning restrictions and plot constraints, are more likely to dictate the details of your design. Factors to consider include:

Pitch
Pitches can vary from 10 degrees to 70. Anything beyond is either a wall or a flat roof. The exact angle will depend on the roof span, the ridge height, the roof covering and the strength of the prevailing wind in your location; a pitch that is acceptable in Sussex, for example, may not be in the Orkneys.

The roof covering will require a minimum pitch to ensure it remains waterproof. Interlocking concrete tiles, for example, can be lain at pitches as low as 12.5 degrees. A traditional clay tile will generally need to be closer to 35

One way of reducing ridge height, while still retaining a steep pitch over much of the roof, is to use a 'mansard' roof, where the pitch changes at ceiling height. Ibstock

degrees, while a thatched roof will require at least 45 degrees.

Ridge Height

The taller the roof, the greater the loft space. On bungalow replacement sites, where planners insist the new house remain single storey, a large roof can incorporate habitable space, creating a chalet-type, 'one and a half storey' design. Doing the same with a two-storey home will effectively add a third storey and maximize the use of the plot. Tthere are always likely to be limits on ridge height – typically determined by those of neighbouring properties.

There are, however, a number ways of reducing roof height, while still retaining a steep pitch. One is to use two ridges, either side by side or one behind the other. Another is to introduce a section of flat roof – invisible from ground level – between front and rear slopes. A 'mansard' roof, meanwhile, has a steep pitch to ceiling height but then changes to a shallow pitch to complete the roof.

Where a roof risks appearing over-large, its impact can be reduced by choosing hipped rather than gable ends, where the roof ends in triangular slopes. Adding dormers will have a similar effect by breaking up large expanses of uninterrupted roof covering.

Cost

The simplest, and cheapest, design consists of two slopes meeting at a ridge between gable ends. Anything that complicates that – hip ends, dormers, the additional wings of an L-shaped or courtyard design – will add to costs, not just in terms of construction but also in maintenance.

Any interruption to a roof surface – such as a valley where slopes meet, or a chimney stack – is vulnerable to water penetration and will eventually need repair or replacement.

Steel-frame construction is still largely confined to the commercial sector, but the inherent strength of steel, its design flexibility, lightness and credentials as a sustainable material give it a promising feature. U Roof

Pros Construction is rapid and easy. High levels of insulation are achieved easily.

Cons They are likely to be a similar cost to attic trusses and they work best with simple designs. They generally require a crane and appropriate lifting gear for installation – the average jobbing builder is unlikely to be familiar with them.

The simplest and cheapest roof design consists of two pitches meeting at a ridge between gable ends; this example has been embellished with decorative bargeboards. Wienerberger

WEEK EIGHT TO NINE: BUILDING THE ROOF STRUCTURE AND GABLE ENDS

Who Needs to Be There
- Bricklayers.
- Carpenter.
- Plumber.
- Scaffolders.

Equipment
- Scaffolding.
- Scaffolding boards.
- Building ladders.
- Wheelbarrows.

Materials
- Trussed rafters (attic trusses/prefabricated panels).
- Truss clips, nails, screws.
- Sawn timber (100mm × 25mm, 50mm × 25mm).
- Exterior quality plywood sheets (9.5mm to 20mm thickness).
- Fascia board.
- Soffit board.
- Lead (Code 4 or higher)/GRP valley components.
- Facing bricks.
- Cement, sand, mortar mix.
- Lime, plasticizer, accelerator, retardant.
- Cavity wall ties.
- Undercloak.
- Lead or preformed fibreglass (GRP) valleys.
- Soffit ventilation strips.

Activities

Erecting the Trussed Rafters
Trussed rafters are typically spaced 600mm apart. This makes it easier to attach the plasterboard sheets that form the upper-storey ceiling and come in multiples of 600mm. Closer spacing will be needed around openings formed by the chimney, loft windows, loft hatch, and so on.

The positions of the rafters are marked on the wall plate. Then each rafter is lifted into place, correctly positioned with temporary bracing and fixed to the wall plate with special truss clips. Once all the rafters are in position, permanent braces (typically 100mm × 25mm) are fitted both longitudinally and diagonally, according to the plans.

L-shaped galvanized steel restraint straps should also

ABOVE: Trussed rafters in the process of being erected; because they are relatively flimsy, they need secure temporary bracing before permanent braces can be fitted to the completed structure.

RIGHT: Roof details. Keymer

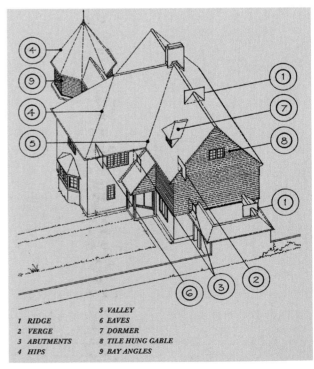

1 RIDGE	5 VALLEY
2 VERGE	6 EAVES
3 ABUTMENTS	7 DORMER
4 HIPS	8 TILE HUNG GABLE
	9 BAY ANGLES

Ordering Trussed Rafters

Trussed rafters are ordered from the manufacturer or a builders' merchant offering a trussed rafter service. They are made on the basis of your plans – not a visit from the manufacturer – so it's wise to leave your order until the foundations are complete and you can check that the dimensions of the walls are as intended.

The manufacturer will need to know:

- the required span (measured between the outside of the wall plates on which the rafter will sit);
- the pitch of the roof;
- the type of eaves planned and how far they will overhang;
- the type of roof coverings and their total weight;
- the size and position of any roof supports, water tanks and openings for chimneys, loft windows, etc.; and
- whether or not you require truss clips, restraint straps, bracing timber or gable ladders (see later for details).

Even after all this, putting the first rafter in place and discovering how well, or not, it fits can be a little nerve-wracking.

be built into the blockwork and fixed across at least three rafters or ceiling joists. Noggins should be added to provide secure fixing points.

Building Dormers, Rooflights and Bay Window Roofs

Once the rafters are in position the carpentry for these items can be done.

Install Water Tank/Hot-Water Cylinder/Thermal Store and Soil Vent Pipes

The cold-water storage tank for a conventional vented hot-water and central heating system is usually sited in

Traditionally, mortar is used to close the gap between the roof cover and the 'undercloak', a strip of tile, slate or, as here, cement-based board, which seals the top of the cavity. Hanson

the loft, as is the expansion tank for the central heating. While access is easy, both can be put it in place on suitably strengthened floor joists.

This can also be an opportunity to place a large hot-water cylinder or thermal store (see Chapter 21 for details), saving space in the main part of the house. In the attic, these items will also be closer to rooftop solar-heating panels, if you plan to use them as a supplementary heat source.

The soil vent pipe, or pipes, which ventilate the indoor drainage system and disperse foul gases from above the roof line, can also be installed at this point, either internally or externally. All of the above are jobs for the plumber.

Building Up the Gable Ends

These triangular constructions, which form either end of the roof, are typically built after the rafters are installed, so that the bricklayers can use them as a guide for their brickwork. Even if you don't intend to make the loft habitable, gable ends are still built as cavity walls to avoid penetrating damp reaching the floors below.

The open top of the cavity is sealed with an 'undercloak', running the length of the verge, from eaves to ridge. It can be made from tile, slate or a cement-based board, which is mortared in position.

The roof covering then overlaps the undercloak and the intervening gap is sealed, traditionally with mortar, to prevent damp from reaching the roof timbers.

Dry Verge Systems

So-called 'dry verge' systems can be fixed mechanically to gable ends. This removes the need both for mortar, which can shrink and crack at this exposed part of the roof, and for the under-cloak beneath it. Dry fix systems of this kind are often specified for exposed locations.

'Dry verge' systems, which are fixed mechanically, allow gable ends to be sealed faster and more reliably with special verge tiles. Redland

Another option is to fit a 'gable ladder'. This is a small timber extension of the roof structure, appropriately ladder-shaped, which is attached to the last rafter and oversails the gable end by several inches. Bargeboards can then be fitted to the outside. They are painted or stained and are sometimes elaborately carved, a practice the Victorians followed widely.

Gable ladders can be built on-site or ordered with the trussed rafters.

Creating the Valleys

Where two downward slopes of a roof meet, a 'valley' is formed. Valleys can be 'open' – effectively sloping gutters – or formed by specially shaped or individually cut tiles. Because they channel large volumes of rainwater, valleys need additional waterproofing. Traditionally, lead lining is used, but fibreglass (GRP), which is cheaper and easier to install, is now more common. Both materials, however, need to be laid over timber

A 'valley' is where two descending roof pitches meet; it can be formed by specially shaped or cut tiles, or simply left 'open', as here, where lead lining effectively creates a sloping gutter.

'valley boards' set between the rafters. Noggins are usually needed to provide it with sufficient fixings.

Building the Roofline
'Roofline' is the collective term for the various parts of the eaves, the lowest point of a sloping roof. It includes the 'fascia' – a board, made of either 20mm-thick planed softwood or PVC, fixed vertically to the ends of the rafters. As well as being decorative, it provides a fixing point for the guttering.

The 'soffit' is another board, attached to the bottom of the fascia and extending horizontally back towards the wall. It can be plywood, PVC or fibreboard.

Normally the ends of the eaves are blocked off, creating a so-called 'boxed eave'. This prevents birds and vermin from entering the roof space.

The eaves are also used to provide ventilation for the roof space, typically by means of a continuous 10mm

'Boxed' eaves are entirely enclosed to prevent birds and vermin entering the roof space; they can be made from plywood, fibreboard or PVC. Hanson

Traditional Eaves

The rafters can also be left exposed at the eaves, a traditional method often seen in barn conversions. The wall is then built up between the rafters.

As an alternative to boxed eaves, the feet of the rafters can be left exposed, a traditional method often seen in barn conversions.
Hanson

wide gap along their length. This can be in the form of a plastic grill, which is either inserted into the soffit, or beneath the last row of tiles so that it vents over the fascia.

WEEK NINE: FELTING, BATTENING AND INSULATING THE ROOF

Who Needs to Be There
- Carpenters.
- Roofers.
- Tilers.
- Plumbers

Roofs were traditionally made waterproof with bituminous felt, but this has largely replaced by 'breathable' membranes, like the one shown here; it, too, is waterproof, but it allows water vapour to pass through, preventing the build up of moisture within the roof timbers. DuPont

A scaffold hoist will speed up the roofing process and make you popular with the roofers.

Equipment
- Hired hoist/elevator.

Materials
- Sawn, treated timber roofing battens (50mm × 25mm).
- Exterior quality plywood sheets.
- Underfelt.
- Undercloak.
- Fascia board.
- Tiles/slates.
- Galvanized steel, aluminium or copper nails.
- Insulation.

Activities

Felting and Battening

This is the point when the roofers arrive. They will expect the scaffolding to be clear, while a hired hoist, ready to lift the tiles or slates to roof level, will make their work quicker and easier.

Unless your roof is especially large or complicated, felting and battening will normally take only a day. Work starts at the eaves where the felt, or underlay, is unrolled across the rafters and nailed or tacked in place. The lower edge should be positioned to overlap the guttering, so that water flowing down is collected there.

Each fresh layer of underlay needs to overlap the one below, usually by around 100mm, to ensure waterproofing. A wider overlap will be necessary on particularly low pitches. The laying continues up and over the ridge and any hip.

The underlay isn't secure until permanently fixed with rows of treated wooden battens, typically 50mm × 25mm, which are nailed across it horizontally. The spacing between the rows – known as the 'gauge' – is determined by the roof covering for which the battens provide fixings.

Insulating – and Ventilating – the Roof

Roofs may be designed to keep the rain out, but that doesn't make them immune to damp. Warm air rising from an occupied and heated home contains water vapour, which can condense in the cool loft, eventually causing the roof timbers to rot and the metal fixings to corrode. Ventilation, then, is essential, both at the ridge and the eaves to ensure a through flow. This is why lofts have traditionally been cold and draughty. When homes were the same, this was more acceptable, but today comfort and fuel efficiency are valued as much as structural integrity, and so roofs are insulated.

The most common method is to lay rolls of mineral wool or fibreglass on the loft floor. When the building regulations only required 100mm of standard insulation, it could fit neatly within the depth of the joists, allowing them to be boarded over for access and storage purposes.

At the time of writing, however, the recommended depth is 250mm, enough to hide the floor altogether and make the space inaccessible. In a low-pitched, trussed rafter loft, that might not be a problem, but many self-builders are acutely aware of the value of internal space and see little point in wasting it.

Making your loft warm and habitable means placing the insulation between the rafters. Typically, rigid foam is used; it's easier to fit into sloping spaces than conventional insulation, not subject to settling and is more thermally efficient in the limited space available. To prevent warm, moist air rising into the roof structure, a vapour barrier is then installed across the undersides of the rafters. The plasterboard for the ceiling will be nailed or screwed over this.

Choosing Underlay

The most common underlay, also known as 'sarking', used to be a bituminous felt, which, though waterproof, would eventually crack and split. This was superseded by more flexible polythene and then by microporous, 'breathable' membranes.

Though equally waterproof, these allow water vapour collecting inside the attic to permeate through them. Breathable membranes are up to three times the cost of traditional underlays but have particular advantages with modern forms of insulation (*see below*).

Alternative

In exposed areas of the UK, the rafters are usually boarded over to strengthen and weatherproof the roof before felting and battening.

In Scotland and exposed areas in general, the rafters are first boarded over before underlay is applied. Though adding to costs, this provides additional weather-proofing and greatly strengthens the roof.

Insulating inside the roof structure creates a 'warm roof' and makes the attic space habitable; here it's done with a combination of mineral wool and a foil vapour barrier, designed to fit between the rafters. Knauf

Counter-battens are now nailed to the tops of the rafters and the underlay laid across them, creating an air space at least 50mm deep between underlay and insulation. This space is ventilated via a continuous 25mm gap at the eaves and a 5mm gap at the ridge, allowing any water vapour that does penetrate the roof structure to be dispersed. The battens for the roof covering are nailed over the counter battens in the usual way.

This, however, assumes you are using conventional felt or polythene underlay. If you opt for a breathable membrane, the extra roof vents, and the effort and expense of adding them, aren't required under the building regulations. The NHBC, however, recommend

---

Alternative Forms of Roof Insulation

1. Reflective film, or multifoil, insulation claims to match the thermal efficiency of other forms of insulation in much less space, typically round 30mm, though it needs a 25mm air gap either side to operate effectively. Unlike mineral wool or foam, which works by slowing down the conduction and convection of heat, multifoil reflects back radiant heat, rather like aluminium foil or the reflective interior of a vacuum flask. It consists of several layers of fibre or foam insulation sandwiched between reflective layers. Available in rolls, it is stapled to the rafters like underlay. The slimness of multifoil makes it popular for loft conversions. Rival insulation manufacturers question its effectiveness but, as temperatures rise, insulation that reflects back external heat, as well as retaining it internally, may be more widely appreciated.

2. One of the disadvantages of rigid foam insulation is that it has to be cut and shaped by hand before fitting between rafters. Gaps, which can cause a dramatic deterioration in thermal efficiency, are virtually unavoidable. Foam insulation, however, also comes in spray form. When applied, it expands before hardening. As a result, the tiniest gaps in the most awkward of spaces can be filled. Applying it from below, once the rafters have been covered with underlay or boarding, may well be worth considering, especially for complex roof shapes.

Radiant film insulation claims high thermal efficiency in just a few millimetres – making it popular for loft conversions. But, for a new build, your local building control department may insist it is combined, as here, with conventional insulation. TLX

Spray foam insulation expands many times on contact with a surface, allowing it to insulate the smallest areas of complex roof shapes.
Biobased Insulation

One of the few new homes in open countryside granted planning permission purely because of its exemplary design, thls features a complex roof covered with hand-made clay tiles, designed to mellow and improve with age. Keymer

the extra ventilation, especially for new builds, which produce extra water vapour as they dry out.

So-called 'warm roofs' of this kind are becoming increasingly popular, partly because of the liberated loft space, but also because they are air-tight, greatly increasing the thermal efficiency of the roof. Their efficiency can be boosted by adding insulation above, as well as between, the rafters, and securing it with special, long, helical nails. You can even use insulated plasterboard with an integral vapour barrier for the ceiling.

WEEK TEN TO ELEVEN: TILING THE ROOF

Tiles and slates are the most popular coverings for pitched roofs and come in a variety of shapes, sizes, colours and materials. Concrete interlocking tiles, however, are the bestsellers, partly because they are cheapest but also because they can reproduce the colour of the traditional clay tile.

They can also be laid at lower pitches than clays, reducing the numbers required. Over time, however, concrete tiles weather and lose colour and, while remaining perfectly serviceable, end up looking decidedly drab.

This is one thing that clay tiles don't do, especially the hand-made variety. They are also machine-made in much the same way as bricks and, originally, with the same local materials, lending them a similar local character. Like bricks, their appearance improves with age and, while an average lifespan of 60 years is often quoted, many survive for much longer.

Clay tiles are more expensive than the concrete version, though the price difference is narrowing. It remains high, however, for hand-mades, just as it is with bricks. Not unsurprisingly, manufacturers argue that their highly individual character more than makes up for the cost with the enhanced kerb appeal – and increased value – they bring to your property.

The popularity of high quality Welsh slate has encouraged the development of more affordable substitutes, made from cheaper materials, such as slate dust and resin, or, like this example, clay. Sandtoft

Like bricks, plain tiles are bonded so that the joints between them are aligned with centres of tiles above and below, preventing water entering at the edges. Sandtoft

Slate, too, is a traditional, equally durable roofing material, originally confined to areas such as Wales and Scotland, where it was found locally. In Victorian times, thanks to the spread of the railways, it became available countrywide and hugely popular. Today, however, Welsh slate, the most prized, is in much shorter supply and as expensive as hand-made clay tiles.

With its sleek lines, blue-black to olive-grey sheen and relatively light weight, slate suits both modern and traditional designs. Less expensive imports are available, though quality can vary. There are also cheaper, synthetic varieties made from slate dust and resin, concrete, fibre cement and even clay.

LAYING PLAIN TILES

Plain tiles – simple, baked-clay rectangles, about 265mm × 165mm, with a gentle camber – are laid across the roof in rows. Like bricks, they are bonded so that the joints between them are aligned with the centres of the tiles above and below. This avoids water entering around the edges.

They also overlap vertically to deter water from above. Each tile is 'double lapped', partly by the tile immediately above and partly by the tile above that, leaving around 65mm of itself exposed.

On the underside of the tile are at least two small projections, or 'nibs', designed to hook over the supporting batten. There are also two holes for corrosion-resistant steel, aluminium or copper nails to fix the tile in position. Typically, only every fourth row is nailed because the weight of the tiles is usually enough to keep them secure. The minimum distance between the battens is provided by the tile manufacturer.

The tiles should be spaced to give a balanced appearance over each expanse of roof. This involves starting at the centre point of the eaves with either a single tile or the joint between two, then moving outwards and upwards towards each verge and the ridge. The bottom row should overlap the gutter by about 50mm to ensure rainwater drops into it and isn't blown back onto the underlay, causing it to deteriorate.

Where tiles need to be trimmed to complete rows, the trimmed tiles are typically laid in the next to last position, so that cut ends aren't left exposed at the verges. Alternatively, extra-large 'tile and halves' can be used.

LAYING INTERLOCKING TILES

Typically about 400mm × 300mm, these tiles lock together at the sides and provide as much water protection as plain tiles using only single lapping, and at a much shallower pitch. This, in turn, reduces the weight of the roof covering and allows wider roof-spans. Special left- and right-hand verge tiles are used to complete rows.

LAYING SLATES

Slates vary in size between 355mm × 180mm and 650mm × 400mm. Generally, the shallower the pitch, the larger the slate required.

They are laid as double-lapped tiles, but natural slates come without nail holes; these have to be made on-site with a special hammer. Typically, every slate is nailed at least once, either just below the head or at the centre; special clips may also be needed.

This larger-format interlocking clay tile combines the convenience and coverage of concrete tiles with the appearance of traditional slate. Sandtoft

Semi-cylindrical ridge tiles, bedded in mortar, are the conventional way of sealing the roof ridge; 'bonnet' tiles add a more traditional touch to the numerous hips of this complex roof. Sandtoft

Most artificial slates are pre-holed and the concrete version comes as an interlocking tile. There is even a clay version, which maintains its slate colour with a similar durability.

LAYING THE RIDGE AND HIP TILES

At the ridge, specialized tiles, usually half-cylindrical in shape, bridge the gap between the two roof slopes. Traditionally, they are bedded in mortar. However, in this most exposed part of the roof, mortar is particularly subject to cracking and failure. As a result, the NHBC now recommends a 'dry fix' system, common in Scotland, where the ridge tiles are attached to the roof timbers with screws or nails and fixing wires. Seals between ridge tiles and roof tiles provide weather-proofing.

Ridges can include special vent tiles for ventilating the interior of a warm roof, as well as providing unobtrusive outlets for gas flue pipes, soil vent pipes and mechanical ventilation systems. They can also include a 'finial', a decorative tile, typically mounted at the apex of a gable, though it can also run the length of the ridge. Popular with the Victorians, finials can range from simple spikes to fleurs-de-lis to elaborate mythical figures.

Hips are effectively sloping ridges, which can be capped with similar semi-cylindrical tiles. If they are mortared in position, the lower end is typically marked

with a hip iron. This is a strip of 6mm-thick galvanized steel, bent into a hook shape with a scrolled end. It's designed to prevent the last tile slipping off before the mortar has set, or if the mortar fails.

'Finials' are decorative tiles, typically mounted at the apex of a gable, though, as in this case, they can also run the length of the ridge. Sandtoft

'Bonnet' tiles add a traditional touch to this hip, while a row of valley tiles complete the look. Redland

For a more traditional look, hips can instead be capped with 'bonnet' hip tiles (tiles with a gentle curve) or 'arris' tiles (where each side lies in the same plane as the adjoining tiles). Another alternative, more common in slate roofs, is a 'close-mitred' hip, which is formed by carefully cutting the existing slates or tiles so that they meet together exactly. This requires a 'soaker', a strip of lead or fibreglass, beneath the joint to keep it waterproof.

All the above are labour-intensive and markedly more expensive than conventional ridge tiles.

LAYING VALLEY TILES

Valleys can be tiled with purpose-made, wedge-shaped tiles, which are held in position by the adjacent plain tiles. Alternatively, a 'laced' valley can be formed by progressively angling plain tiles upward as they meet, creating a slope made of single, overlapping tiles lying on their side. This is particularly effective with a so-called 'eyebrow' dormer.

A 'swept' valley is effectively the reverse, where the tiles of the opposing roof slopes are angled downward. The slopes need to be of equal pitch.

The same applies for a 'mitred' valley. Here, plain tiles or slates are cut to form the valley. Like the mitred hip, they need a soaker beneath the joint to keep it waterproof.

INSERTING THE FLASHINGS

Wherever there is a break in a roof, where it meets or abuts another wall, or is penetrated by a chimney or a soil vent pipe, metal or fibreglass (GRP) 'flashing' is needed to make the joint waterproof. With chimney stacks and abutting walls, the flashing is secured beneath the tiles or slates on one side and, on the other, chased into joints in the brickwork.

As with valleys, GRP is quicker, easier and cheaper to use, but lead will last a great deal longer; 'Code 4' is the type to use.

TOPPING OUT

Tying a leafy branch to the chimney and enjoying a short alcohol break might not seem the most logical activity for a building site, but this ceremony traditionally marks the completion of a building's structure, which you have now achieved with the finishing of the roof.

Originally from Scandinavia, topping out marked the raising of the highest beam in a timber-frame building. The leafy branch may be optional – though a good picture for your build album – but a few beers will undoubtedly go down well with your workforce.

Another major stage has been completed, and that's well worth celebrating.

How to Buy Tiles or Slates

First, use your plans to calculate the total area of your roof in square metres. The elevations will provide the degree of pitch. With these figures you can work out a number of tiles or slates you will need from manufacturers' or suppliers' brochures or online calculators.

Depending on the slate or tile, add between 5 and 8 per cent for breakages. Veer towards the higher figure for hand-made clay tiles, where you will need to blend different batches to balance out variations in colour caused by the firing.

You will also need to allow for ridge, verge and other specialist tiles or slates, depending on your design, as well as the appropriate fixings. Stockists and manufacturers' technical departments will be able to help with this and provide estimates.

Or you can opt for a supply and fix service and choose from a selection recommended – and usually supplied at a discount – by your roofing company.

CHAPTER 20

Windows, Doors and Rainwater Goods

Hugely satisfying though it is to complete the structure, it's important to appreciate that the build is barely half-way through, and the next stage is the most intense.

From now on there are times when virtually all the trades involved can be on-site, often working in close proximity and often relying on each other to complete tasks in the right sequence and at the right time. In practice, they form an ad hoc team. If they've worked together successfully before, life becomes a lot easier. If not, your role (or that of your project manager), becomes more important.

Co-ordination is key, both in supervising the workforce and ensuring that everything they need – from power sockets to sanitaryware to complete kitchens – is chosen, ordered and, most importantly of all, delivered in time to be used when required,

First, there are a few details to finish on the exterior.

WEEK ELEVEN TO TWELVE: WINDOWS, DOORS AND RAINWATER GOODS

Who Needs to Be There
- Carpenters.
- Glazier/window fitters.
- Plumber.
- Decorator.

Equipment
- Scaffolding.

Guttering needs to be fixed as high as practicable on fascias, partly to capture the maximum amount of run off from the roof, but also to allow sufficient fall to the downpipes. Redland

Materials
- Primer, undercoat, top coat/stains.
- Knotting solution.
- External doors.
- Windows.
- Mastics and sealants.
- Guttering, downpipes and fittings.

Activities

Painting/Staining the Fascias,
Soffits and Bargeboards
While the scaffolding is still up, and the guttering has not yet been fitted, it's a good opportunity to paint or stain the external woodwork of the roof.

Timber boarding will need knotting solution to prevent resin leaking from knots, followed by primer, undercoat and one or two exterior topcoats; fascias and bargeboards will need the extra protection. Alternatively you could use two coats of exterior wood stain. Microporous paints and stains will allow the wood to breathe and prevent moisture becoming trapped and eventually causing rot.

Too many drainpipes can mar a façade, but the effect can be minimized by hiding them around corners on less conspicuous sides, as here. Sandtoft

Buying Rainwater Systems

To specify the right system for your roof, you need to calculate the likely volume of run-off and rate of flow. For that you'll need the roof area, its pitch and your local rainfall intensity. Part H of the building regulations contains details of the latter, while rainwater goods' manufacturers provide information on how best to meet your requirements. Once that's established, there's plenty of choice in terms of the shape, colour and materials.

Half-round guttering is the most common. Square guttering will take a higher volume of rainwater and can be less obtrusive. Semi-elliptical 'deepflow' guttering is designed to cope with heavy volumes from particularly large or steep roofs. Ogee, where the external side is angled outward in a decorative curve, was a Victorian favourite and suits traditional designs.

The most popular construction material is uPVC. It's inexpensive, comes in permanently coloured black, white, grey and brown, is lightweight and easy to install. Its main disadvantage is that it deteriorates in sunlight, becomes brittle and will need renewing after about 15 years.

Cast iron, once ubiquitous, is still available. It can cost up to three times the price of uPVC and will need re-painting every 5 to 7 years, but can last the lifetime of your house.

Other, similarly expensive and durable alternatives include aluminium, galvanized steel – both available in a variety of colours – and copper. Being recyclable, all three have good green credentials.

Though more expensive than plastic, galvanized steel guttering offers similar lightness but with greater durability and much less thermal movement.

You might get the decorators in early to do this, or use the roofers or carpenters, depending on their skills and inclination; or you could do it yourself.

Fitting the Gutters and Downpipes

This is another relatively easy job while the scaffolding gives full access to the eaves. Essentially, guttering should be fixed as high on fascias as practicable, partly to capture the run-off from the roof efficiently, but also to allow a sufficient fall to the downpipe; a minimum drop of 6mm for every metre of guttering is typical.

Tiles or slates shouldn't overhang guttering by more than 50mm, or no more than half the width of large gutters. Underlay should overlap the inner edge of the gutter.

Straight runs are the most efficient, though your house design may make this difficult. Too many downpipes can mar a façade, but it's possible to hide them just around corners on less visible sides. Where a valley discharges, a downpipe should be fitted, if possible, to cope with the volume of water.

Fitting the Windows

Windows can be installed by the suppliers, carpenters or even the bricklayers. However, an installer registered with the Glass and Glazing Federation's FENSA scheme (short for Fenestration Self-Assessment) can certify his own work, which won't then need the approval of the building inspector. FENSA certification also includes an insurance-backed warranty.

Windows need to be fitted level and plumb. A cavity closer (see Chapter 20) ensures that the window is positioned precisely and allows it to be clicked into place. Expanding foam and sealant are then used to seal the gaps between the window and brickwork.

Which Material?

UPVC windows are the cheapest, provide good insulation (see below) and can easily be custom-made to fit virtually any opening. UPVC isn't as strong, however, as its main rival, timber, which results in obtrusively bulky frames. Though low-maintenance, the surface will discolour irreversibly if not kept reasonably clean, repair is difficult and uPVC degrades in sunlight; it's unlikely the windows will last the lifetime of the house. UPVC disposal also results in the release of toxic chemicals, though recycling is increasing.

Timber, meanwhile, is a natural, sustainable material and a reasonable insulant. Its innate strength allows

Choosing Windows

Composite windows combine the visual appeal of timber on the inside with a low-maintenance exterior in uPVC, fibreglass or, in this example, aluminium. Jeld-Wen

Like roofs and brickwork, windows can make or mar the appearance of your house. Getting them right, however, isn't made particularly easy, for three main reasons:

1. While the heights of standard windows are usefully made in multiples of 150mm – the depth of two brick courses – their widths are not. They include 488mm, 630mm, 915mm, 1200mm and 1770mm. These dimensions are far from the 'golden ratio' favoured by the Georgians (see Chapter 21), which made their windows and houses so beautifully proportioned and are the reason why so many modern windows look oddly squat.

2. Windows today are almost universally set flush with the brickwork. This is convenient with modern cavity walls, because it avoids having to make a deep external reveal both watertight and suitably insulated. Brick, however, is a textured, three-dimensional material, unlike, say, the smooth curtain walls of skyscrapers. Windows set back into brickwork reinforce this three-dimensional quality and give the sense of depth we admire in Georgian and Victorian houses. A deep reveal also helps to protect the window fabric from the elements.

3. Modern windows are universally double-glazed, with the panes now up to 24mm apart. The depth and weight of glazing demand much broader and sturdier frames than those of our predecessors. That said, windows are generally better made and in wider variety than ever before. Routinely, they come factory glazed, complete with locks, handles, integral sill, draught-proofing (for opening windows) and either a partial or full finish, ready for immediate fitting.

frames to be slimmer and more elegant. Bespoke timber windows, however, will cost a lot more than uPVC. Timber windows now come pre-treated with preservatives, but they will need regular repainting or restaining, though less frequently with more expensive hardwoods. Properly maintained, however, they can last a lifetime.

Composite windows combine the low maintenance of uPVC with the design flexibility of timber. The frames are wooden on the inside with a more durable coating on the outside, usually powder-coated aluminium, uPVC or fibreglass. New, stronger forms of fibreglass, sometimes combined with uPVC or wood fibre, promise similar design flexibility with even higher thermal efficiency.

Energy Efficiency

Windows are governed by a range of building regulations, including the means of escape in case of fire and ventilation. For example, unless your house is mechanically ventilated, habitable rooms must have opening windows with 'trickle vents' – small, closable slots, usually part of the frame, which allow fresh air to enter when the window is shut.

However, it's in relation to energy efficiency where matters become complicated. Windows lose heat through the glass, the fabric of the frame and even tiny gaps where air escapes, but they also gain warmth from the sun. All these factors are now taken into account under an A to G energy rating system, rather like electrical goods.

At the time of writing, Band C is the minimum requirement, giving a total U-value of 1.6 (see Chapter 8 for an explanation of U-values). It's achieved by a mixture of low-emissivity coatings on the inside of the glass, which retain internal warmth and repel solar heat, an insulating gas, usually argon, between the panes and warm edge 'spacer bars'; these hold the two panes together and, by using an insulation material, prevent heat leaking out the sides.

Improving on this will almost certainly mean choosing triple-glazing, which can achieve U-values down to 0.8. This is the thermal efficiency required by the Passivhaus system (see Chapter 7 for details), the best-established energy-efficient form of building.

Is It Worth It?

It depends how energy efficient you want, or can afford, to be. Energy costs will continue to rise, and so will the demands of the energy-efficiency regulations, if the government continues in its aim to make all new houses 'zero carbon' by 2016. Triple-glazing will not only cut your fuel bills, but increase the value of your property in an increasingly energy-sensitive market.

On the other hand, as well as being more expensive than double glazing, a triple-glazed window is markedly heavier and will need to be suitably sturdier. The

Glazing for all seasons: the blue-tinted glass in the roof of this orangery provides solar control, reflecting back around 60 per cent of the sun's heat, while a low-emissivity coating on the inner pane retains warmth generated inside the house during colder periods. Pilkington

Triple-glazed windows like these can achieve U-values as low as 0.86. Green Building Store

amount of daylight it allows through is also between 5 and 15 per cent less, depending on the coatings applied to the glass.

Fitting Exterior Doors

Exterior doors need to be as weather-proof and thermally efficient as windows and even sturdier, both to handle constant use and to provide security. They are also conspicuous design statements. Ideally, they should be in proportion to the windows and either match their style, colour and material, or provide a pleasing contrast, especially the front door.

Confusingly, standard dimensions are in feet and inches, typically 6ft 6in × 2ft 9in (1,981mm × 838mm) or 7ft 6in × 2ft 8in (2,032mm × 813mm).

The simplest and quickest method of installation is to use a pre-hung door, supplied within a factory-made frame with all hardware fitted, including handles, letter box, any glazing and locks.

Choosing Exterior Doors

Outside doors use the same materials as windows, though solid timber, once the traditional material, now shares the market with uPVC, fibreglass (GRP) and steel.

As well as needing regular maintenance, solid timber suffers from a tendency to bow and warp through the seasons, making adjustments necessary and draught-proofing difficult. But, above all, it is increasingly difficult to meet the demands of energy-efficiency regulations.

As a result, more and more 'engineered' wood is being used. This is wood that is either laminated or reconstituted under factory conditions to make it dimensionally stable.

This composite front door combines a rigid polyurethane core with a fibreglass skin, providing good heat and sound insulation, dimensional stability and impact resistance. Jeld-Wen

Pickled Wood

Accoya wood is a new Dutch treatment, which effectively pickles timber in a form of vinegar. It claims to make wood rot-proof, dimensionally stable and a better insulator.

Like the windows, uPVC doors need to be braced internally and can be bulky and visually unappealing; they are rarely mistaken for anything else, despite manufacturers' fondness for reproducing design from traditional timber doors.

Steel and fibreglass doors are composites. They combine sturdy frames with a foam insulation interior and a low-maintenance exterior. Fibreglass can provide a convincing woodgrain, while steel gives the greatest strength. Both can achieve U-values down to 0.55, four times the thermal efficiency of solid timber.

Patio doors, French doors and folding, sliding doors use timber, uPVC and aluminium.

Security

All exterior doors should follow the recommendations of the Association of Chief Police Officers' Secured by Design scheme, which are now part of the NHBC's warranty requirements. These include fitting doors with a solid core at least 44mm thick, partly for strength but also to incorporate a mortice deadlock. A minimum five-lever mortice deadlock made to British Standard 3621:1980 is recommended (look for a BSI kite mark). Only the key hole and covering plates should be visible from outside.

Other measures include mortice rack bolts at top and bottom of the door, hinge bolts and protective metal strips along the sides of the frame. Even the strongest door is only as strong at the frame that supports it.

For maximum security, choose a door set certified to British Standard PAS 24-1 'Doors of enhanced security'. The door, frame, locks and fittings will have been attack tested; the Secured by Design website (*see* Contacts) has details of suppliers.

Once in place, the windows and doors will still need a degree of protection from damage while the scaffolding is removed and heavy work, such as floor laying and plastering, is carried out inside.

Folding sliding doors, together with a level but well-drained threshold, allow the garden to become a temporary extension to the home.
Apropos

CHAPTER 21

First Fix

You can now concentrate on the interior, a process that occurs in two main stages:

- 'First fix' covers the underlying support structure. It includes the studwork, flooring, screeding, sound-proofing, door linings, staircases, plastering (and/or dry-lining), pipework and wiring – essentially, everything that will be hidden from view, if only under carpeting or coats of paint or stain.
- 'Second fix' follows with the fitting out, final finishes and the connection and commissioning of all the services.

The order in which first-fix activities are carried out will vary according to your design details, convenience and, to a degree, the availability of the various trades.

Meanwhile the bricklayers can move on to completing any brickwork for the fireplace and/or building any masonry boundary walls or retaining walls needed for landscaping.

WEEK TEN TO TWELVE: FIRST-FIX CARPENTRY

Who Needs to Be There
- Carpenter.
- Bricklayer (for fireplace/landscaping/detached garage, as required).
- Plumber.

Equipment
- Concrete mixer.

Materials
- Tongued and grooved (t&g) moisture-resistant chipboard panels/floor boarding.

- Studwork timber (100mm × 50mm softwood).
- Timber door linings.
- Windowboard.
- Nails, screws.
- Underfloor central heating pipework (if required).
- Insulation.
- Staircase.
- Garage door and frame.
- Bricks, sand, mortar (for fireplaces, garden walls, landscaping).

Activities

Laying Timber Floors
Typically, the upper floors in a brick and block house are timber, and usually consist of either plywood or, more commonly, moisture-resistant chipboard panels. These come in 2,400mm × 600mm sheets and are either 18mm deep, for joists 450mm apart, or 22mm thick for 600mm spans.

You may have chosen to lay them earlier, protecting them with plywood or heavy plastic sheeting. If not, it can be done now to provide a base for the studwork walls upstairs

Tongued and grooved panels are easiest to lay. The long edges lie across the joists, with the cut ends resting mid-joist. PVA wood adhesive is applied to the joints before they are pushed together and the panels screwed or nailed in place. Normally noggins are only required at the edges of a room where the boards are cut to fit and an expansion gap is left. The skirting will hide this later.

The same can be done for a suspended timber ground floor. However, ensure that the plumber and electrician install any underfloor wiring or pipework while there is still easy access from above.

Planning for Maintenance

Commercial developers tend to glue and screw down chipboard floor panels without paying much attention to the services beneath. This is rather like selling cars with the bonnets welded shut. If there is a problem later, both the floor covering will need to be removed and the flooring ripped up to find the source of the trouble. You can avoid this by building in removable service panels above joints in under-floor pipework or wiring junctions. They are likely to require noggins between the joists. If edged with raised metal or plastic, the panels can be infilled with the eventual floor covering.

If you are laying a 'floating' floor on a solid sub-base, perhaps covering rigid foam insulation and a damp-proof membrane, this can also be done now.

If you have a solid floor and plan to lay floorboards, battens for attaching them can be fitted over a damp-proof membrane. If possible, though, leave the laying until the house has dried out and been heated for a while, so that the boards can acclimatize to the interior atmosphere. Otherwise, they can absorb moisture, causing them warp and twist.

Whatever the flooring, once in place, it will still need to be protected from damage.

Erecting the Studwork

Despite the solidity and superior sound-proofing of blockwork internal walls, timber studwork is often used for upper storeys. Typically, it consists of a 100mm × 50mm softwood frame, secured to the ceiling joists and floor, and then lined on both sides with plasterboard. The acoustics, however, are minimal. They can be boosted by using double layers of plasterboard, particularly of dense acoustic plasterboard, and by filling the hollow studwork with conventional insulation.

Once the floors are down, studwork can also be erected for airing cupboards, built-in wardrobes, bath stands and any fitted furniture.

Fitting the Door Liners

Timber door linings can be bought in standard sizes to fit standard doors, or be made up on-site. As with exterior doors, doors are available pre-hung in a frame, though it's advisable to leave fitting them until second fix to avoid damaging them.

Fitting the Window Boards

Window boards provide the finish for internal window sills. They have a stepped edge along the back, designed to fit into the window frame, while the front edge is rounded.

Cut on-site from lengths up to 3m, they should be fixed into the blockwork with frame cramps, which attach to the underside of the board, leaving the top smooth. Where the ends of the board protrude from the wall, they can be rounded for a more attractive finish.

Installing the Staircase

The simplest and cheapest form of staircase is a single, straight flight, generally of thirteen treads. At the bottom it rests on the floor. At the top it's fixed to a trimmer – one edge of a rectangle of timber that provides the opening for the staircase.

One side of the staircase – known as the inner 'string' – is attached to the adjacent wall. A 'newel post' at the start and the end of a staircase provides the support for the string and a handrail.

Staircases are ordered or custom-made on the basis of the house plans; the key measurements are the finished floor to finished floor heights. Typically, stairs arrive only partially assembled. Since the actual dimensions of the build are unlikely to reflect the plans precisely, the stairs are usually assembled 'dry', i.e. without gluing, to check the fit and make necessary adjustments.

The balustrading and finishing components are usually left until the second fix.

For reasons of economy and weight reduction, timber studwork walls are often used for upper stories.

Choosing a Staircase

Timber remains the most popular material, ranging from simple MDF to the most enduring hardwoods, with prices to match. If you plan to carpet the stairs, however, it may be more cost-effective to opt for engineered wood or softwood and concentrate your attention and cash on the balustrading. Even 'off-the-shelf' examples offer this most conspicuous part of the staircase a huge variety of styles, finishes and materials, including stainless steel and toughened glass.

Other Points to Consider

DESIGN

A straight flight may be simple, but it's not the most space efficient. Adding a quarter- or half-landing, to create an extra flight, which turns back over the stairway, maximizes the use of the stairwell space. It also allows more flexibility in the first-floor layout. Alternatively, 'winders' – tapered treads – can be used at the turns.

One method of reducing the impact of a single flight is to use 'cut' strings, where the sides of the staircase are shaped to fit the steps. Another is to make the treads 'open', where the risers are removed and the stairs become see-through. Even more effective, though considerably more expensive, is to build the entire staircase out of toughened, laminated glass.

A spiral staircase can save between a third and a quarter of the space of single flight stairs and takes up relatively little space on the ground floor, but the stairwell needs to be square or circular to accommodate it. To use one as a main staircase, a minimum diameter of 1,830mm is required, simply to get beds and all but the bulkiest furniture upstairs.

Where a narrow staircase is unavoidable, however, a demountable balustrade can make furniture moving a lot easier.

Sound-proofing can be an issue when timber stairs dry out and begin to creak. If your house has masonry floors, consider a concrete staircase. It can be bought precast, though you will have to crane it into position before the roof is built; or it can constructed *in situ*, using specially built formwork. It can even be clad with timber to disguise its underlying structure.

Adding one or more turns to a flight of stairs maximizes the use of the stairwell space and allows more flexibility in the first floor layout. Richard Burbidge

BUILDING REGULATIONS

These are concerned with safety issues, ensuring that stairs aren't too steep, the treads too shallow or too high, and that the surroundings, including the space above a staircase, don't obstruct users.

The main points are:

- No staircase should be steeper than 42 degrees.
- No tread should be shorter than 220mm.
- No 'riser' – the vertical front of a step – should be higher than 220mm.
- There should be at least 2m of headroom above any stair or landing.
- The space at top and bottom of stairs should be clear of any obstruction for the width of the stair and for the same distance beyond the stair.

LEFT: The ultimate in staircase rigidity: a precast concrete staircase. Hanson

RIGHT: A spiral staircase takes up relatively little space on the ground floor, but needs a square or circular stairwell. Bisca

Erecting Garage Door Frame and Doors
Once the studwork is up and floors are down, enabling electricians and plumbers to get to work, the carpenters can move on to this job.

Miscellaneous Carpentry
This can include fitting timber bases for heavy objects, such as attic water tanks and hot-water cylinders, installing battens between ceiling joists to ease the application of plasterboard, installing a loft hatch and boxing in pipework that can't otherwise be hidden in a cupboard or within a partition wall.

WEEK ELEVEN TO TWELVE: FIRST-FIX PLUMBING

Thanks to plastic pipework and 'push fit' joints, domestic plumbing is a lot easier than it used to be, and well within the ability of an experienced DIYer. Work, however, on central heating boilers, unvented hot-water cylinders and gas pipework can only be carried out by suitably qualified engineers.

Who Needs to Be There
- Plumber/gas safety registered engineer.
- Specialist trades for whole-house ventilation and central vacuuming systems.
- Carpenter.

Equipment
- Provided by trades.

Materials
- Copper and polybutylene 'push-fit' pipe, 15mm, 22mm and 28mm diameter, as required.
- Waste-water pipe, 32mm, 40mm and 50mm diameter, as required.
- Related fittings, including connectors, isolating valves, stopcock, pipe clips, etc.
- Foam insulation sheathing.
- Copper indirect cylinder or steel unvented cylinder plus expansion vessel.
- Plastic water tanks.
- Ducting, ventilation unit and related components for mechanical whole-house ventilation system.
- Underfloor heating pipework and manifold (if needed).

Garages

Building a garage at the same time as your house enables you to reclaim the VAT on the costs of construction and materials, including prefabricated models (see Chapter 24 for full VAT details).

A detached garage is relatively free of building regulations. To allow for a variety of future uses, however, it would be wise to build in a solid floor with a damp-proof membrane, insulation and a mains water and electricity supply.

Integral garages, meanwhile, are covered by the regulations governing the house. They are chiefly concerned with preventing the spread of fire and insulating the garage space thermally from the rest of the house. The main points are:

- Any shared wall, ceiling or door must offer at least 30min of fire-resistance. A masonry wall is sufficient, but the ceiling will need a double thickness of plasterboard.
- Entrances into the house must be self-closing fire doors, classed FD30 or FD60.
- The garage floor must be at least 100mm lower than the ground floor of the house, or slope away from any shared door.
- An integral garage is required to meet the thermal-efficiency requirements of the house. Since the garage door will not be insulated, this will mean insulating the ceiling and internal walls, as well as the floor.

Plastic 'push fit' plumbing is cheaper and easier to work with than traditional copper, which is usually reserved for areas where pipework will be on show.

Activities

Laying Pipework

One of the first tasks is to fit an internal stopcock to the mains water supply pipe, enabling you to shut off the entire system in case of emergency. It should be sited for easy access, typically in the kitchen, utility room or integral garage.

The pipework from this point can be traditional copper or plastic (usually polybutylene) or a mixture of the two. Copper makes neat, compact connections, either soldered or using compression fittings, which are closed with a wrench. The metal is pliable yet strong, highly durable and aesthetically pleasing. Water freezing inside a copper pipe, however, can split it, while hot pipework can burn you.

Plastic is more flexible, enabling it to be run like electrical wiring in continuous lengths of up to 100m. It's a better insulator, making burst pipes much less likely, and it can be cut easily and connected with simple 'push fit' joints, saving a lot of time. Most significantly, it's cheaper. As a result, it's used more and more for hidden pipework with copper reserved for pipework on show and for the first metre run from boilers.

First-fix pipework largely involves this concealed aspect. It includes pipe runs from where the boiler will be sited to the positions of the hot-water cylinder, hot and cold taps, showers, radiators and water tanks, if any. Typically, each run terminates in a copper 'upstand', an upright length of pipe rising out of the floor and topped with an isolating valve. This allows you to change or repair the attached appliance without having to drain the entire system.

If I-beam floor joists are used (*see* Chapter 17 for details), running pipework of any kind is relatively easy. Engineered wood can be drilled safely more or less where needed; metal web I-beams are largely open space already.

Solid timber joists will need to be drilled or their tops notched to receive pipework. Since this weakens their structure, the building regulations impose limits on the positions and amount of timber that can be removed.

Pipework running through concrete screed should be laid in galvanized steel ducting, plastic piping or custom-made ducting using formwork made up on-site. Any connections should have access panels. This not only makes repairs easy, but allows the system to be renewed with minimum disruption. The same goes for pipework inside walls. Ducting can be chased into blockwork and covered with paintable screw-in panels; or, if it can be done unobtrusively, pipes can be surface mounted and boxed in.

Drainage pipework also needs to be run from WCs, hand-basins, baths, showers, the kitchen and utility room. Connections are made to the soil and vent pipe, or 'stack'. This tall, 110mm-diameter pipe provides access to the external drains through the ground floor and ventilates the system at roof level.

Toilets are connected through a 110mm soil pipe. Everything else uses 32mm, 40mm or 50mm plastic pipework. The joints use push-fit, compression fittings or solvent-weld, a form of glue that fuses the plastic together. All connections to the stack need to be protected by a water trap, a U-bend, which puts a watery barrier between you and the distinctive odour of the drains.

The standard fall for the pipework is between 20mm and 40mm per metre run, but there are also limits to the length of the connecting pipework. For WCs, it's around 6m, 3m for baths and showers and 2m for hand-basins; beyond that, siphonage can occur. This is when the pressure of retreating water becomes so great it sucks the water out of the water trap.

If all the discharge outlets can't fit within these limits, there are options. You can add another stack, discharge to a separate drain outside or fit an internal stack with an air admittance valve. This uses a one-way valve, which only opens when pressure builds up in the pipe. It can be sited anywhere above the highest water-level in the house.

The gas supply will normally run from the meter to the central heating boiler and/or any gas fires and any gas-fired tumble dryer. For safety reasons only copper pipework can be used.

All pipework should be secured with appropriate pipe clips to prevent it moving, and to reduce noise when water surges through it. Pipework in a cold attic should be always be carefully insulated. Insulating all pipework, if possible, will minimize heat loss.

Any openings made in external walls and into cold attics to accommodate pipework must be carefully sealed to maintain the required air-tightness of the house.

Siting the Hot-Water Cylinder

Traditionally, this is in the airing cupboard. With today's factory-insulated cylinders, however, most of the warmth will come from the associated pipework, assuming it's left uninsulated inside the cupboard. If you

Distributing Heat

Radiators made from pressed steel are the most common, and generally cheapest, form of heat distribution. They come in standard sizes, with double and finned versions to increase their output. More elegant, and more expensive, versions are available in stainless steel, aluminium and traditional cast iron.

All radiators, however, take up room on the walls, restricting the layout of furniture – a good reason why the size and position of radiators should be worked out with the plumber before pipework is laid.

They are also not the most efficient of heat emitters. Despite their name, they work chiefly by convection, warming air, which rises to the ceiling before circulating through the room, cooling as it goes. This not only leaves cold spots, but helps to distribute dust. There are several alternatives.

Underfloor Central Heating (UFH)

While radiators concentrate heat, rather like traditional fires, underfloor heating systems distribute it over the entire floor area, effectively turning it into a giant radiator. As a result, satisfactory warmth can be produced with relatively low temperatures – around 50°C compared to the 60°C plus of radiator systems. Even better, the heat is concentrated between floor and head height, just where human beings need it.

UFH works by circulating warm water through a continuous loop of plastic piping embedded in the floor. The hub of the system is the manifold, where up to a dozen separate loops can be connected, creating individually controlled temperature zones in different parts of the house.

Typically, UFH is fitted in solid ground floors, where the pipework is laid above the rigid foam insulation. It is then covered with a minimum 65mm-deep sand and cement

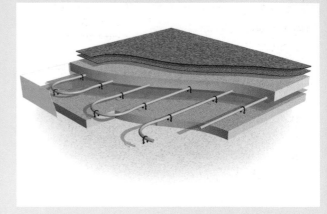

Ground floor underfloor heating typically consists of loops of plastic pipework laid over rigid foam insulation and then covered with a sand and cement screed.

screed. This warms up slowly but acts as a thermal store, needing little extra heat to maintain its temperature.

UFH also works with floating floors and suspended timber floors; in the latter, the pipework rests on aluminium plates which direct the heat upwards.

The system is most effective on solid floor coverings, such as tiles, slates or flagstones. But laminated wood flooring under 22m thick is also suitable, as well as carpet and underlay with a total 'tog' value below 2.5; carpet manufacturers should be able to provide this information.

UFH is like central heating itself; once experienced, few wish to go without it. It allows you to place furniture where you wish, reduces dust and is ideal for homes with high, vaulted ceilings, which would otherwise swallow up the heat of radiators.

More importantly, its low running temperatures suit modern, energy-efficient condensing boilers and also newer, sustainable forms of heat production, particularly heat pumps (*see* Chapter 22 for details).

UFH, however, has two main drawbacks. Its price is high compared to conventional systems – one reason why many self-builders opt for UFH downstairs and radiators upstairs. It also responds slowly. But if you are predominantly home-based, perhaps as a home worker, a young family or a retiree, this is much less of a problem.

Skirting Radiators

These take the place of conventional timber skirtings and provide a more even heat distribution than radiators.

Stoves

Wood-burning and multi-fuel stoves are increasingly popular as supplementary forms of heating – for convenience, aesthetic appeal, the enhanced atmosphere they create and their use of sustainable fuel, but mainly for the sheer

Traditional cast iron and modern 'designer' stainless steel radiators are visually appealing, though expensive, variations on the standard pressed steel variety. Aestus

In suspended floors the pipework of underfloor heating systems is usually run beneath aluminium plates, which disperse the heat. Robbens Systems

enjoyment of a living fire. In super-insulated houses, they are often the only conventional form of heating and only needed on the coldest days. Before buying one, however, check that it is exempt from Smokeless Zone restrictions.

The fact that the building regulations continue to demand higher and higher levels of insulation and air-tightness will mean that less and less space heating will be needed. That doesn't necessarily mean that your choice of heating system will be less important, but it's advisable to take into account other factors, such as the likely availability and cost of your chosen fuel in future and the ability of a system to cool as well as warm the home. This will be discussed in more detail in Chapter 22. Also, *see below.*

Woodburning and multi-fuel stoves are increasingly popular as both supplementary forms of heating and design features. Euroheat

Using a Thermal Store

Natural gas is still the most popular home heating fuel but, as prices continue to rise, so will the demand for cheaper alternatives, such as solar heating, heat pumps and biomass boilers (see Chapter 22 for details). Some of these energy sources, however, only become cheaper at certain times of the year, or when alternative fuel prices drop.

A good way of future-proofing your home is to install a heat store that can be fed easily from a variety of sources. This is what a 'thermal store' does.

A thermal store, like this Xcel Heat Bank from Thermal Integration, can take heat from a variety of sources, including a conventional boiler, woodburning stove and solar heating panels, while providing mains pressure to all hot and cold outlets.

It's a form of hot-water cylinder that allows mains pressure throughout the house but works in the opposite way to an unvented system. There, the water in the cylinder remains under pressure while it's heated by means of a heat exchanger containing hot water from the boiler. In a thermal store, it's the heat exchanger that contains the pressurized water from the mains, while the water in the cylinder is heated directly by the boiler. As the mains supply passes through, it's warmed by the surrounding hot water.

Since the cylinder isn't under pressure, it can be lightweight copper, just as in a vented system, and it doesn't have to be fitted by an engineer qualified in unvented systems.

Even better, it can be fitted with extra heat exchangers, taking water heated by other sources, such as a solar heating panel or the back boiler of a wood-burning stove that you might only use infrequently.

The main drawback of the thermal store is the size of the cylinder, which needs to be large to function efficiently, but, as with an unvented cylinder, storage tanks aren't needed in the attic.

How Plumbing Systems Work

Plumbing systems have three functions: to supply clean, fresh water for drinking and cooking; hot water for heating and washing; and drainage for disposing of 'grey water' from cooking and washing and 'blackwater' from toilets.

There are two basic types of system: low pressure or 'open vented' and pressurized or 'unvented'.

Open Vented System

This is the traditional plumbing arrangement. Water enters via a main supply pipe, which branches in two inside the house. One supply goes to the cold-water tap over the kitchen sink and, perhaps, an outside tap. The other, thanks to mains pressure, rises to the attic, where it fills a large cold-water storage tank and a smaller expansion tank sited next to it.

The large tank feeds all the other cold-water outlets and the hot-water cylinder, which supplies the home's hot taps.

The expansion tank feeds the central heating boiler and keeps the radiators topped up. It also provides an outlet for expanding water if the system overheats – in effect, an 'open vent', hence the term for the system. (The tank also has an overflow pipe to the outside in case its capacity is exceeded.)

Water heated by the boiler is pumped to the hot-water cylinder, where it passes through a heat exchanger – a spiral of metal pipework, which warms the water inside the cylinder – then returns to the boiler. The heated water in the cylinder then feeds the hot taps.

Meanwhile, electrically operated diverter valves enable a second supply of heated water to be pumped through the central heating radiators, warming the house. Each radiator has 'return' pipework, which carries the cooling water back to the boiler to be reheated.

Advantages Most of the system is low pressure, which reduces its noise and the chances of serious leaks or foul water being siphoned back into the mains supply. If the mains fail, the system will continue functioning until the attic tanks are emptied.

Disadvantages Water pressure depends on the 'head', the distance between the attic tank and an outlet. As a result, a first-floor shower is only likely to have a feeble flow and need an electrically powered shower pump to boost its performance.

If you have a cold attic, you will need to insulate the cold-water tanks and all the associated pipework to avoid burst pipes in winter. If your attic is habitable, space must be made for the water tanks and pipework.

Unvented System

The disadvantages of the traditional system can all be avoided by this increasingly popular alternative. Here, everything is under mains pressure. This gives you high pressure in showers throughout the house and drinking water from every cold tap. Even better, cold-water tanks are no longer required, enabling full use of a habitable attic.

HOW IS THIS ACHIEVED?
In two ways:

- One is to fit a 'combination' boiler (*see later* for full details), which only heats water on demand, direct from the mains. Consequently, no storage is required and mains pressure ensures water is constantly available.
- The second method is to fit an unvented hot-water cylinder. Instead of being topped up from an attic tank, it is fed directly from the mains. To withstand the increased pressure, it is made of stainless steel, which makes it more expensive than the lighter copper cylinders used in vented systems. In place of the expansion tank is a metal expansion vessel, which simply contains overheated water. If its limits are approached, a safety valve known as a 'tundish' releases water to the outside. Some systems include the boiler and the hot cylinder within one unit, simplifying the installation process.

WHAT ARE THE DISADVANTAGES?
- Your local mains need to have sufficient operating pressure, measured in 'bars'. One bar is the force exerted by a 10m 'head' of water. The UK average is about three bars. If the local pressure is over four bar, you may need to fit reducing valves to reduce wear and tear on the system.
- Unvented systems can only be installed by a suitably certified plumber or heating engineer.
- If the mains supply fails, you are without water.

See Chapter 16 for details of drainage systems.

Pipework for underfloor heating is usually secured by clipping to a grid or pressing into plastic formwork, as here. Worcester Bosch Group

are using a combination boiler, there is, of course, no hot-water cylinder.

Installing Underfloor Heating Pipework

The pipework is pinned or clipped in position over rigid foam insulation, using a grid or plastic formwork, according to the manufacturer's instructions. Perimeter insulation is also needed to the depth of the covering screed and, on large areas, a perimeter gap to allow for the expansion of the covering screed.

Once the pipework is connected to the manifold, a connection is made to the water supply and the system pressure tested. The floor is then ready for screeding or the laying of a floating floor.

Installing Ducting for Whole-House Ventilation

Mechanical whole-house ventilation requires a double set of flexible ducting: one rising from wet areas to a fan unit in the attic; the second from the unit to the habitable rooms. Shorter ducts expel the air and draw in a fresh supply, typically via the eaves. (*See* Chapter 7 for a full explanation.)

The ducting accesses rooms through holes, which are cut in the ceiling and covered by vents at second-fix stage. However, installing the ducting itself is a first-fix task.

Passive stack ventilation is a non-mechanical alternative, where ducts rise vertically from wet areas to terminals in the roof. Typically, rigid ducting is used inside, within habitable parts of the house, easing the

natural tendency of warm air to rise. Flexible ducting is used only when necessary in the attic space. Like mechanical whole-house ventilation, the ducts are accessed through ceiling openings.

It's advisable that both types of systems are fitted by specialist installers.

Installing Ducting for Central Vacuuming

Here, typically, two ducts, one upstairs and the other down, connect to a powerful vacuum cleaner motor in a utility room or a garage. Once a pipe is attached to an outlet, the motor starts automatically and the dust is collected at a distance; it can even be deposited straight into a dustbin.

It may sound like pure luxury, but conventional vacuum cleaners can re-circulate as much dust as they extract. It also removes the need for the elderly or infirm to manhandle a portable model.

Again, the ducting needs to be installed at first fix, preferably by the specialist supplier.

Boxing-In

The carpenter will box in any exposed pipework or ducting, ready for the plasterers to start work.

WEEK TWELVE TO THIRTEEN: FIRST-FIX ELECTRICS

Unlike much of plumbing, the bulk of electrical work is restricted to qualified persons under Part P of the building regulations, so your electrician will install the electrical system specified in your plans.

Now that the internal layout is visible, however, it's important that you confirm with the electrician the positions of switches, power points, light fittings, TV and telephone points, etc. What seems sensible on a plan may be totally impractical in actuality, or you may simply have changed your mind.

Points to watch for include:

- **Power points** – review the numbers you believe you need. Is one bedroom now likely to become a home office, or a TV/games room? You need to at least double the three or four double sockets typically used in a bedroom. Are the positions of the power points right? Furniture layouts will change over time. Concentrating sockets on one or two walls will eventually result in a highly visible tangle of cables.
- **Two-way/three-way switches** – are there any flights of stairs, long hallways or large rooms with two entrances that are not covered by sufficient switches?
- **Doors** – they normally open into a room but, in some rooms, opening the opposite way may be more convenient. The position of the light switches will need to reflect this.
- **5-amp circuits** – using small round-pin sockets, these allow portable sidelights to be operated, and dimmed, from a single switch, a much more flexible arrangement than installing fixed wall lights.
- **Eyesight** – at the age of sixty you need three times as much light to do basic tasks as you did at twenty. If you're retiring and downsizing, check you're not under-estimating the light levels you've specified.
- **Extra lights** – have you allowed for worktop illumination in the kitchen? Or a light in the attic, the airing cupboard or other storage area?
- **LED lighting** – LEDs (light emitting diodes) offer a cool, ultra-low energy, environmentally friendly and extremely long-lived form of lighting. Currently, they are expensive and not widely available, but that is changing, so do check them out before making lighting decisions.
- **Extra services** – ethernet cabling, wiring for speakers, internal and external security systems, supplies for electrically powered blinds and skylights and for a garden office or workshop may, or may not,

have been considered at design stage. If not, this is a convenient opportunity to include them.
- **Building regulations** – at the time of writing, between 70 and 100 per cent of fixed light-fittings must be energy efficient. Power sockets should be no lower than 450mm off the floor and light switches no higher than 1,200mm (*see Chapter 11 for details*).

Who Needs to Be There
- Electrician.

Equipment
- Trades supplied.

How Electrical Systems Work

The mains electrical cable terminates in a service head then passes through a meter. Both are installed by the service provider in the meter box, which is sited on an outside wall.

Two meter leads and an earth connection then pass through the wall inside a conduit and are connected to a consumer unit. This distributes the supply to the various circuits within the house.

Each circuit is protected by a miniature circuit breaker (MCB), a small switch that shuts off the supply if the current is earthed or overloaded. Capacity typically varies between 10 and 12 circuits (making it a '12-way' unit), but it's sensible to specify a unit with spare circuits for future needs.

Some circuits can also be protected by residual circuit devices (RCDs), which instantly cut the supply when there's an imbalance between positive and negative currents. This is usually caused by current flowing to earth, e.g. when someone accidentally severs a cable.

Typically, each floor has a power circuit, or 'ring main', which links the various power points and returns to the consumer unit. The kitchen, where the power drain is usually highest, has its own power circuit.

Appliances that draw a large amount of power, such as electric cookers, immersion heaters and electric showers, have individual 'radial' circuits, which run directly from the appliance to a dedicated MCB in the consumer unit.

Similarly, the ground and upper floors have their own lighting circuits.

Materials

- Cables and wire, 5amp to 30amp, two core and earth, three core and earth, co-axial cable, electric bell wire, telephone wire, speaker cabling, etc.
- Green and yellow earth sleeving.
- Cable clips.
- Steel or PVC back boxes.
- Galvanized steel or PVC conduit.
- Consumer unit (10–12-way)

Activities

Installing the Cabling and Back Boxes

Power cables are normally run vertically to the back boxes from the floor, while lighting cables are dropped to the switches from the ceiling. With masonry walls, both should be covered with a protective plastic channel, which will then be covered by plaster or plasterboard. Some electricians may choose to chase out a groove in the blockwork, particularly if conduit is used; this is relatively easy with aircrete, but hard work with standard concrete blockwork.

As with plumbing pipework, running cabling through conduit throughout the house, especially through solid floors, makes repair and replacement infinitely easier and less disruptive.

Space for back boxes is typically chiselled out so that, when the cover plate is fitted, it lies flush to the wall.

Power supplies for appliances that are not accessed easily, such as central heating controls, washing machines, dishwashers and waste disposal units, will need individual 'fused spurs'. These are radial circuits taken off a power point or joint box and run via a connection unit, which contains a fuse and often a switch and an indicator light to show the power is on.

Cabling for smoke detectors and carbon monoxide alarms are typically included in lighting circuits.

It's a good idea to photograph the cable runs. A record of their final positions will be invaluable when you come to make repairs or alterations.

Earth Bonding

As a safety measure, exposed metalwork in the house needs to be earthed in case it inadvertently comes in contact with an electric current. The process is known as 'bonding'. A small strip of metal called an 'earth clamp' is attached to the metal then linked by an earth wire – identified by its green and yellow plastic sleeving – to the nearest earth connection.

All domestic electrical fittings contain an earth connection, which returns to the main consumer unit and then to the mains gas and water supply pipes. In bathrooms and shower rooms, all metal pipework must be 'cross bonded', i.e. linked together by earth wires before being attached to an earth connection.

Installing Openings and Ducting for Ventilation

If you don't specify a whole-house ventilation system, individual extractor fans, venting to the outside, will be needed for kitchens, utility rooms, bathrooms and toilets.

The building regulations require minimum rates of power for each location, measured in litres extracted per second (ltr/sec). They are:

- Kitchen (cooker hood) and utility rooms: 30ltr/sec.
- Bathrooms: 15ltr/sec.
- Toilets: 6ltr/sec.

The electrician will usually make the openings for these in an outside wall and install the ducting, which may run between ceiling joists or be boxed in if that isn't possible.

As with the plumbing, any opening made in the external walls or into a cold attic must be carefully sealed.

Boxing-In

As for plumbing, any necessary boxing in is done by the carpenter.

CHAPTER 22

Plastering, Dry-Lining and Screeding

This is transformation time. From a rather bedraggled skeleton of a building, with many of its vital organs still on display, your project will turn into a recognizable house, and usually with astonishing speed.

The magic is down to the plasterers and dry-liners, who dry-line or 'tack out' the ceilings and any timber studwork walls with plasterboard – thin sheets of gypsum plaster sandwiched between paper lining.

Plasterboard is also used to dry-line the blockwork of the inner leaf, though the traditional method of finishing new masonry walls is to 'hard plaster' them with an undercoat of either sand, cement and lime or a mixture of sand and gypsum, known as 'browning'. A top, or finish, coat of gypsum is then added.

Plasterboarded ceilings and walls can also be 'skim plastered' with a similar top coat.

Meanwhile, any floating floors are laid and solid floors given a final screed, ready to receive the floor covering.

Hugely encouraging as it is to see the walls, ceilings and floors finished, the major downside to this stage is that the plaster and concrete now need to dry out before further progress can be made. This is why commercial house-builders usually prefer to dry-line all the internal walls, virtually eliminating drying out time. But, for those who want to enjoy the full benefits of a masonry home, careful planning can exploit this enforced delay.

If the drains have not yet been installed, this is a good time to do it (see Chapter 16 for details). Open service trenches can also be back-filled. If a mechanical digger is used, it can then be employed to complete the driveway or carry out any necessary landscaping.

WEEK FOURTEEN TO SIXTEEN: CEILINGS, WALLS AND FLOORS

Who Needs to Be There
- Plasterer/dry-liner.
- Carpenter.

Equipment.
- Mixer.
- Power float.

Materials
- Plasterboard sheets, 2,400mm × 1,200mm, either 9.5mm or 12.5mm thick, square-edged or tapered.
- Sand, cement, lime/gypsum 'browning'.
- Scrim or jointing tape, filler.
- Fixings.
- Dry-line adhesive.
- Galvanized steel or uPVC beading.
- For floating floors: moisture resistant chipboard flooring, wood glue.
- Liquid screed.
- Rigid insulation.

Planning Ahead
Contact utility companies to confirm dates for gas, electric, water and telecom services to be activated.

Activities
Tacking Out Ceilings and Timber-Studwork Walls
Tacking out is typically done by screwing or nailing sheets of plasterboard to timber supports. These are either the joists of the floor above or the studwork of timber-frame walls. For joists or uprights spaced at

'Tacking out' involves nailing or screwing sheets of plasterboard to ceiling joists or, as here, timber studwork; these square-edged boards will later be skim plastered for a smooth, glossy finish.

600mm, 12.5mm thickness plasterboard is usual; 9.5mm can be used for 400mm spacings.

Plasterboard is either square- or tapered-edged. If you plan to decorate the surface directly, specify tapered edge. The joints, along with recessed nail or screw heads, are taped over then filled with jointing compound. Before decoration, the surface is sanded to an overall matt finish.

For a smooth, glossy finish, use square-edged board. Here, the joints are covered with a fine, woven mesh know as 'scrim' before the whole surface is skim plastered to a minimum depth of 3mm.

Jointing tape is also applied to where the walls and ceilings meet to help bind all the surfaces together.

Tapered-edge boarding is quicker and less likely to produce cracks as the house dries out, but skim-plastered, straight-edged boarding produces a finer, more attractive finish.

Laying a Floating Floor

If you are laying a floating floor over rigid insulation, it's advisable to do so before the ceiling is plasterboarded, to protect the insulation and provide the plasterers with a working surface.

If your floating floor is going onto a concrete screed, however, it's wiser to leave it until the ceilings and walls are plastered. This will save the floor surface from damage and also allow the concrete longer to dry out.

All floating floors should be laid over a damp-proof membrane as a precaution.

Plasterboarding Steels

Any exposed steel beams should be covered with fire-resistant plasterboard. Though steel won't burn, it can buckle and warp, with unpredictable consequences for whatever it supports.

Hard Plastering or Dry-Lining Blockwork Walls

Commercial house-builders typically dry-line blockwork walls. They use a technique known as 'dot and dab', where a special adhesive is used to fix the plasterboard sheets to the blockwork. Its main advantage is speed – not only is the wall finished quickly, it can

Specialized Wallboards

Fire-resistant plasterboard Identified by its pale-pink colour, it's used in areas where fires could be particularly dangerous, such as the walls and ceilings of integral garages, ceilings below attic accommodation and for fire-proofing steel beams.

Vapour-resistant plasterboard It has a foil backing, which acts as a vapour barrier. For ceilings below cold attics it will prevent warm, moist air reaching the unheated space above and condensing out.

Moisture-resistant plasterboard Pale-green in colour, this is useful for bathrooms, shower rooms and kitchens.

Insulated plasterboard Backed with various thicknesses of foam insulation, it can provide a final layer of insulation for the interior of a warm roof or the internal surface of an outside wall.

Cement-based board If it becomes saturated, standard plasterboard will break down, and eventually rot. Cement-based wallboards are reinforced with fibreglass and are unaffected by water, making them ideal for tiled walls, floors and work surfaces.

Gypsum fibreboard is a stronger alternative to standard plasterboard; reinforced with cellulose fibres it can support weights up to 50kg. Fermacell

Gypsum fibreboard This is reinforced with cellulose fibres, enabling it to carry weights up to 50kg – well in excess of unsupported plasterboard. It also has superior sound, moisture and impact resistance.

---

be decorated within the hour. Serious cracking is also minimized as the wall dries out.

The main disadvantage is that it lacks the solidity found in a hard-plastered masonry wall. Dot and dabbed plasterboard should have a continuous line of adhesive around its edges, but voids still remain on the underside. These can also create problems with air leakage, as well as being a potential location for mould.

Hard plastering overcomes these problems by forming a continuous bond with the blockwork. A basecoat around 10mm deep is applied by trowel, followed by a 2–3mm finish coat. Skilled plasterers can do this work at dazzling speed – well worth a short break in your schedule to watch. Hand application means that every nook and cranny of a wall can be covered, ensuring good air-tightness.

The main disadvantage is lack of speed. Each coat needs to dry out before the next is applied, while the large volume of water used soaks into the wall, which can take several weeks to dry out, especially in cold, damp weather. This, in turn, delays decoration. In addition, as the blockwork dries, it shrinks, causing fine

cracking in the plaster, which will need filling; lightweight aircrete blocks are particularly prone to this.

If all this seems a lot of trouble, the payback is that nothing beats hard plaster for solidity, durability, ease of repair and a dazzling glassy smoothness. It also has the ability to absorb and release both heat and coolness, helping to even out the interior temperature.

For both hard plaster and dry-lining, corners, window reveals and door openings require galvanized steel or

Professional Tip

Effective as hard plastering is at providing high levels of air-tightness, it will only work if the entire inner leaf is plastered. That includes spaces below and beside stairs, inside built-in cupboards and behind anything else that stands against an external wall. Depending on your design, this may mean delaying some carpentry, and perhaps staircase installation, until all the plastering is finished.

LEFT: 'Dot and dab' is a fast way of plastering masonry walls by attaching plasterboard sheets with a special adhesive. British Gypsum

RIGHT: Walls can also be dry-lined by fixing the plasterboard to steel profiles; this technique can be useful for creating a void for services or insulation. British Gypsum

uPVC corner 'beading'. These are strips of angled mesh used to provide protection and a straight edge where surfaces meet, and which can be hidden by the skim plaster.

Screeding Floors

A finishing layer, or screed, is laid over a solid floor to create a smooth, level surface. Typically, it's a mix of cement and sharp sand in a ratio of 1:3.

If laid over rigid insulation, a damp-proof membrane is first placed on top. This will prevent moisture rising from the concrete slab, and also allow the screed to cure faster. A thin layer of insulation the depth of the screed is also run around the perimeter to prevent cold-bridging. The covering screed should have a minimum screed depth of 65mm. If laid over concrete that already has insulation embedded in it, then 50mm is sufficient. Where underfloor heating pipework is installed, 75mm is typical. Any greater depth will provide a longer-lasting thermal store, but it will also take the system longer to respond to changes of temperature.

This is also the time to lay conduit and access points for underfloor plumbing and electrics.

For covering large areas, ordering a ready mixed screed makes the work easier, faster and guarantees a more consistent mix. Large areas may also require reinforcement, typically in the form of polypropylene fibres, added to the mix, and possibly expansion joints to allow for movement. It's up to your designer, or the screeder, to specify these.

The finishing surface can be done by hand or mechanically, using a power float, which can be hired.

Once laid, a screed needs to be left for up to 48 hours to cure. No floor covering, however, can be put down until it is fully dry. This can take several weeks, depending on its thickness and local weather conditions.

Tempting though it sounds, underfloor heating can't be used to speed up the process. Moisture leaving the screed at an accelerated pace will only weaken the structure.

Liquid Screeds

'Flowing', or liquid, screeds, which are pumped through a hose, will greatly speed up the laying process. They can be laid at shallower depths than traditional screeds and completely enclose underfloor heating pipework, so increasing its efficiency. They also don't need reinforcement.

They are, however, more expensive than traditional screeds and can be damaged by water, making their use inadvisable in areas liable to flooding.

CHAPTER 23

Second Fix

This is that heady stage when it all starts to come together, light fittings sprout from ceilings, radiators from walls, doors turn spaces into rooms and finally, improbably, an end seems in sight.

True though that is, part of the joy is undoubtedly in reaching familiar territory. Most of us have experience of decorating and refurbishment, and there's reassurance in that; but there are also dangers.

One is the urge to become more hands-on – perhaps to save time or money or both. It may succeed, but it's easy to forget that this is DIY on a bigger scale and a far tighter schedule than most of us have ever experienced before. The end result could well be a disruption of the activities of tradespeople, extra snagging and an even longer build schedule.

The other, more common danger, is second thoughts. You may have meticulously researched every fixture and fitting, but viewing it in a brochure or a showroom isn't always the same as seeing it *in situ*. You may be delighted; you may be appalled.

At this stage, however, sudden switches in major items like baths, kitchen layouts and lighting systems can be hugely disruptive, and trigger budget-busting bills for 'variations'. If you genuinely feel you have made an horrendous mistake, talk to your designer and main contractor before making a decision; they may well come up with a solution that's faster or more cost-effective.

Even if they don't, don't assume you have to resolve everything now. This may sound odd after you've gone to so much trouble to get exactly what you want, but even the most perfect home isn't static. Its fabric will weather and mature; eventually it will need re-painting, repairing, renovating. More importantly, as you get to know it, your attitudes will change, too. In six months' time, today's horror could be a memory, or a lifesaver.

On the other hand, if you've still got cash available and your schedule is flexible, go for it. Do get an estimate in advance, and in writing. There's no point in being silly about it.

WEEK SIXTEEN TO EIGHTEEN: SECOND-FIX CARPENTRY AND FLOOR TILING

Who Needs to Be There
- Carpenter.
- Decorators.
- Kitchen fitters.
- Bedroom furniture fitters.
- Ceramic or stone flooring fitters.

Equipment
Tools supplied by tradesman.

Materials
- Skirting.
- Architrave.
- Picture/dado rail.
- Internal doors and door furniture.
- Staircase balustrading.
- Floor boarding/laminated flooring.
- Nails, grab adhesive.
- Ceramic/stone flooring.
- Adhesive, spacers, grouting compound.
- Kitchen units, worktop, sink, oven, hob (electric/gas), cooker hood, white goods.
- Mastic and sealants.

Planning Ahead
Contact the utility companies to re-confirm that services will be available when promised.

Activities

Laying Ceramic or Stone Flooring

Typically this is confined to the kitchen, bathrooms and shower rooms, and perhaps the utility room. It is, however, ideally suited to underfloor heating, and can be used wherever it is fitted.

Incidentally, if you are using floor of this kind in the kitchen, consider laying it before the kitchen is fitted. This not only makes the job easier and quicker now, but makes it much easier to change the layout in the future. It also guards the subfloor against unseen leaks beneath or behind the units.

Fitting Skirtings, Architraves, Dados and Picture Rails

Dados and picture rails may be essentially Victorian but even in a contemporary hallway, a dado can usefully divide the decorative upper half of a wall from a more

Laying a stone or ceramic tile floor before a kitchen is fitted will make future layout changes much easier; it will also protect the subfloor from hidden leaks. Limestone Gallery

robust lower half, subject to bumps from buggies, bikes and wheelchairs.

Picture rails, too, make life a lot easier if you like to change pictures, photographs and other wall decorations frequently, but it's safer to attach them with nails rather than grab adhesive, which can be used for skirting and architraves.

Fitting Internal Doors and Door Furniture

Hanging doors accurately is skilled and fiddly work, but can be speeded up considerably by specifying door sets, which come complete and fitted to the frame.

Care needs to be taken that sufficient room will be left beneath for your chosen floor covering. With solid floor coverings, such as tiles, slates or flagstones, it can be easier to postpone the door hanging until after the floor is laid.

Don't forget that, in a house of more than two storeys, any door opening on to the stairwell should be a fire door (graded FD30 or FD60), fitted with an intumescent seal; this expands in a fire, sealing the gap between door and frame.

A self-closing fire door should be fitted between the house and an integral garage.

Fitting Newel Posts and Balustrading

The most decorative, and most vulnerable, parts of your staircase can now be installed.

Pre-hung door sets will make door hanging a lot faster and often more accurate. Premdor

If a top-end designer kitchen turns out to be a budget item too far, it's useful to remember that kitchens of all kinds use much the same carcassing; one way to reduce build costs is to fit basic doors and panels initially then upgrade to higher end versions at a later date. Stoneham

Fitting the Kitchen

For most people the kitchen is the single most important room in the house and the one on which most design effort and expense are lavished. For this reason, many go to a kitchen specialist who provides a full design and fitting service, as well as the kitchen itself. This will simplify matters, though the work of the fitters will still need to be co-ordinated with that of your existing tradesmen, especially the electrician and plumber. It's unlikely, however, to be the most economical option, which is buying a flat-pack kitchen from a DIY warehouse and assembling it yourself. However, unless you'd done this successfully before and are flexible about your schedule, the pressure to complete other aspects of the build won't make this easy.

One alternative is to give the job to your carpenter, if you are managing your own project, or your main contractor. The safest way to do this is allow them to supply the materials from builders' merchants or joinery centres. Both will have trade catalogues you can study and the discounts the professionals obtain can be close to flat-pack prices. Otherwise, if there are any problems, the tradesman may be tempted to avoid responsibility by blaming your poor choice of materials.

If your carpenter is sufficiently skilled, it may be worth getting them to build the units from basic materials. Even expensive kitchens use much the same MDF or chipboard for the 'carcassing' – the basic structure of the units – as cheaper versions.

In fact, if your budget is being pinched at this point, you might be wise to invest in sturdy carcassing and fit either basic site-made or flat-pack doors, which can be replaced with more expensive versions later. Kitchen units come in standard sizes and, if your carcassing remains sound, swapping doors and drawer fronts is an easy and economical way of upgrading a tired kitchen.

Installing Vanity Units, Fitted Wardrobes and Other Items of Fitted Furniture
Vanity units in bathrooms will need to be in place ready for second-fix plumbing. Fitted wardrobes may wait until decoration is finished.

WEEK EIGHTEEN TO TWENTY: SECOND-FIX PLUMBING AND ELECTRICS

Be warned – this is the most hectic part of the most hectic part of the build. You may well be juggling the activities of kitchen fitters, fitted-bathroom installers, possibly even fitted-bedroom or home-office installers, as well as existing plumbers, central heating engineers, electricians and carpenters, and all will be bombarding you with questions.

Invariably it's at this point that the importance of preparation imprints itself indelibly on a self-builder's mind.

Who Needs to Be There
- Plumber/central heating engineer.
- Electrician.
- Carpenter.

Equipment
Tools supplied by tradesman.

Materials
- Plumbing.
- Central heating boiler.
- Motorized valves and pumps.
- Radiators.
- Thermostatic radiator valves.
- Programmer.
- Room thermostat.
- Shower pump(s), if needed.
- Gas hob, gas oven, gas tumble dryer, waste-disposal units, water softener.

- Baths, shower trays, shower heads, sinks, hand-basins, taps.
- WCs and cisterns.
- Sealing trim, silicone mastic sealant.
- Electrics.
- Switches, power sockets, light fittings, TV, satellite, telephone, ethernet and speaker points.
- Lighting (ceiling lights, downlighters, wall lights, strip lights external security lighting, etc.).
- Extractor fans.
- Door bell and transformer.
- Smoke detector, heat and carbon monoxide alarms.

Activities

Plumbing
INSTALLING THE BALANCED FLUE
Central heating boilers require a balanced flue about 100mm in diameter and consisting of two concentric tubes. Air for combustion is sucked in through the outer tube, while the inner vents the combustion gases.

Typically, the flue projects from the back of the boiler through the external wall to which it's attached. Alternatively, a fan-assisted flue can extend several metres. This is useful if you're unable to site the boiler on an outside wall, or the space immediately behind the boiler doesn't meet the requirements of the building regulations. For example, according to Part J, the flue terminal should be no closer than 2.5m from a facing wall, fence or boundary.

As with any opening in an outside wall, its edges should be carefully and thoroughly sealed to avoid air leakage.

FITTING THE CENTRAL HEATING BOILER
Modern gas boilers can be remarkably compact and many are designed to fit snugly between, or inside, standard kitchen wall units. A system boiler, which includes hot-water storage, may need a full-height cupboard,

Siting the boiler elsewhere, however, will save kitchen storage space and reduce the background room temperature in summer. In a utility room, for example, that warmth may be more useful in drying clothes. Any leaking gas or combustion fumes will also be confined to a non-habitable space (a good reason to fit a carbon monoxide detector).

The latter also applies to installation in an integral garage.

Choosing a Boiler

Under the current energy-efficiency requirements of the build-ing regulations, condensing boilers are, to all practical purposes, compulsory, if you are using the main fuels of gas, oil or liquefied petroleum gas (LPG). They promise efficiencies of over 90 per cent. You can check the figures for your chosen boiler on the government's Boiler Efficiency Table website (see Contacts).

This performance is achieved by including an extra heat exchanger to extract heat from the flue gases, which would otherwise be lost to the atmosphere. It preheats the cold water feeding the boiler and so reduces the amount of fuel needed to raise it to the required temper-ature. It also makes the flue gases cooler, which is why the water vapour they contain condenses and creates a characteristic white plume.

These benefits, however, aren't without cost. Traditional cast-iron boilers were only moderately efficient but very reliable and could last for years. Condensing boilers are more complicated, much more expensive and tend not to be so long-lived.

In addition, maximum efficiency is only achieved in what is known as 'condensing mode'. This occurs when the water returning to the boiler is at about 55°C or lower, enabling the water vapour in the flue gases to condense out and release significant amounts of latent heat.

The good news is that this makes condensing boilers ideal for heat-ing systems, which operate at relatively low temperatures – notably underfloor heating. As houses become better insulated, tempera-tures for space heating will fall.

Modern condensing boilers are compact, reliable and capable of very high efficiency, especially when used with low-temperature heating systems. Worcester Bosch Group

Even if a condensing boiler isn't working at peak efficiency, however, it will still perform at least as well as an effi-cient non-condensing model. There are also other ways of improving boiler performance. One is to opt for a model with 'gas burner modulation'. This automatically adjusts the gas and air mix for optimum efficiency, depending on the demand placed on the system.

A more radical approach is to fit a micro-CHP appliance. 'CHP' stands for combined heat and power. It's a standard-sized gas boiler, but it also contains a Stirling engine, a motor that runs on heat and which produces up to a kilowatt of electricity per hour whenever the boiler is firing.

At the time of writing, only one appliance – Baxi's Ecogen – is commercially available and it's expensive, but at least one rival is reported to be on its way.

Baxi's Ecogen is currently the only micro-CHP (combined heat and power) boiler available to domestic users; whenever gas is burnt, the heat operates an internal Stirling engine, which produces electricity for the home.

Grants for Renewables

Feed-In Tariffs (FITs)

If you generate your own electricity through an eligible renewable technology, you can claim a feed-in tariff from your electricity supplier for every unit you produce. That includes both electricity you use yourself and any surplus that you don't.

The eligible technologies are:

- Photovoltaic panels.
- Microchip (see above).
- Wind turbines.
- Small-scale hydroelectric power.

Renewable Heat Premium Payment

This is a one-off grant to encourage the purchase of an eligible renewable energy source, such as solar heating panels, a ground- or air-source heat pump system or a biomass boiler.

Renewable Heat Incentive (RHI)

In a scheme similar to FITs, this allows you to claim for every kilowatt of heat generated by an eligible technology. At the time of writing, both renewable heat schemes are under review.

The Green Deal

This is a loan scheme, enabling householders to upgrade the energy efficiency of existing homes, a process that can include renewable technologies, as well as measures like whole-house mechanical ventilation and heat recovery. The idea is that the savings in fuel costs must equal or exceed the loan repayments.

Details are still being worked out at the time of writing, but there are suggestions that the scheme may eventually be extended to new homes.

Grants, and their funding, are subject to regular change. Check out the current arrangements at the Department of Energy and Climate Change website (see Contacts).

Photovoltaic roof panels will not only provide useful electricity for the home but enable you to claim a tariff from your provider for every unit produced. Sandtoft

Solar heating panels can provide up to 50 per cent of your domestic hot water over the course of a year.

Choosing Fuel

Gas

Even with ever-rising fuel prices, this remains the cheapest, most convenient fuel and usually the first choice for the 85 per cent of the UK with a main gas supply.

Oil and LPG

For areas without piped gas, the traditional alternatives have been electricity, oil, LPG and solid fuel. Oil and LPG both require on-site storage facilities, good access for delivery vehicles and strict safety arrangements, all of which can be problematic on a small plot, as well as adding to overall costs.

LPG users are also tied into exclusive contracts with suppliers who own the storage tanks, though swapping to better deals has recently been made easier. Oil may become cheaper and more sustainable with the introduction of biofuels. Both oil and LPG, however, have suffered dramatic price rises in recent years.

Coal and Biomass

Coal, which used to dominate the solid-fuel market, is still widely available, but now more often used as an occasional alternative for multi-fuel stoves. Cheaper and much more convenient to use is biomass, which, for all practical purposes, means wood in the form of logs, chips or pellets.

Wood's big advantage is that, if obtained from a sustainable source, it's virtually carbon-neutral. This is good for the environment and even better for the wallet since wood-burning appliances attract government subsidies.

The most efficient boilers and stoves burn pellets of compressed wood about 20mm long and 8mm in diameter. Because of their regular size and shape, they can be loaded automatically from a hopper and ignited electronically via a

Wood-pellet stoves and boilers burn pellets of compressed wood which are loaded automatically from a hopper, providing a degree of control usually only found in gas and oil burners.

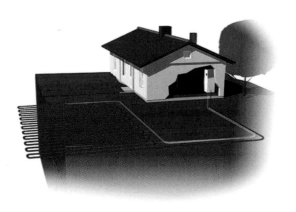

A ground source heat pump works like a refrigerator in reverse; liquid, pumped through buried pipework, extracts heat from the earth and delivers it indoors, via a compressor.

thermostat and timer, just like a gas boiler. As a result, boilers can last up to week before refuelling, and stoves almost as long. Their main drawback is that woodburners can't be turned off as rapidly as gas or oil-fired boilers. The contents of the combustion chamber have to be consumed first, producing heat that may not be needed. The solution is to install a large, well-insulated thermal store (see Chapter 21 for details) to soak up the surplus heat and release it when required. This also allows the boiler to work in the most efficient way – at high temperatures for continuous periods.

Sufficient space is therefore needed for the boiler, a fuel hopper and a large hot-water cylinder. Pellet boilers and stoves are also expensive, another reason for the government subsidy.

After installation, biomass and solid-fuel boilers and stoves need to be issued with a certificate showing they have been fitted according to the building regulations. This can be provided by an engineer registered with HETAS (see Contacts), whose website lists accredited suppliers of biomass and solid fuels.

Electricity

The high cost of electrical heating has largely confined it to back-up immersion heating for hot-water cylinders, heated towel-rails and the occasional top-up fan or panel heater. It's also been popular for background or short-term underfloor heating in the form of mats or films laid under tiles in bathrooms, kitchens or conservatories.

There are, however, very compact electric boilers, which don't require flues and so can be sited anywhere. They are useful for non-gas areas, where oil or LPG is impractical and space is limited.

The main growth area for electricity is in 'heat pumps'. They operate on the principle that the ground, air and large bodies of water all retain heat from the sun, which, with the right equipment, can be extracted and used to heat our homes.

The equipment used is effectively a fridge in reverse. In ground- and water-source heat pumps, water mixed with antifreeze, is pumped through a closed loop of pipework, gathering heat from the surrounding medium. It's then passed through a compressor, which releases the heat.

Electricity is needed to power the compressor and the pump, but between two and a half and four times the energy used will be extracted – a difference known as the 'coefficient of performance' (CoP). While it's enough to provide both central heating and hot water, it's at low temperatures best suited to underfloor heating and very well-insulated homes.

Typically, ground-source heat pumps need an area about two and half times the footprint of the house in which to run the pipework. It's buried about a metre down, where the ground temperature remains more or less constant throughout the year. The excavation can be done with the mechanical digger used for the foundations.

If your plot doesn't have enough space for this, the loop can be sunk vertically. Since this involves calling in borehole engineers, it's inherently more expensive; but if your foundations are piled, you might ask your piling company to drill an extra borehole and use that. Masterbuilder Bob Harris, who installed London's first ground-source heat pump for a block of flats, employed this method with great success.

Air-source heat pumps work in the same way but extract heat from the atmosphere. Since air temperature fluctuates much more than that of the ground, the yield of heat is lower and more variable, but installation is much easier and cheaper. The unit can sit in the garden or against an outside wall. The incoming air can be used either to heat a water-based central heating system or provide warm air heating.

Air-source heat pumps are cheaper to buy than ground-source and water-source versions, but all are expensive, though government subsidies are available. Once installed, however, maintenance is minimal. Running costs can be reduced by using cheap rate overnight electricity or electricity from photo-voltaic panels or wind turbines.

In some heat pump systems, the cycle can be reversed in hot weather, allowing heat to be extracted from the house and dispersed outside.

An air-source heat pump extracts warmth from the atmosphere via an external unit, which can be sited on an outside wall or tucked away, unobtrusively, in the garden. Inside the heat can be distributed by a fan, or a conventional central heating system, using a heat exchanger.
Worcester Bosch Group

Fitting Appliances

Appliances (such as radiators, thermostatic radiator valves and heated towel rails, sinks, handbasins, baths, taps, shower trays, shower heads, WCs and cisterns) are now installed and connected to the hot and cold feed upstands and the various waste pipes. Showers with one or more tiled walls will need to wait for tilers to complete their work before they are fully water-proofed with strips of sealing trim or silicone mastic sealants.

The same applies where baths, hand-basins and sinks abut tiled surfaces.

Installing Electrics

Fixing light fittings, switches, power sockets, cooker point and cooker hood, kitchen, bathroom and toilet extractor fans, wiring up immersion heater, fixing smoke, heat and carbon monoxide alarms, TV aerial points, telephone points, speaker points, etc. – all these will be connected to the consumer unit. The following can be done in conjunction with the heating engineer, or left to the engineer:

- Installing central heating programmer and thermo-stat and wiring to boiler, along with motorized valves and pumps.
- Connection of gas and mains electricity by arrange-ment with the relevant providers.
- Commissioning and testing of central heating boiler and heating system. This involves checking the oper-ation of the boiler and its controls, the security of pipework joints and the functioning of each radia-tor's thermostatic valve. The system is also flushed

to remove any debris left after installation and traces of mineral oil used in radiators during the manufac-turing process; this can damage rubber parts within valves and pumps.

- Consider fitting an in-line magnetic filter to minimize the accumulation of sludge in radiators, pumps and valves. Caused by dirt in the water and corrosion within pipework, sludge can cause pumps to fail and cold spots within radiators.
- Adding corrosion inhibitors to the system will reduce it, but filters, which can be cleaned annually, are a cheaper and more convenient option than the alter-native, often recommended by plumbers – draining and power flushing the entire system.
- Issuing of commissioning certificates for central heat-ing and hot-water systems is the job of the central heating engineer. If you have hired your own engi-neer, or specialist company, no final payment should be made before the certificate is issued.
- Issuing of electrical safety certificate – final payment depends on receiving a suitable certificate.

Taking Note

Contact numbers for the central heating engineer and electrician may well be in your build diary, and included in the invoices they supply, but if a main contractor has sub-contracted their work – as often happens – it's wise to ask for a business card or contact details in case problems arise later.

CHAPTER 24

Completion and Snagging

The lights work, water gushes from the taps, the radiators warm up and you can lock the front door – you have, to all intents and purposes, a new home. For most self-builders this is a heady moment, mingling joy, relief, pride and a good deal of exhaustion.

With the final flurry of the second fix complete, the house can seem eerily quiet and the urge to simply pay everyone off and get back to normal life positively overwhelming. The process of completion, however, requires just as much attention as the rest of the build.

The first question to ask is: have I now finished? The answer is more complicated than it may seem.

Normally, the next stage would be decoration, along with any remaining tiling and a degree of landscaping. Your agreement with a main contractor, or sub-contractors, may well include this, but many self-builders choose to do it themselves. This is likely to take a great deal longer than the professionals, especially if you plan to move in immediately, but there are practical advantages to delaying the final touches.

Leaving decoration until the house is fully dried out, and all cracks have appeared and been filled, means the job will only be done once. Deep floor screeds can also take up to six months to be completely dry, which they should be before carpeting and wood floor covering goes down. If you can put off the fitting of internal wooden doors until this time, they are much less likely to warp, twist or stick.

That's for the future. For now, the issue is 'practical completion', usually regarded as the point at which you can occupy the house without being disturbed by armies of tradespeople. Achieving that triggers the final-stage payment from your lender, which, in turns, enables you to pay your main contractor or sub-contractors.

Completion, however, depends on passing final inspections by the local building control department and your warranty provider's surveyor.

Part of that process is an air-leakage test, demonstrating that the house has met the requirements of Part L of the building regulations. The results are used to re-run the SAP calculations originally made at the design stage (see Chapter 11 for details). These will tell you if your home, as built, has matched, or improved upon, the energy efficiency and carbon dioxide emissions predicted.

Assuming the figures are favourable, they are then used to produce a compliance report and an Energy Performance Certificate (EPC).

Once the inspections are passed, completion certificates can be issued by building control, and by your architect, project manager or other building professional. You can then move on to the main contractor's final account.

A major part of this is the 'snagging' process. This involves thoroughly examining the house for any defects or blemishes. A snagging list is agreed with your main contractor, or sub-contractors, and final payment shouldn't be made until all the items on the list have been dealt with.

Even so, the final account should include a retention, which is kept for a further 6 months to ensure that any lingering snags, or any new ones that arise, will be remedied. Retentions are typically 2.5 per cent of the contract sum. Incidentally, they need to be written into the initial contract to be enforceable at this stage.

Completion also means you can now apply for your VAT refund. This allows you to reclaim the Value Added Tax paid on all the building materials and many of the services used to construct your house. Twenty per cent – the current rate – of a large part of your budget can go a long way towards the cost of decoration, floor coverings and landscaping.

Meanwhile, if decoration, tiling and landscaping are part of your contract with a main contractor, or you have organized sub-contractors to do the work, you have a further 3 to 4 weeks to go.

WEEKS TWENTY-ONE TO TWENTY-THREE: TILING, DECORATING AND LANDSCAPING

Who Needs to Be There
- Tilers.
- Decorators.
- Groundworkers.
- Landscape gardener.
- Air-tightness tester.
- Warranty provider surveyor.
- Building inspector.

Equipment
- Tiling and decorating tools supplied by tradesmen.
- Dehumidifier.
- Mechanical digger.
- Skip.
- Garden roller.
- Concrete mixer.
- Rotavator.

Materials
- Emulsion and gloss paint/natural or eco paint, primer, undercoats, stains, varnishes.
- Fillers, sandpapers, knotting solution, brush cleaner.
- Wall and floor tiles, adhesive, spacers, grouting compound.
- Geotextile fabric, hardcore, paving/gravel.

Activities

Completing the Tiling
Typically, this involves tiling walls in bathrooms, showers and between worktops and wall units in kitchens, but can include other areas, such as boxed-in waste pipes, vanity units and worktops themselves.

Most adhesive and grout is waterproof, but flexible varieties should be used on non-masonry surfaces, such as plasterboard, blockboard and plywood. Heat-resistant adhesive and grout is advisable around hobs

---

Professional Tip

When sealing the edges of a bath with mastic where it abuts a wall, always fill the bath first to allow for the effects of the extra weight. With a shower, always stand in the tray to do the same.

---

and cookers; epoxy-based grout, which resists stains and bacteria, is good for tiled worktops.

Clearing and Tidying Up
Clearing up at the end of the build should be part of the contract with a main contractor. Left to their own devices, building workers have been known to bury rubbish that won't fit into the final skip, or can't be burnt.

Persuading sub-contractors to tidy up after themselves is harder to enforce. You are more likely to end up doing it yourself, and quickly, if painters and decorators are due. They will expect their areas of work to be empty of rubbish, swept and dusted.

Painting and Decorating
One major advantage of using professionals is that skilled workers can 'make good' an enormous number of minor blemishes, from cracks, dents and scratches in plaster to proud nails to annoying gaps where woodwork should join seamlessly.

In fact, the bulk of their work, as DIYers quickly discover, is in preparation. Painted woodwork will need rubbing down, then an application of knotting solution – to avoid knots leaking resin and causing stains – followed by primer, undercoat and topcoat.

For best results, paint the back as well as the front of skirting, architraves and mouldings, ideally before the carpenter starts to cut and fix them. Alternatively, persuade the carpenters to fit these items loosely, allowing the decorators to remove then replace them more securely.

Alternatives to paint are wood stain or varnish, neither of which require knotting solution and can cover more quickly.

Emulsion is standard for walls and ceilings. Prepared plasterboard can take it immediately. Skim-plastered plasterboard will need to be touch dry first – this typically takes a couple of days. For hard-plastered masonry walls, it can take several weeks.

Arranging the Air-Tightness Test
Under Part LIA of the building regulations, all new homes need to pass a test for air permeability, the rate at which air, and therefore heat, leaks through the external fabric of the building. The current requirement is a maximum air-leakage rate of $10m^3/m^2/h@50Pa$.

In English this means that, for a pressure difference of 50 pascals (a measure of force against a given area)

Healthy Paints

Generally speaking, oil-based paints should be avoided, if possible. They provide a high-gloss finish and generally the best protection, but they also contain chemicals known as volatile organic compounds (VOCs). These can cause nausea, dizziness and skin irritation and have been linked to allergies, asthma and 'sick building' syndrome. VOCs also continue to 'offgas' into the atmosphere for up to five years after application.

VOC symbol protected, used under licence

Exposure to paints high in volatile organic compounds (VOCs) can cause nausea, dizziness and skin irritation and has been linked to asthma and allergies.

An alternative is so-called organic or 'eco' paints. These are based on water and plant or vegetable oils, rather than petrochemicals, and use as many natural and renewable ingredients as practicable. Their big advantage is they don't give off the characteristic new paint smell – or the hazardous fumes that go with it; a newly painted bedroom can be slept in immediately without discomfort. They are also microporous, allowing water vapour to pass through easily, a useful quality in a newly built masonry home.

Their disadvantages are a colour range dominated by pastel shades, high price and limited distribution; the Eco Decorators' Association (*see* Contacts) lists suppliers and manufacturers.

If your budget can't justify them, look instead for water-based paints (which will also make brush-cleaning easier) and paints labelled as zero or minimal VOC content. Allergy UK (*see* Contacts) also publishes a list of allergy-friendly paints and varnishes.

Organic or 'eco' paints are based on plant or vegetable oils rather than petrochemicals; though more expensive, they allow newly painted rooms to be occupied immediately without smell or discomfort. Earthborn

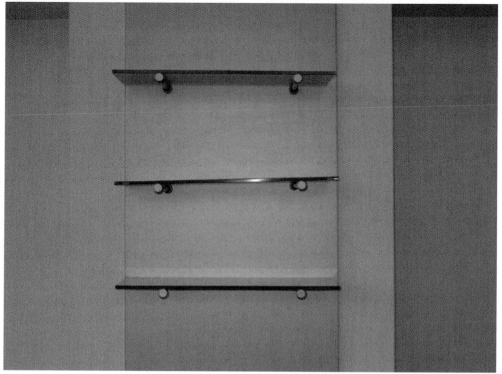

Spot the non-deliberate mistakes: snagging is an essential part of the completion process.

between interior and exterior, $10m^3$ of air will leak through every $1m^2$ of the external fabric every hour.

Since this is roughly the equivalent of a 10p-sized hole for every $1m^3$ of the outside envelope of the house, the test isn't exactly demanding. By comparison, Swedish homes routinely achieve air-tightness of $3m^3/m^2/h@50Pa$ and the Passivhaus system demands $1m^3/m^2/h@50Pa$.

Typical leakage points are leaky windows and doors, gaps around services penetrating outside walls and points where joists break through the inner leaf of a cavity wall.

Testing is done by closing all windows, vents and external doors, except the front, to which a large fan is attached. Air is then blown inside to increase the internal pressure. The rate at which it falls is then measured by a variety of instruments. If the house fails the test, leaks can be traced using smoke tests and thermal imaging cameras.

Approved testers are listed on the website of the Air Tightness and Measurement Association (see Contacts), though warranty providers offering building control services also provide air-tightness testing and SAP assessment.

Snagging

Snags come in two forms. First, they are the minor items you have noticed in the last weeks of the build – sealant missing from door frames, lopsided power sockets, patches of poor paintwork.

Second, they are the problems that arise as the house dries out and settles in: cracks in plaster, creaking stairs and floors, sticking doors. Brick and block homes, built, as they are, with large volumes of water, are particularly prone to these. Defects in the plumbing, heating and electrical systems may also become obvious through daily use.

The latter snags should be covered by the normal 6-month retention in the contract. The former are noted and discussed as you walk round the house with your main contractor and designer or project manager.

Don't be tempted to deal with a main contractor on your own. An objective, professional eye will pick up on details you may miss, or not identify correctly, and provide perspective on problems that may not be as serious as they first appear.

If your designer is unwilling to get involved, and you don't have a project manager, consider hiring a surveyor

A Guide to Snagging

The twin perils of snagging are either getting over-picky or being too tolerant. The first can simply annoy your contractor, who may believe that he has been generous enough to you already. The second may make you kick yourself later when you realize you can't live with something and your contractor complains, not unreasonably, that you should have raised the issue earlier when it could have been dealt with more easily.

If you are unwilling or unable to engage professional help in the process, the warranty providers can give you a hand, but not in the way you might think.

Providers like the NHBC and LABC may have approved your build, but their main concern is the structure of your home, the roof and the foundations. As long as the house is technically habitable, the fact that a door sticks or there's a minor leak is generally regarded as irrelevant.

That said, both the NHBC and LABC provide guides to standards and tolerances, which can be downloaded free from their websites (see Contacts). According to the NHBC, for example, external walls should vary horizontally from plumb no more than plus or minus 10mm for lengths up to 5m. The LABC, meanwhile, suggests that window frames up to 1.5m in height can be a maximum of 6mm out of plumb.

This may seem reasonable or outrageous to you – usually depending on how you view your own walls and windows. But they do give an indication of what the average contractor is likely to believe is acceptable.

Generally, however, if you are basically happy with the end result, you're more likely to get the snagging done to your satisfaction if you act in a way you, and the contractor, find reasonable. Unless, of course, something really rankles.

Establishing a position for a crossover to your driveway should be an early priority; it may affect the siting of manholes and services. Wienerberger

New front garden driveways over 5m² in area should now be either permeable, or designed to drain into a lawn or border. Wienerberger

or other building professional, or a specialist snagging company (*see* Contacts).

If you are managing your own build, snagging with individual sub-contractors is likely to be more complicated – unless you are dealing with companies or individuals who are members of trade organizations with warranty schemes. This is all the more reason to ensure you are happy with their work before payment is made, and that you retain contact details in case any follow-up is needed.

Installing Crossovers
Facilities for parking will normally form part of your planning application and, in most roadways, will include creating a dropped kerb to provide access to your driveway. Otherwise, you will need to approach your local authority and relevant highways authority for permission.

Some authorities will allow you to use your own contractor for the work, as long as you, or they, have public liability insurance (which will be the case if you have had to make a connection to a public sewer). Others will insist you use a contractor from a local authority approved list, which is likely to cost a lot more.

Creating a crossover also involves strengthening the pavement and can affect the positioning of new or existing manholes, or other services. It's important, then, to check the location of your driveway as early as possible.

Building a Driveway
Since 2008 in England, any new driveway over 5m² in area in a front garden must be either 'permeable' or so arranged that rainwater can drain into a lawn, border or soakaway. In Scotland, similar requirements now apply to any new paving between a house and the street.

These new planning rules are a response to Britons' habit of paving over front gardens for free parking and minimal garden maintenance. As a result, large amounts of rainwater have been flowing into sewers, causing rivers and streams to flood and become polluted.

There are numerous ways to comply:

- Gravel: the simplest form of driveway (and a handy auditory warning of visitors, welcome or otherwise); 50mm of gravel over a 200mm-deep aggregate sub-base will support vehicles, but won't suit wheelchair users.
- Conventional paving with appropriate drainage: here, the run-off is directed away from the road onto a lawn, flowerbed or soakaway.
- Porous paving: this consists of porous asphalt, concrete or clay blocks, which allow water to soak into it and around the edges.
- Reinforced grass: buried plastic or concrete blocks allow grass to grow on the surface, but provide support for vehicles.

All driveways should be installed over a permeable geotextile fabric to stabilize the sub-base, while still allowing water to pass into the soil.

Final Accounting
Unless you have been usually scrupulous in keeping your accounts, your main contractor's final bill may contain a few surprises, not to say shocks.

Common causes for this are 'variations', which were either not fully priced when they were requested, or not priced at all; PC or prime cost sums for items such as kitchens and bathrooms, which turn out to cover only a fraction of what you actually fit; and provisional sums where the figure first suggested, and budgeted for, bears little relation to the actual cost of the work.

It's at this point that the value of a well-maintained build diary becomes obvious. It may provide the evidence that certain prices were agreed, 'extras' asked for or materials used, or not.

If you're still genuinely puzzled by some of the final account figures, it's reasonable to ask for more details, including copies of invoices. You may find, for example, that material suppliers have mistakenly added VAT, or not applied agreed discounts.

From all this you'll gather that a degree of negotiation is involved. Here, again, a review of your build diary can

help you maintain a balanced view, reminding you, for example, of favours done – on both sides.

If this doesn't appeal to you, you can arrange for your architect, designer or project manager to negotiate the final account on your behalf – the job a quantity surveyor does on a large construction project. You will, of course, be charged for this service.

Reclaiming Your VAT

Unless they are in the happy position of achieving a turnover of £77,000 a year as a self-employed individual or the owner of a business – the current threshold for registration – the mysteries of Value Added Tax are unknown to most people. The current 20 per cent surcharge added to a variety of goods and services is largely disregarded, unless, of course, the government raises or lowers it.

The exception, perhaps, is in dealing with trades people, who will sometimes offer, or be asked, to leave VAT off all or part of their bill in exchange for cash payment. This is illegal for the tradesperson, though not for the customer. If there are problems later, however, getting redress in the absence of an invoice may be a problem. All this assumes the tradesperson was registered for VAT, anyway.

Thankfully, most of these problems disappear with house-building, which, in large part, is zero-rated. This means that a main contractor or sub-contractor shouldn't add VAT to their bills.

HM Revenue and Customs give self-builders a special dispensation, recognizing them as temporary members of the construction industry for the period of their build. For just 3 months after completion you can make a one-off claim for the refund of the VAT paid on most building services, and for all building materials and fixtures that form a permanent part of your new home.

That includes heating, plumbing and electrical systems, fitted kitchens, fireplaces, curtain poles, per-manent flooring and boundary fencing. It excludes white goods, carpeting and furnishing – since they are not permanent fixtures. As with all good bureaucracies, however, there are anomalies. Here are the main ones, and suggestions on how to bypass them.

Professional Fees
Services provided by an architect, project manager or structural engineer, etc. include VAT at the standard rate.

TOP: **Plant hire isn't zero-rated for VAT, but, if the hire charge includes an operator, the VAT on labour charges can be reclaimed; make sure the invoice separates the two.**

BELOW: **If you build a swimming pool inside your new home, or inside an attached building constructed at the same time as the house, the VAT paid on its construction costs can be included in your one-off reclaim.** Sandtoft

VAT cannot normally be reclaimed on cookers, unless they form part of the central heating system, like this woodburning example. Wamsler

Remedy If your house is built by a design and build company, or a main contractor, who includes design and other professional services as part of their contract, their bill will be zero-rated – but only if any professional services are not specifically mentioned or itemized on their invoice.

Plant Hire
Scaffolding, mechanical diggers, cranes include VAT in their hire charges.

Remedy If the hire includes operators, as it usually does with the above items, ask for the invoice to itemize hire and labour charges separately. The labour element will be zero-rated.

Swimming Pools, Conservatories and Outbuildings
Standard-rated.

Remedy If the pool is inside the house, or inside a building attached to the house, it is zero-rated. This also applies to conservatories or outbuildings, such

> ### What Counts As a 'Self-Build' for VAT Purposes?
>
> 'Self-builds' also include houses built for relatives and as holiday homes, conversions of non-residential buildings, such as barns, stables and oast houses (but only if they have never been lived in, or not within the last 10 years) and partly completed houses. These can include shells built by a developer and intended specifically for the buyer to fit out.

as garden offices, studios and workshops, which are similarly attached and built at the same time as the main house.

Fitted Furniture
Standard-rated.

Remedy If you build in storage cupboards, using existing walls, ceiling and floor, the materials used are zero-rated. A large cupboard can, of course, be later turned into a wardrobe space.

Cookers
Standard-rated.

Remedy If your cooker has an integral boiler that forms part of the heating system, as in a range cooker, it is zero-rated.

Buying Elsewhere in EU
This isn't so much an anomaly as a potential perk. If you buy qualifying materials in another European Union country, you can reclaim the sterling equivalent of the VAT paid. When sterling was strong in relation to the Euro and VAT rates higher in Europe, bargains could be had. France was so popular for this that builder merchants in Channel ports specifically targeted British buyers. If you are making a day trip, it can be worth checking the current situation.

A Warning Regarding Sub-Contractors
If sub-contractors charge VAT and you pay it inadvertently, you will be unable to make a reclaim on their behalf. All you can do is persuade them to adjust their next VAT return – which is usually made quarterly – and reimburse you personally. Good luck with that.

If in doubt about any of these points, do check with the VAT helpline that they still apply (*see* Contacts).

Brick can be as effective in landscaping as it is in house-building, from attractive and durable paths, walls and planters, to elaborate garden features that give full rein to the bricklayer's skills.

Ibstock

How Do You Make a Claim?

At the time of writing, the form you need is VAT431NB, which you can download from the HM Revenue and Customs website. The accompanying booklet explains exactly what you have to do, but the crucial point is being able to supply original VAT invoices. Copies are not acceptable.

A VAT invoice should include:

- The supplier's VAT registration number.
- A description of the services or goods supplied, including quantities.
- The price of each item.
- Your name and address if the total value is over £100.
- The VAT amount may not be separated out, but you can do that yourself by dividing by 1.2 to find the VAT-free figure and subtracting it from the total.

Once you have totted up the full amount due, pop the completed form in the post along with your invoices, a full set of approved plans and evidence of completion.

Assuming there are no problems, you should receive your refund within 30 days.

THE END

The build schedule may be complete, but in reality few self-builds reach a definitive conclusion. There are now gardens to create, furniture to install, heating systems to fathom, until it all merges into general on-going maintenance.

For the moment, however, simply enjoy the feelings of relief, disbelief that it's all finally over and, most of all, huge pride. Self-build is still unusual enough in this country to represent an extraordinary achievement and a genuine milestone in the lives of those who take it on.

The reward is extraordinary, too – a unique home, better tailored to your needs, and your bank balance, than any mere developer could provide, and a uniquely personal contribution to Britain's housing heritage. Something to ponder while the elements work their magic on the brick that surrounds you, moulding it ever closer and more attractively to the landscape that produced it.

Contacts

TRADE BODIES AND ASSOCIATIONS

Aircrete Products Association (www.aircrete.co.uk)

AECB 0845 456 9773 (www.aecb.net)

Air Tightness Testing and Measurement Association
0202 253 4514 (www.attma.org)

Allergy UK 01322 619 898 (www.allergyuk.org)

Architectural and Specialist Door Manufacturers
Association 01494 447 370 (www.asdma.com)

ASBA (Association of Self Build Architects)
0800 387 310 (www.asba-architects.org)

Association of Brickwork Contractors 020 7692 4000
(www.associationofbrickworkcontractors.co.uk)

Association of Consultant Approved Inspectors
(www.approvedinspectors.org.uk)

Association of Plumbing and Heating Contractors
0121 711 5030 (www.aphc.co.uk)

Association of Project Management
(www.apm.org.uk)

Basement Information Centre 01276 331 155
(www.basements.org.uk)

Boiler Efficiency Database (www.boilers.org.uk)

Brick Development Association, The Building
Centre, 26 Store Street, London, WC1E 7BT
020 7323 7030 (www.brick.org.uk)

British Hydropower Association
(www.british-hydro.org)

British Structural Waterproofing Association
020 8866 8339 (www.thebswa.plus.com)

Building Control in Northern Ireland
(www.buildingcontrol-ni.com)

Building and Engineering Services Association
020 7313 4900 (www.hvca.org.uk)

Brick Directory (www.brickdirectory.co.uk)

British Association of Landscape Industries
024 7669 0333 (www.bali.co.uk)

British Flue and Chimney Manufacturers Association
0118 940 3416 (www.feta.co.uk)

British Ready Mix Concrete Association
www.brmca.org.uk

British Research Establishment (BRE) 01923 664 000
(www.bre.co.uk)

British Woodworking Federation 0844 209 2610
(www.bwf.org.uk)

Centre for Alternative Technology (CAT)
01654 705 950 (www.cat.org.uk)

Chartered Institute of Architectural Technologists
020 7278 2206 (www.ciat.org.uk)

Chartered Institute of Building 01344 630 700
(www.cbcschemes.org.uk)

Chartered Institute of Plumbing and Heating
Engineering 01708 472 791 (www.ciphe.org.uk)

Clay Roof Tile Council 01782 744
(www.clayroof.co.uk) – good website information.

Communities and Local Government 0303 444 0000
(www.communities.gov.uk)

Community Build 0117 924 1263
(www.communitybuild.org.uk)

Community Self Build Agency 01795 663 073
(www.communityselfbuildagency.org.uk)

Concrete Block Association (www.cba-blocks.org.uk)
– good explanation of blocks and how to use them.

Confederation of Roofing Contractors 01206 306 600
(www.corc.co.uk)

Council of Mortgage Lenders 0845 373 6771
(www.cml.org.uk)

Custom Electronic Design and Installation Association
(CEDIA) 01480 213 744 (www.cedia.co.uk)

Department of Energy and Climate Change
0300 060 4000 (www.decc.gov.uk)

Design Council 020 7420 5200
(www.designcouncil.org.uk)

Eco Decorators Association
(www.ecodecorators.org)

Ecology Building Society 0845 674 5566
(www.ecology.co.uk)

ePlanning Scotland (www.eplanning.scotland.gov.uk)

Electrical Contractors Association 020 7313 4800
(www.eca.co.uk)

ELECSA 03333 218 220 (www.elecsa.co.uk)

Environment Agency 03708 506 506 (www.
environment-agency.gov.uk)

Federation of Plastering and Drywall Contractors
020 7634 9480 (www.fpdc.org)

Fenestration Self-Assessment Scheme (FENSA)
020 7645 3700 (www.fensa.co.uk)

Gas Safe Register 0800 408 5500
(www.gassaferegister.co.uk)

Glass and Glazing Federation 020 7939 9101
(www.ggf.org.uk)

Ground Source Heat Pump Association
(www.gshp.org.uk)

Guild of Bricklayers 01623 554 582
(www.guildofbricklayers.org.uk)

Health and Safety Executive (www.hse.gov.uk)

Health Protection Agency (www.hpa.org.uk.)

Heating and Hotwater Industry Council
(www.centralheating.co.uk)

Heat Pump Association 0118 940 3416
(www.feta.co.uk)

HETAS (Heating Equipment Testing and Approval
Scheme) 0845 634 5626
(www.hetas.co.uk)

HM Revenue & Customs 0845 010 9000
(www.hmrc.gov.uk)

Hot Water Association 01274 583 355
(www.hotwater.org.uk.)

Interpave (Precast Concrete Paving and Kerb
Association) 0116 253 6161 (www.paving.org.uk)

Joint Contracts Tribunal (www.jctltd.co.uk)

Kitchen Bathroom Bedroom Specialists Association
01623 818 808 (www.kbsa.org.uk)

Kitemark 0845 0809 000 (www.kitemark.com)

Institute of Carpenters 0844 879 7696
(www.instituteofcarpenters.com)

Institute of Domestic Heating and Environmental
Engineers 02380 668 900 (www.idhee.org.uk)

Institution of Structural Engineers 020 7235 4535
(www.istructe.org)

Insulating Concrete Formwork Association
01403 701 167 (www.icfinfo.org.uk)

Interlay (Association of Block Paving Contractors)
0116222 9840 (www.interlay.org.uk)

Kitchen Bathroom Bedroom Specialists Association
01623 818 808 (www.kbsa.org.uk)

LABC 020 7091 6879 (www.labc.uk.com)

Land Registry 0844 892 1111 (www.landreg.gov.uk)

Metal Gutter Manufacturers Association
01633 891 584 (www.mgma.co.uk)

Microgeneration Certification Scheme 020 7090 1082
(www.microgenerationcertification.org)

Mineral Wool Insulation Manufacturers Association
020 7935 8532 (www.mima.info)

Mortar Industry Association 020 7963 8000
(www.mortar.org.uk)

National Access and Scaffolding Confederation
020 7822 7400 (www.nasc.org.uk)

National Association of Professional Inspectors and
Testers (NAPIT) 0845 543 0330
(www.napit.org.uk)

National Building Specification (NBS) 0191 244 5500
(www.thenbs.com)

National Energy Foundation 01908 665 555
(www.nef.org.uk)

National Federation of Glaziers 020 7404 3099
(www.nfoglon.org.uk)

National Federation of Roofing Contractors
020 7638 7663 (www.nfrc.co.uk)

National House Building Council (NHBC)
0844 633 1000 (www.nhbc.co.uk)

National Insulation Association 08451 636 363
(www.nationalinsulationassociation.org.uk)

National Self Build Association 0145206100051
(www.nasba.org.uk)

National Self Build and Renovation Centre
0845 223 4455 (www.buildstore.co.uk)

National Specialist Contractors Council
0844 249 5351 (www.nscc.org.uk)

National Inspection Council for Electrical Installation
Contracting (NICEIC) 0870 013 0382
(www.niceic.com)

Oil Firing Technical Association (OFTEC)
0845 658 5080 (www.oftec.org)

Painting and Decorating Association 024 7635 3776
(www.paintingdecoratingassociation.co.uk)

Passivhaus Trust 020 7704 3502
(www.passivhaustrust.org.uk)

Plastics Window Federation 01582 456 147
(www.pwfed.co.uk)

Quantity Surveyors International (www.theqsi.com)

Precast Concrete Paving and Kerb Association
0116 251 4568 (www.paving.org.uk)
Precast Flooring Federation 0116 253 6161
(www.precastfloors.info)
Renewable Energy Centre 01926 865 835
(www.therenewablenergycentre.co.uk)
Royal Institute of British Architects (RIBA)
020 7580 5533 (www.architecture.com)
Royal Incorporation of Architects in Scotland
0131 229 7545 (www.rias.org.uk)
Royal Institute of Chartered Surveyors
0870 333 1600 (www.rics.org)
Royal Society of Architects in Wales
029 2022 8987 (www.architecture.com)
Royal Society of Ulster Architects 028 9032 3760
(www.rusa.org.uk)
Royal Town Planning Institute 020 7929 9494
(www.rtpi.org.uk)
Scottish Environment Protection Agency
01786 457 700 (www.sepa.org.uk)
Scottish Government (www.home.scotland.gov.uk)
Secured by Design (www.securedbydesign.com)
Solar Trade Association 020 7925 3575
(www.solar-trade.org.uk)
Solid Fuel Association 0845 601 4406
(www.solidfuel.co.uk)
Steel Window Association 0844 249 1355
(www.steel-window-association.co.uk)
The Building Centre 020 7692 4000
(www.buildingcentre.co.uk)
The Concrete Centre 01276 606 800
(www.concretecentre.com)
The Planning Portal
(www.planningportal.gov.uk)
Tile Association 020 8663 0946
(www.tiles.org.uk)
Timber Research and Development Association
(TRADA) 04194 569 600
(www.trada.co.uk)
Timber Trade Federation 020 3205 0067
(www.ttf.co.uk)
Trussed Rafter Association 020 3205 0032
(www.tra.org.uk)
Trustmark 01344 630 804
(www.trustmark.org.uk)
UK Copper Board www.ukcopperboard.co.uk
UK Rainwater Harvesting Association
0845 026 240 (www.ukrha.org.uk)
Valuation Office Agency www.gov.uk

CONSTRUCTION INDUSTRY CONTACTS

Bathrooms
Aqualisa 01959 560 020
(www.acqualisa.co.uk)
Bathstore (www.bathstore.co.uk)
Simon Taylor Furniture 01296 488 207
(www.simon-taylor.co.uk)

Beam and Polystyrene Block Manufacturers
Charcon 01249 463 244
(www.charconflooring.com)
Hanson 01628 774 100 (www.heidelbergcement.com/
uk/en/hanson/home.htm)
Litecast Homefloors 02476 356 161
(www.litecast.co.uk)
Rackham Housefloors 01924 455 876
(www.rackhamhousefloors.co.uk)

Block Manufacturers
Cemex 0800 667 827
(www.cemex.co.uk)
Hanson 01628 774 100 (www.heidelbergcement.com/
uk/en/hanson/home.htm)
H+H Celcon 01732 886 444
(www.hhcelcon.co.uk)
Tarmac 0800 1 218 218 (www.tarmac.co.uk)
Thomas Armstrong 01900 68211
(www.thomasarmstrong.co.uk)

Bricks
Coleford Brick & Tile 01594 822 160
(www.colefordbrick.co.uk)
Ketley Brick 01384 78361
(www.ketley-brick.co.uk)
Hanson 01628 774 100 (www.heidelbergcement.com/
uk/en/hanson/home.htm)
H.G. Matthews 01494 758 212
(www.hgmatthews.com)
Ibstock 0844 800 4575
(www.ibstock.co.uk)
Northcot Brick 01386 700 551
(www.northcotbrick.co.uk)
Wienerberger 0844 303 2524
(www.wienerberger.co.uk)
York Handmade 01347 838 881
(www.yorkhandmade.co.uk)

Builders' Merchants Offering Self-Build Services

Buildbase (www.buildbase.co.uk)
E.H. Smith 0121 713 7100 (www.ehsmith.co.uk)
Elliotts 023 8022 6852 (www.elliotts.uk.com)
Jewson (www.jewson.co.uk)
Robert Price 01873 858 585 (www.robert-price.co.uk)
Travis Perkins (www.travisperkins.co.uk)
WBS 01244 288 202 (www.wbsltd.eu)

Central Heating Boilers

Baxi 0844 871 1525 (www.baxi.co.uk)
Glow-Worm (www.glow-worm.co.uk)
Vaillant 0844 602 0262 (www.vaillant.co.uk)
Worcester Bosch 0844 892 3000
   (www.worcester-bosch.co.uk)

Chimneys

Anki 01983 527 997 (www.anki.co.uk)
Isokern 01202 861 632 (www.isokern.co.uk)

Contracts

Federation of Master Builders 020 7242 7583
   (www.fmb.org.uk)
JCT 0845 082 1080
   (www.home-ownercontracts.co.uk)
Scottish Building Contracts Committee (SBCC)
   (www.sbcconline.com)

Design and Build Companies

Design & Materials 01909 531 454
   (www.designandmaterials.uk.com)

Doors

I.G. Doors 01633 486 860 (www.igdoorsltd.co.uk)
J.B. Kind 01283 554 197 (www.jbkind.com)
Jeld-Wen 0845 122 2890 (www.jeld-wen.co.uk)
Premdor 0844 209 0008 (www.premdor.co.uk)

Estimating Services

Best Estimating Service to the Trade 07802 725 715
   (bestestimating.co.uk)
Estimators-Online 0845 650 2208
   (www.estimators-online.com)
Estimating Service 01562 750 430
   (www.estimatingservice.co.uk)
HXBL 0845 1234 065 (www.hxbl.co.uk)
Quanti-Quote 01931 716 810 (www.quantimate.co.uk)
Sirca Home Developer (rightproperty.com/sirca)

Foundations

Abbey Pynford 0870 085 8400
   (www.abbypynford.co.uk)
Roger Bullivant 01283 511 115
   (www.roger-bullivant.co.uk)

Heat Pumps

Danfoss 0114 270 3900 (www.ecoheatpumps.co.uk)
Ice Energy 0808 145 2340 (www.iceenergy.co.uk)
Kensa Heat Pumps 0845 680 4328
   (www.kensaengineering.com)
Worcester Bosch 0844 892 3000
   (www.worcester-bosch.co.uk)

Home Automation

AMX 01904 343 100 (www.amexeurope.com)
Control4 www.control4.com
Konextions 0844 870 7701
   (www.konextions.co.uk)
Lutron 020 7702 0657 (www.lutron.com)
SMC 020 7819 1700 (www.smc-uk.com)

I-Beam Manufacturers

Eco-Warm 0151 708 1400 (www.ecowarm.net)
Lynx Trussed Rafters 0193902340149
   (www.timberframe.co.uk)
Oakworth Timber Engineering 01142 611 150
   (www.oakworthtimberengineering.co.uk)

Insulating Concrete Formwork

BecoWallform 01652 653 844
   (www.becowallform.co.uk)
Logix 0845 607 6958 (www.logix.uk.com)
Polarwall 0845 838 2181 (www.polarwall.co.uk)
Polysteel 01242 692 335 (www.polysteel.co.uk)
Quad-Lock 01952 884 931 (www.quadlock.co.uk)

Insulation

Expanded Polystyrene
Jablite 0870 600 3666 (www.jablite.co.uk)
Kay-Metzeler 01245 342 100
   (www.kay-metzeler.com)
Springvale 01457 863 211 (www.ecobead.com)

Extruded Polystyrene
Dow 020 3139 4000
   (www.Building.dow.com)
Knauf 08444 800 0135 (www.knauf.co.uk)

Polyurethane (PUR), Polyisiocyanurate (PIR) and Phenolic
Celotex (www.celotex.co.uk)
Kingspan 0870 850 8333
 (www.insulation.kingspan.com)

Mineral Wool
Isover 0800 032 2555 (www.isover.co.uk)
Knauf 08444 800 0135 (www.knauf.co.uk)
Rockwool 01656 862 621 (www.rockwool.co.uk)
Superglass 01786 451 170 (www.superglass.co.uk)

Radiant Film
Actis 01249 462 888 (www.insulation-actis.com)
TLX 01204 695 666 (www.webdynamics.co.uk)

Spray Foam Insulation
BioBased Insulation (www.biobasedinsulation.ie)
Renotherm 0800 389 2104 (www.renotherm.co.uk)
Walltite 0778 737 278 (www.walltite.basf.co.uk)

Kitchens
Blum (www.blum.com/gb/en)
Nolte (www.nolte-kitchens.com)
PWS (www.pws.co.uk)
Simon Taylor Furniture 01296 488 207
 (www.simon-taylor.co.uk)
Stoneham 020 8300 8181
 (www.stoneham-kitchens.co.uk)

On-Site Accommodation
Ashwood Timber 01823 251 488
 (www.ashwoodtimber.co.uk)
Static Caravans for Temporary Accommodation
 07803 290 687 (www.selfbuildcaravans.co.uk)
The Caravan Warehouse 01656 744 889
 (www.thecaravanwarehouse.com)
Worcestershire Caravan Sales 01299 878 872
 (www.worcestershirecaravansales.com)

Panelized Roofing
Excel 01685 845 200 (www.excelfibre.com)
Pasquill 0800 169 1113 (www.pasquill.co.uk)
Smart Roof 01675 442 345 (www.smartroof.co.uk)

Plotfinding Services and Plot Prices
BuildStore 0845 223 4888 (www.buildstore.co.uk)
Rightproperty 020 7193 9914
 (www.rightproperty.com)

SelfBuild & Design magazine Plotbrowser (free to readers)

Plumbing and Drains
Hepworth 0844 856 5152 (hepworth.waivin.com)
Hunter Plastics 020 8317 1551
 (www.hunterplastics.co.uk)
Marley 01622 852 695
 (www.marleyplumbinganddrainage.com)
Polypipe 01709 770 000 (www.polypipe.com)

Rainwater Goods
Hunter Plastics 020 8317 1551
 (www.hunterplastics.co.uk)
Lindab 0121 585 2780 (www.lindab.co.uk)
Marley 01622 852 695
 (www.marleyplumbinganddrainage.com)

Roof Tile and Slate Manufacturers
Dreadnought Tiles 01384 77405
 (www.dreadnought-tiles.co.uk)
Forticrete 01525 244 900 (www.forticrete.co.uk)
Keymer Hand Made Clay Tiles 01444 871 852
 (www.keymer.co.uk)
Marley Eternit 01283 722 588
 (www.marleyeternit.co.uk)
Redland 08705 601 000 (www.monier.co.uk)
Sandtoft 0844 9395 900
 (www.sandtoft.co.uk)

Self-Build Mortgage Lenders and Brokers
Aston Mortgage Services 0800 9774 732
 (www.ownbuild.co.uk)
BM Solutions www.bmsolutions.co.uk
BuildStore 0845 223 4888
 (www.buildstore.co.uk)
Leeds Building Society 08450 505 062
 (www.leedsbuildingsociety.co.uk)
Mary Riley Solutions 07808 094 014
 (www.maryrileysolutions.co.uk)
Norwich and Peterborough Building Society
 0845 300 2522 (www.nandp.co.uk)
Progressive Building Society 02890 244 926
 (www.theprogressive.com)
Scottish Building Society 0131 313 7700
 (www.scottishbs.co.uk)
Worldwide Financial Planning 0800 011 2825
 (www.wwfp.net)

Self-Build Television
SelfBuilder.tv Freesat 402, Sky channel 231 and
  www.selfbuilder.tv

Self-Build Warranties
Build-Zone 0845 230 9874 (www.build-zone.com)
LABC 0845 054 0505 (www.labcwarranty.co.uk)
National House-building Council (NHBC)
  0844 633 1000 (www.nhbc.co.uk)
Premier Guarantee 0151 650 4343
  (www.premierguarantee.co.uk)

Sewerage
Epurbloc 0800 907 0051 (www.epurbloc.co.uk)
Klargester 01296 633 000 (www.klargester.com)

Snagging
Brickkickers 0845 226 6036 (www.brickkickers.co.uk))
New Build Inspections 0845 226 6486
  (www.newbuildinspections.com)
Site Snagging 07814 838 314 (www.sitesnagging.co.uk)

Solid Fuel Heating
Construction Resources 020 7232 1181
  (www.constructionresources.com)
Euroheat 01885 491100 (www.euroheat.co.uk)
Stovax 01392 474000 (www.stovax.com)
Stoves Online 0845 226 5754
  (www.stovesonline.co.uk)
The Logpile Website www.nef.org.uk/logpile

Specifications
NBS 0845 456 9594 (www.thenbs.com)

Stairs
Bisca 01439 771 702 (www.bisca.co.uk)
Jeld-Wen 0845 122 2890 (www.jeld-wen.co.uk)
Richard Burbidge 0161 678 300
  (www.richardburbidge.com)
Stairplan 01952 608 853 (www.stairplan.com)

Steel-Frame Roofing
U Roof 01422 237 922 (www.u-roof.co.uk)

Stone and Ceramic Flooring
Ceramica and Stone 01491 412 455
  (www.ceramicaandstone.co.uk)

LimeStone Gallery 0207 828 6900
  (www.limestonegallery.com)
Topps Tiles 0800 783 6262 (www.toppstiles.co.uk)

Thermal Store
Chelmer Heating Solutions 01245 471 111
  (www.chelmerheating.co.uk)
Gledhill 01253 474 550 (www.gledhill.net)
Thermal Integration 0845 241 1441
  (www.heatweb.com/xcel)

Tradespeople
Fairtrades 08707 384 858 (www.fairtrades.co.uk)
HomePro (www.homepro.com)
HouseProfessionals (www.houseprofessionals.com)
The Construction Centre 01926 865 825
  (www.theconstructioncentre.co.uk)

Underfloor Heating
Invisible Heating Systems 01854 613 161
  (www.ihsenergy.co.uk)
Nu-Heat 0800 731 1976 (www.nu-heat.co.uk)
Polypipe 01709 770 000
  (www.homesolutions.polypipe.com)
Robbens Systems 01424 851 111
  (www.underfloorheating.co.uk)

Wallboard
British Gypsum 0844 800 1991
  (www.british-gypsum.com)
Fermacell 0870 609 0306 (www.fermacell.co.uk)
Knauf 08444 800 0135 (www.knauf.co.uk)

Windows and Glazing
Apropos 0845 434 8901
  (www.apropos-conservatories.com)
Green Building Store 01484 461 705
  (www.greenbuildingstore.co.uk)
Jeld-Wen 0845 122 2890 (www.jeld-wen.co.uk)
Pilkington www.pilkington.com
Velux 01592 778 225 (www.velux.co.uk)

Ventilation
EnviroVent 0845 27 27 807
  (www.homeventilation.co.uk)
Nuaire 08705 121 400 (www.nuaire.co.uk)
Vent-Axia 0844 856 0590 (www.vent-axia.com)

Index